An Aesthetics
for
Art Educators

AN AESTHETICS
FOR
ART EDUCATORS

E. F. Kaelin

Teachers College • Columbia University
New York • London

Published by Teachers College Press, 1234 Amsterdam Avenue,
New York, NY 10027

Library of Congress Cataloging-in-Publication Data

Kaelin, Eugene Francis, 1926–
  An aesthetics for art educators / E.F. Kaelin.
    p. cm.
  Bibliography: p. 217
  Includes index.
  ISBN 0-8077-2961-2. —ISBN 0-8077-2960-4 (pbk.)
    1. Art teachers—Training of—United States. 2. Aesthetics—Study
and teaching—United States. I. Title.
N88.3.K34   1989
701—dc20   89-32571
                                                    CIP

ISBN 0-8077-2961-2
ISBN 0-8077-2952-3 (pbk.)

Manufactured in the United States of America

94 93 92 91 90 89   1 2 3 4 5 6

To
Young Dave Ecker,
who never seemed to grow old in the service

CONTENTS

Foreword *by Stanley S. Madeja*   ix

Preface   xiii

Acknowledgments   xix

PART I: AESTHETICS IN ART EDUCATION   1

1 Aesthetics Yesterday and Today   3

2 The Educational Function of the Fine Arts   14

3 Isness and Oughtness: Reasoning about Values   28

4 Aesthetics and the Teaching of Art   36

5 Why Teach Art in the Public Schools?   54

PART II: THE PHENOMENOLOGICAL METHOD
IN ART EDUCATION   63

6 Aesthetic Education: A Role for Aesthetics Proper   65

7 *Epochē* and Relevance in Aesthetic Discourse   84

8 An Existential-Phenomenological Account of
   Aesthetic Education   107

9 Between the Innocent Eye and the Omniscient Mind:
   Phenomenology as a Method for Art-Critical and
   Aesthetic Analysis   138

10 Three Themes for Determining a Measure of
   Aesthetic Literacy   163

Afterword   193
Glossary   207
References   211
Annotated Bibliography   217
Index   223
About the Author   233

FOREWORD

Barnaby Keeney, the first Chairman of the National Endowment for the Humanities, when asked in a congressional hearing to summarize in one sentence the difference between the arts and the humanities, answered in this way: "If you think about it or study it, it's a humanity, if you do it, it's an art."[1]

The humanities use discourse and language to describe, analyze, document, compare, and evaluate ideas. The arts use processes and techniques in each of the art forms to make the art object or create the art event. Consequently, the arts and the humanities may be separate tables, but they also may have a common leaf or two between them. In this collection of essays by Gene Kaelin, philosopher and aesthetician, he addresses the sometimes simple, but more often complex relationships between the arts and the humanities. These essays demonstrate Kaelin's knowledge, but also his intellectual commitment to the integration of the domains of aesthetics, art criticism, studio arts, art history, and art education.

Art education, within the time span of Kaelin's papers (1962 to the present), has been attempting to expand its domain of knowledge beyond study and involvement in the artistic process to other areas such as aesthetics, art history and art criticism. As Kaelin aptly documents, the study and inclusion of aesthetics in the teaching of art is not a new concept. Proponents of this idea, Kaelin among them, existed long before the idea of teaching art as a discipline was ever discussed in the art education literature. Further, the expressive content of a work of art, and the relationship to the artistic idea and the art object, are also ideas which had their groundings in aesthetics.

---

[1]Bittle, Livingston. *Our Government and the Arts,* New York: A.C.A. Books, p. 145.

The value in reading Kaelin's works is that they act as a historical mirror in which is reflected the development of current trends in the field of art education, and the way philosophers and philosophy have contributed to the now-expanded domain of knowledge in the visual arts. The other, and probably more important, idea addressed by the essays is the question: Why teach art as part of the general education of every student? Most writings in art education have been concerned with how to teach art, and for the most part, are woefully lacking a rationale as to why art should be taught at all. What Kaelin accomplishes for the reader is to define a societal need and a philosophic base for why art exists and why it should have an important place in our educational system. Within this discourse he addresses another issue that has plagued the art educator for most of this century; that is, the conflict between whether art should be taught as a subject that is part of every student's general education, or whether it should be limited to the development of artistry.

Another important and dominant thread running through Kaelin's essays is the concept of *aesthetic* education. Not well-understood by the field of *art* education, it remains, as Kaelin aptly argues, the most powerful idea for organizing the art curriculum. The substance of aesthetics can be the starting point for the teaching of art as it defines its content, its rationale for existence, and its structure. The art program can be organized around the traditional questions that Kaelin and other aestheticians pose as central to critical discourse, such as: What is the nature and structure of art? What are the aesthetic and creative qualities that determine the worth or value of art to an individual or a culture? What is the nature of aesthetic discourse? How does aesthetic discourse effect the artistic process? How does one describe, analyze, and determine the aesthetic merit of a work of art?

As Kaelin has suggested, if the student can engage in this kind of discourse then we have expanded the content and domain of the visual arts. The argument in the art education literature to expand that content base in art education has been very forceful in the last two decades. Consequently, Kaelin's essays are extremely relevant to this ongoing dialogue between proponents for the general education in art for every student and those who advocate a specialized training modeled after the professional artist. The significance of Kaelin's work is that he addresses these issues very specifically, enabling the reader to gain insight into how the visual arts can be structured to meet the general education needs of the student without compromising the content or integrity of the discipline or the artistic process. What these essays call for is the use in the art program of a broader philosophic stance based in aesthetics. To my thinking, if accomplished, this can do nothing but improve the teaching of art at all levels.

STANLEY S. MADEJA
DEAN, College of Visual
and Performing Arts
Northern Illinois University

PREFACE

William James once shocked the philosophical world by suggesting that the meaning of any idea—philosophical or otherwise—could be ascertained by calculating its "cash value." While the crassness of the metaphor might be expected of someone like John Dewey, James's use of the expression seemed at odds with his Brahmin upbringing. What he meant to tell us, of course, was that any idea meant only what it could be applied to—what circumstances of possible use would fulfill any of its claim to truth. In the essays collected in this volume, I have tried throughout the years to show the range of the use-values attributable to a philosophical aesthetics.

As a preview of the conclusions to be drawn from these essays, allow me to list a few of the cash-values one might expect from an investment in speculative aesthetics. First, coming to know anything at all still has its charms. It makes no difference whatsoever whether, in attempting to know something, we learn that no theory of our subject is possible—although the claims made for this position have always been greatly exaggerated—as long as our inquiry succeeds in building a set of concepts (James's ideas once again) that may be applied to categorize our aesthetic experiences. I shall call these "aesthetic categories" and shall plead for their acceptance on the basis of their use in making clear some aspect of those very experiences we call "aesthetic" because they constitute the value it has been the wont of aestheticians from time immemorial to investigate.

Nor should the introduction of a value designation seem out of place here. Whoever enters into scholarly discourse about values must get used to both the descriptive and the evaluative sense of more than one aesthetic concept, beginning with that of the common adjective *aesthetic* itself. It is for this reason that this term, in its ordinary uses, has two opposites: either *nonaesthetic*, designating a set of circumstances under which it is improper to make aesthetic judgments of any kind; or *unaesthetic*, designating a negative judgment on a particular subset of the circumstances that permit the proper use of the descriptive concept. And, if we continue reflecting in this vein for a moment, we should be able to convince ourselves that the terms *moral* and *logical* function in the same way: our conduct, which is properly designated *moral*, may be evaluated as good or bad, indeed moral or immoral; and when it is not within the descriptive purview of a possible moral judgment, then it is simply *amoral*. Finally, when it is proper to consider our behavior as logical, that is, our thinking or analyzing, then it, too, is either good or bad, logical or illogical, while other human behaviors are descriptively nonlogical.

If making the distinction between a descriptive and a normative aesthetics is one of the first fruits of philosophical reflection upon our aesthetic experiences, then applying the concepts of the two kinds of investigations is the expected cash-value of the ideas gained in the inquiry. The most obvious of the further uses of aesthetic reflection derives from this distinction. For example, the categories we may devise for a normative aesthetics may be turned into a means for evaluating any critical concepts employed by practicing critics, whose language in turn may be either descriptive or normative: either describing the properties of particular works of art or evaluating the same. When aesthetic categories are used in this way they are used as metacriticism, which, again, may function either descriptively or normatively, depending upon whether the metacritic is describing a critic's behavior or evaluating it as good or bad, effective or ineffective, pertinent or impertinent, and the like.

The two previously mentioned functions of aesthetic reflection make it possible to conceive of aesthetics as providing a foundation for art educational theory and practice—the third return on our original investment in philosophical thought. It was to promote this function that the original essays and addresses of this text were written. Although the theory is here, it was originally manifested in many different contexts; and so, in re-editing the essays I have been careful to remove any undesirable repetition, which was caused, in the main, by the diversity of the educational problems addressed. Whatever the results of my revisions, some reader is sure to see in them a "retrospective" of my work in aesthetics; and for this I offer my apologies, in advance.

In our own time there is a movement afoot to incorporate aesthetics into a curriculum of instruction in the arts, along with three other disciplines—studio production, art history, and art criticism. Pro-

moted by the Getty Center for Education in the Arts, which is supported by the J. Paul Getty Trust, the movement goes by the name of
discipline-based art education (Clark, Day, & Greer, 1987). The Center is
currently engaged in seeding institutes across the country, preparing
the teachers for introducing DBAE, as it is called, into selected school
districts. If the plan succeeds, it shall go far to reformulate the discipline of art education itself.

But as I look upon this curious social phenomenon—the dispersal
of private foundational funds to revolutionize the theory and practice
of public art education—I am struck by a certain diffidence on the part
of the Getty Center to recognize what has already been done in the
field, since the middle of the 1950s, to use the tools of philosophical
aesthetics to structure an art educational curriculum. I may be able to
shed some light on this puzzle by suggesting where some of the missing pieces may be found.

Integrating aesthetics, along with art history and criticism, into the
art educational curriculum was an accomplishment achieved by Fred
Logan at the University of Wisconsin (Madison) during the less radical
years of his chairmanship there. After publishing his *Growth of Art in
American Schools* (1955), he was looking for ways of contributing to the
kind of growth he had already found in modern progressive education. He made his contribution by sending all his students, both graduate and undergraduate, to the department of philosophy for their
background training. I learned as much about art and art education
from those students as they learned about philosophy from me. Indeed, it was there I learned the lesson that a classroom is a locus of social interaction and not a negative space enclosed by a set of walls, and,
incidentally, that both philosophy and art are tools, and not the end,
of education.

Dave Ecker and Bill Krueger were a part of that group, and they
took their experience to the Ohio State University, where Manuel Barkan had already begun to take an interest in the movement following
the 1965 Seminar in Art Education for Research and Curriculum held
at the Pennsylvania State University under the auspices of the Arts and
Humanities Program of the U.S. Office of Education. That seminar,
uniting all the named players within the discipline, was the second
great push toward a reformulation of the art educator's job of work. It
was there the debate over "child centeredness," "problem centeredness," or "discipline centeredness" came to a head, with Manny Barkan stressing the importance of the latter orientation.

Finally, in the summer of 1966, at OSU, Dave Ecker served as director of an Institute for Advanced Study in Art Appreciation, which

included simultaneous seminars in art history (taught by Matthew Baigell, then of osu), art criticism (by Edmund Burke Feldman, of the University of Georgia), and aesthetics (by myself). Besides participating in all three seminars, each member of the Institute was asked to choose one of the areas for a fourth course of study in special problems in the discipline. As I see it, this was the true beginning of the multidisciplined approach to art education in this country. The Institute was supported by the federal government operating under the provisions of the National Foundation on the Arts and Humanities Act of 1965.

As the Central Midwestern Regional Educational Laboratory (Cemrel) in St. Louis began, in cooperation with the School of Art at the Ohio State University, to develop its program in aesthetic education (which included curriculum development in the visual arts, music, drama, dance, and literature), Manny Barkan headed Phase I of the program. It eventuated in the publication of a set of guidelines for curriculum development in aesthetic education (Barkan, Chapman, & Kern, 1970). Laura Chapman's later work in art education (1978) owes much to her exposure to the aims of a general aesthetic education while working on phase I of Cemrel's program. Phase II of the program was headed by Stanley Madeja, now dean of the College of Fine Arts at Northern Illinois University.

Although the movement toward a general aesthetic education failed to take hold in the public schools, it should not be forgotten that it was never designed as a replacement for instruction in the particular arts, especially the visual arts and music, which were already more generally recognized, if poorly understood, as staples of the general educational curriculum. Some superintendents of public instruction and some school administrators could not understand why public funds should be found both for the arts *per se* and for an aesthetic education devoted to an understanding of aesthetic experiences considered as experiences, just as they could not, in John Dewey's time, understand the educational value of experience as contributing to the growth of individuals and their cultures.

Between the seventies and the eighties, some school boards have been inveigled into settling this paradoxical problem by redesigning their curricula of instruction in art education. And that is the role being filled by the Getty Center program—a project that may yet succeed, if only the discipline of aesthetic education is itself modified in both theory and practice in the graduate schools of this country.

In these pages I have assembled a number of essays that I hope will throw some light upon the role of philosophical aesthetics in the discipline of art education, in an effort to help bring about the necessary reformulation of the regnant theories.

The division of my subject matter is laid out in two parts, each containing five essays. The first part, Aesthetics in Art Education, attempts to show the possibility of applying philosophical aesthetics as a foundational study for art education, but the field is defined in traditional terms. It is for this reason that this section begins with the chapter entitled "Aesthetics Yesterday and Today." By the time the reader has progressed to the fifth article in this section, philosophical aesthetics will have begun to display the characteristics of my own idiosyncratic thought patterns.

The second part, The Phenomenological Method in Art Education, covers much of the same ground as the first but is much less eclectic in theory. The five essays included therein pass as somewhat difficult, since they were worked out in a foreign idiom. Although it is not unknown in this country, phenomenological philosophy and its cognate discipline of psychology are not generally practiced in American academic circles. From my own point of view, this neglect of one of the dominant movements in recent continental European philosophy is both inexcusable, because it is parochial in the extreme, and prejudicial, since it has precluded the everyday use of some very powerful analytical techniques, such as bracketing the world of appearances (the better to allow their aesthetic properties to appear), phenomenological description of our conscious experiences of aesthetic properties (the better to describe the language of criticism), and the joint use of the same techniques to develop the categories necessary for determining the relevance of aesthetic concepts.

As I see it, the strangeness of the phenomenological terminology hardly causes enough pain for us to continue our disregard of its therapeutic uses in an educational setting—especially in light of the fact that the insights gained from the method are, for the most part, compatible with those of American pragmatism. But that can only be understood by carefully reading both pragmatic and phenomenological aesthetics.

A common thread, running through the 10 articles, has come of late to be called "the institutional theory of art" (Danto, 1964; Dickie, 1979). My own view is institutional in the sense that works of art are described as created, preserved, and appreciated in a set of overlapping social institutions designed to liberate the human impulses that drive us to creative expression of feeling. Indeed, art, aesthetics, art criticism, and art history are such institutions, each related to the other in specific ways not yet worked out in the Getty program. I offer the following essays in an attempt to suggest just what these specific relationships might be—the better to structure a curriculum of instruction in art for our public schools. The journey, as any reader may discover, has been long and hard.

The introductions to the chapters have been added to suggest the continuity of the topics addressed in the included essays.

I wish to thank all those generations of my own students who have accompanied me on this journey, in particular that group from the department of art education at the University of Wisconsin who, in 1960, moved out across the country into other similar departments to spread the effects of the movement to incorporate aesthetics within the institutional nexus of art education. Foremost among these has been Professor D. W. Ecker of New York University, who did not even seem to mind when I tried to explain to him that all critics must function as something between an innocent eye and an omnisicent mind, since quite obviously no man or woman is either of these. Because he was my student, he taught me that thinking in another person's categories may be the most rewarding, if the most difficult and trying, of educational objectives. Owing to his seemingly unbounded enthusiasm for his work, some of us will always remember him as "young Dave Ecker," as he was baptized by Manny Barkan himself. When I came to know Barkan, he was already suffering through the last stages of his terminal cancer; and it was Laura Chapman and Evan Kern who brought phase I of the Cemrel project to its successful conclusion.

ACKNOWLEDGMENTS

For their kind permission to reprint copyrighted material, the author wishes to express his sincere thanks to the following persons and agencies:

To Professor Harve Thompson, Chairman, Department of Continuing Education in the Arts, and Dean John W. Schmidt, Division of General Extension, at the University of Wisconsin-Madison, for permission to publish a re-edited version of my article, "The Educational Function of the Fine Arts," that appeared in *Arts-in-Society* (vol. 1, no. 4, pp. 47–61, 1960).

To T.H. Hatfield, Excutive Director, National Art Education Association, for permission to publish a re-edited version of my "Isness and Oughtness" that first appeared in the NAEA journal, *Art Education* (vol. 21, pp. 6–10, 1968), and a version of my "Aesthetics and the Teaching of Art," from *Studies in Art Education* (vol. 5, no. 2, pp. 42–56, 1964).

To Ralph A. Smith, editor, and the University of Illinois Press, for permission to reprint two of my essays published previously in *The Journal of Aesthetic Education:* "Aesthetic Education: A Role for Aesthetics Proper," (in vol. 2, pp. 51–66, 1968), and "Why Teach Art in the Public Schools?" (in vol. 20, pp. 64–77, 1986).

To Ralph A. Smith, editor, and the University of Illinois Press, for permission to reprint my "Epochē and Relevance in Aesthetic Discourse" from their 1970 volume, *Aesthetic Concepts and Education* (pp. 135–163).

To Dean Harlan Hoffa, College of Arts and Architecture, The Pennsylvania State University, for permission to publish a revised version of my "An Existential-Phenomenological Account of Aesthetic Education," which first appeared in the *Penn State Papers in Art Education* (no. 4, 1964).

To Professor David W. Ecker and Dean Jerrold Ross, Division of the Arts and Arts Education, New York University, who were, respectively, editor and publisher of my "Between the Innocent Eye and the Omniscient Mind," as it appeared in an institute report titled, *Qualitative Evaluation in the Arts* (pp. 19–60, 1980).

To Frances A. Phelps, editor of publications, the Florida Art Education Association, for permission to reprint my "Three Themes for Determining a Measure of Aesthetic Literacy," from the FAEA *Forum* (pp. 3a–12a, 1987).

To the Oxford University Press, for permission to quote from Benjamin Jowett's translation of Plato's "Symposium," in *The Dialogue of Plato*, vol. I, p. 334 (New York: Random House, 1937), and for permission to cite Ingram Bywater's translation of Aristotle's *Poetics*, in Richard McKon (ed.), *The Basic Works of Aristotle*, p. 1462 (New York: The Random House Lifetime Library, 1941).

To Donald W. Crawford, editor of the *Journal of Aesthetics and Art Criticism*, and Roger A. Shiner, Secretary-Treasurer of the American Society of Aesthetics, for permission to reprint the photograph of the five stages of a painting by Saul Horowitz, analyzed by David W. Ecker (see Figure 4.1 p. 50, this volume). It appeared in *The Journal of Aesthetics and Art Criticism* (vol. 21, no. 3, Spring, 1963) and is used with the permission of the American Society for Aesthetics.

To the Board of Directors, Service Photographique de la Réunion des Musées Nationaux de France, for permission to use their black-and-white photograph of James McNeill Whistler's *Arrangement in Grey and Black, No. 1* (The Artist's Mother). (See Figure 10.1, p. 169, this volume.)

To the Glasgow (Scotland) Art Gallery and Museum, for permission to use their black-and-white photograph of James McNeill Whistler's *Arrangement in Grey and Black, No. 2* (Thomas Carlyle). (See Figure 10.2, p. 170, this volume.)

AN AESTHETICS
FOR
ART EDUCATORS

PART I

AESTHETICS IN ART EDUCATION

Five essays from 1960 to the present, illustrate the efforts of one aesthetician to participate in the processes of education in the arts. The first four supply the premises for an argument that would warrant the inclusion of the arts as a necessary component of a well contrived general education, the topic of the fifth essay.

Why include the arts in a general educational curriculum? Because if we don't, we leave our children uneducated; and leaving them uneducated in the way only the arts can educate them can only impoverish our national democratic cultural—and political—institutions. And they are already poor enough.

1

AESTHETICS YESTERDAY AND TODAY

This essay was originally a radio address delivered at station WHA ("The Oldest Station in the Nation"), Madison, Wisconsin, in the 1962 series Music in Context. *It traces a brief history of philosophical aesthetics, relating the study to the dominant art of the historical epoch and ending with the distinction between the sensuous and conceptual elements found in these arts. Music is noted as differing from literature or figurative painting in emphasizing the sensuous over the intellectual components of the aesthetic experiences that each affords.*

Aesthetics, like most other intellectual disciplines, had its beginnings in the speculations of the Greeks on the nature of things and ideas. Unlike most of the other disciplines that are still taught in institutions of higher learning, it has not achieved a status independent of philosophy, now, as always, the mother of sciences. Nor is there good reason to suppose that it should attain to independence. For wherever men and women have experiences that tease their curiosities, there we shall find philosophy. Experience, reflection, criticism; renewed experience, reflection, and criticism describe the never-ending round of the philosophical enterprise, which begins in a relatively confused experience and, if it attains to any degree of felicity, ends in a richer, clearer, more enjoyable experience of the values to be found in living. Philosophy calls for, and sometimes produces, a life more replete with direct consummatory values.

It used to be said that philosophers were dedicated to the pursuit of the true, the good, and the beautiful, that holy triad of human values whose possession made for the wholeness of man. Being whole, the person who possessed these values would be rich in spirit however otherwise poor. And having traded in that aspect of his Christian heritage, his poverty of spirit, for fuller experience of his own humanity here and now, an aesthete would have yielded any claim he may have had to gaining the kingdom of heaven. His consolation for this disappointment would be considerable nonetheless, for in the process he would have become truly wise.

Any synthesis of the classical Greek with our Hebraic-Christian religious tradition must appear at first glance to blend into an uneasy mixture of confused ideals, and any one metaphor embodying the points of view of the three cultures will of necessity exhibit a cubistic character. Under the influence of too many cultural sources, our vision becomes blurred and we may end up seeing only empty space. To the intellectually curious person, however, wisdom is the proper reward. For the Greeks, the philosopher was a lover of wisdom; and it was a Christian, imbued with the ideals of chivalry, who insisted that a true gentleman ought never to brag about his conquests. Love wisdom we might, but talk about the affair and we sin against the dictates of good taste.

As is well known, Plato learned everything he knew from Socrates, who never wrote a word in his life. He preferred to talk and to ask questions of others who listened only more or less well. In the end, it was always the same: the interlocutors talked too much, and Socrates proved he was the wisest of men because he knew that he knew nothing, while his opponents in discourse continued to believe whatever prejudices their minds had already conceived. In the *Symposium*, the most charming of the Socratic dialogues, Plato has Socrates recount his initiation into the art and science of love. Oddly enough for a Greek of his time, he has a woman, Diotima by name, explain to Socrates the connection between love and beauty. Listen to her words:

> These are the lesser mysteries of love, into which even you, Socrates, may enter; to the greater and more hidden ones which are the crown of these, and to which, if you pursue them in a right spirit, they will lead, I know not whether you will be able to attain. But I will do my utmost to inform you, and do you follow if you can. For he who would proceed aright in this matter should begin in youth to visit beautiful forms; and first, if he be guided by his instructor aright, to love one such form only—out of that he should create fair thoughts; and soon he will of himself perceive that the beauty of one form is akin to the beauty of another; and then if beauty of form in general is his pursuit, how foolish would he be not to recognize that the beauty in every form is one and the same. (Jowett, 1937a, p. 334).

For those who have never heard nor heeded them, her words are long— yet worth hearing for both their content and their form. She continues:

And when he perceives this he will abate his violent love of the one, which he will despise and deem a small thing, and will become a lover of all beautiful forms; in the next stage he will consider that the beauty of the mind is more honorable than the beauty of the outward form. So that if a virtuous soul have but little comeliness, he will be content to love and tend him, and will search out and bring to birth thoughts which may improve the young, until he is compelled to contemplate and see the beauty of institutions and laws, and to understand that the beauty of them all is of one family, and that personal beauty is a trifle; and after laws and institutions he will go on to the sciences, that he may see their beauty, being not like a servant in love with the beauty of one youth or man or institution, himself a slave mean and narrow-minded, but drawing towards and contemplating the vast sea of beauty, he will create many fair and noble thoughts in boundless love of wisdom; until on that shore he grows and waxes strong, and at last the vision is revealed to him of a single science, which is the science of beauty everywhere. (Jowett, 1937a, p. 334).

In those words, written so long ago, we find perhaps the most cogent statement of the aims and the scope of the discipline called "aesthetics." When Keats wrote, "Beauty is truth, truth beauty, that is all/ Ye know on earth, and all ye need to know" (Quiller-Couch, 1939, p. 746), he was echoing the words of Diotima. And once again it was no accident, since he was writing an ode inspired by a personal experience of a Grecian urn wrought to that degree of perfection that inspired Plato's reflections on aesthetics in the first place. Platonism enjoyed a tremendous vogue among the English romantic poets and continues to flourish in the minds of those who look upon aesthetics as the science of beauty. The facts of our aesthetic life, however, indicate that this is a mistake.

Plato himself started the reaction. Although no one in the history of Western culture understood art and artists more—if the perception of value, the force of vision, and the perfection of style are taken as evidence—no one mistrusted or feared them more. Recognizing the power of the poets to stir up the passions of the populace, he suggested their banishment from the ideal state and only on second thought considered their admission to the halls of the just—provided they submit to the decree limiting their discourse to a small number of approved topics. Moreover, men soon became disillusioned with a Beauty said to inhabit a nether region to which only an intellectual elite could attain. In the *Republic* itself, Plato disparages imitative artists as dealers in copies of the copies of real forms; in third-rate realities, if you will.

Minds of sterner stuff, however, began to insist that beauty is in the thing, not an idea floating in a limbo somewhere beyond the pale. Listen now to Aristotle's matter-of-fact description of a beautiful form, as delivered to his students, who recorded them:

> We have laid it down that a tragedy is an imitation of an action that is complete in itself, as a whole of some magnitude. . . . Now a whole is that which has beginning, middle and end. A beginning is that which is not itself necessarily after anything else, and which has naturally something else after it; an end is that which is naturally after something else, either as its necessary or usual consequent, and with nothing else after it; and a middle, that which is by nature after one thing and has also another after it. A well-constructed plot, therefore, cannot either begin or end at any point one likes; beginning and end in it must be of the forms just described. (McKeon, 1941, p. 1462).

It must be remembered that Aristotle's students were trailing behind him in an uneasy walk and therefore not very well placed for objecting to the obviousness of this pronouncement. If they had objected, no doubt they would have received a masterly rebuke: just as obvious, the wise one would have said, is the fact that beginnings, middles, and ends do not present themselves as such before the fact of poetic creation. Critics may perceive the parts of a plot once it has been constructed, but poets must discover them in the depths of their own experience.

As to the power of artists to move the masses, Aristotle was less pessimistic than Plato—or optimistic, as the case may be. The purpose of the tragic poem he considered to be the arousal of emotions, such as pity and fear, which are then purged from the souls of the audience. So runs his theory of catharsis. A modern aesthetician has likened this explanation to the experience of a man who deliberately puts on a shoe that is too tight for the pleasure of taking it off once again. Poetry for constipated souls is not a very delicate image, nor a fair and noble thought. However, whatever the condition of their souls, it is estimated that the Athenians had access to their purge at most twice a year. Instead of a hindrance or a blight of imperfection on the form of the state, the purging poets were conceived by Aristotle as an instrument of its smooth functioning. Neither deceivers, nor clowns, nor fools, nor perverters of the public morality, the poets—and by extension all artists—were saved from perdition by a closer examination of the facts of our aesthetic life.

But if Aristotle's decision was right, his reasons were wrong; just as Plato's decision to ban the poets was wrong even though some of his reasons were right. A paradoxical state of affairs, if ever there was one. The explanation is as follows: there actually is no reason why art and artists should be excluded from a well-run state; to say the least, life would be rather dull without them. But to say they should not be banished from the polis because their activity helps keep order in the house is as wrong-headed as to say that they should be banished because their activity creates disorder there. The application of both these principles by the commissars of culture in various people's republics in our own time indicates that if politics gains, art suffers by being tied to an extrinsic function. And we know, too, that even in the Soviet Union a mere generation ago there were renegades who found the orthodox Socialist Realism impalatable and who practiced the decadent art of the West—predominantly abstract and expressionist between 1945 and 1960—in the secret confines of cellars and attics. Moreover, when art in America did change in the sixties, it was to a mode of expression highly critical of the culture approved by the establishment.

The point to be made here, I believe, is that art, like any other of the institutions in a freely functioning and democratic society, must be allowed to work within a social context as it can and for what it is, rather than as it can be made to work when it is put into the service of a function extrinsic to its own nature. The job of the aesthetician in our own time, then, seems to be the reconsideration of the nature and functioning of art considered as an institution that in its own sphere relates an artist and an appreciative audience in an act of creative communication, while outside its own sphere it interacts with the other institutions of society in determining the life patterns of the individuals living together within that society. If this could be done—and I can see no reason why not, although most certainly I shall not be able to show how in a single short chapter—it would be found that Diotima's words to Socrates were prophetic indeed.

In this volume of essays, I shall be pursuing the steps necessary for the universalization of the impulse to art through its institutionalization within the general society. The prime medium for such a universalization is through the reformation of art education in our public schools.

Of all the changes to be made, we may begin with those in aesthetics itself. Beauty is no longer the ideal pursuit of the aesthetician because it is no longer the ideal pursuit of artists. Artists criticize the established order when in a satirical or iconoclastic mood, boiling over when frustrated and screaming when angry. Pop art was the new *vox populi*, and unless we arrogate to ourselves the privilege of denying someone else's democratic rights—I mean the artist's freedom of expression—there is no way of keeping this anger and frustration and satire from showing up in their works. The grotesque has an expressive power undreamed of by a Plato, and no entirely lucid person would call a truly grotesque work either beautiful or unsuccessful art. Plato clearly feared a grotesque society much more than he respected human freedom of expression; had he respected the latter more, he would have feared the former less. Clearly, an artist is doing something other than imitating reality, which is Beauty itself; on this score, Plato was absolutely right: no matter how he try, the artist would never succeed in duplicating any real thing, whether it be beautiful or ugly when considered in its own context.

The two themes of Platonic idealism and Aristotelian naturalism run throughout the history of aesthetics as thinkers of greater or lesser courage and greater or lesser insight have tried to face up to these same facts of our aesthetic lives. Some, like the Platonist and romantic Schopenhauer, were guilty of forcing the facts into a Procrustean bed— into a theory that preceded their observation. Others, like the Aristotelian and classicist Lessing, were guilty of judging works of their own age by applying rules fixed in the past. It is significant to note that Lessing took the rules of Aristotle's poetic to be as binding upon the dramatists of his own time as were the rules of Aristotelian logic for anyone engaged in discursive thinking. Little did he realize that shortly Aristotle's logical "rules" were to be superseded by the discovery of much more powerful logical techniques.

The intellectual battles of the romantics and the classicists seem as futile to us today as some of the medieval discussions on the locus and quantitative distribution of disembodied spirits. How can one decide the question of what is more important to art, expressive feeling or expressive form, when the problem is that of understanding just how a given form expresses precisely the feeling it does? If and when this task is performed, then only may we proceed to the aesthetician's wider social aim of showing how such expressions may function to improve the lives of people living in a democratic society of interacting institutions.

For the nonce, I shall try to concentrate on clearing the way for a useful conception of how feelings become expressed in artistic forms. The aesthetic works of two other German philosophers will be useful for this purpose. The first is Friedrich Nietzsche, whose essay "The Birth of Tragedy from the Spirit of Music" contains a general theory of aesthetics as well as a short course in the history of Hellenic art. The theory of tragedy it contains is one of the first significant divergences from the Aristotelian tradition. Foreshadowing some of Freud's later discoveries, Nietzsche postulated two distinct principles of human existence. The one is said to aim at complete individuation, wholeness of form, and clarity of appearance. This is the Apollonian, from the god Apollo, who embodied all the characteristics of light, beauty, and prophecy. The connection the Greeks saw between light and prophecy will be better understood when all the meanings of the mystical expression "to see" are comprehended; one might as well write "seen in one act of comprehension" as "comprehended in one act of poetic vision." Both these acts, the seeing and the understanding, are fused into one appearance in the great works of Greek sculpture, a predominantly Apollonian art form. Form, clarity, vision, and understanding—all there for those of us with the eyes to appreciate them.

The second principle, opposed to the clarity of the Apollonian and deriving from man's addiction to strong drink and its resultant exhilaration, is said to give vent to pent-up feelings, too primitive to be classified and too urgent to be passively contemplated. In such a mood, the Dionysian, man gives way to an impulse to action, to song, and to dance and excessive sexual activity. We should all know the end of this story: Dionysus, the god of the grape, is torn apart by the women he has stimulated, as all predatory males are possessed by the very beings they would have possessed; and in the process, peace and balance are restored to nature. Nietzsche found this principle in its purity to be predominant in the musical arts and embodied in all the other arts to which music may add the effects of its rhythms. He found this latter to be the case in the old Attic tragedies from which Aristotle had inferred his rules. In making tragedy the cause of spiritual purgation, Aristotle, according to Nietzsche, was making cause with the enemies of art, whose true purpose he himself conceived as the intensification of life. Attic tragedy was the last of the type: after the Greek dramatists poets began to take themselves too seriously as thinkers; the errors of Socrates, which are only foolish in philosophy, became fatal to art—until the spirit of tragedy was reborn in nineteenth-century German music. What did Nietzsche find there? In his translated words:

Nature, as yet unchanged by knowledge, maintaining impregnable barriers to culture—that is what the Greek saw in his satyr, which nevertheless was not on this account to be confused with the primitive cave-man. On the contrary, the satyr was the archetype of man, the embodiment of his highest and intensest emotions, the ecstatic reveler enraptured by the proximity of his god, the sympathetic

companion in whom is repeated the suffering of the god, wisdom's
harbinger speaking from the very heart of nature, which the Greek
was wont to contemplate with reverence and wonder. (Nietzsche,
1871/n.d., p. 985).

Between the two periods—the early Hellenic and the nineteenth-century German—the Western world became Christianized and the man-
goat was traded off against the man-God, who as the sacrificial lamb
took upon himself the sins of the world. Whether lamb or goat, Christ
is said to have relieved the suffering of humanity by taking away the
sins of the world. In the same suicidal act, he likewise took away
whatever claim man may have had to any measure of dignity. Western
man may still suffer, but he may no longer lay his claim to human dignity on that fact; he must now be satisfied with a promise of better
things to come. For this reason, some critics have maintained that there
is only one Christian tragedy, and that was the crucifixion of Christ,
which is celebrated today only symbolically and in bloodless fashion
on the altars of the world.

What happens to an artist in the Christian view of the world was
celebrated in art by James Joyce (1916/1956), who revived the myth of
Daedalus, the artificer who fashioned wings with which to escape from
the Labyrinth, also by happenstance of his own design. Minos, the ty-
rant of the place, had been cuckolded by a bull who bequeathed him
a stepson, half-man, half-bull. To escape exposure of his disgrace, Minos ordered the Labyrinth built and Daedalus complied; but when the
latter fell out of favor with the ruler, he, too, was imprisoned. Daedalus and his son, Icarus, winged for flying, soared away; but the boy,
emboldened by his new-found power, flew too close to the sun, which
melted the wax binding his wings. As is well-known, Icarus fell into
the sea and drowned, bequeathing his name to the waters that claimed
his body.

In Joyce's portrait of the artist, the hero is given the name of Stephen Daedalus. Stephen, the artificer, looking for a rational explanation of the life of creation, will find it in making works of art. It is not
insignificant, of course, that this Daedalus bears the forename of the
first Christian martyr or that the description he gives to the qualities
of works of successful art contains the threefold set of characteristics
found in the aesthetic writings of Thomas Aquinas (himself canonized
as a Christian saint). According to Aquinas, the marks of beauty are
integritas, consonantia, and *claritas*. Stephen translated them: wholeness, harmony, and radiance. We may see the significance, however,
if we render them as "wholeness, of harmonic proportion in the parts,

and bearing a unique significance in the act of our perception." It is the uniqueness of the significance, I believe, that has frustrated centuries of aesthetic speculation. Stephen's own interpretation is not far from the truth: he opted for *quidditas*, or the "whatness" of the object constructed; in older or more modern terms, the essence of the thing. Although we should be happier with some other term, say, *haecceitas*, or the "thisness" of a thing, it should be clear that we mean by this its individuality. All we need add is that the individuality of a work of art is the discovery of the artist, not a gift from God or the muses.

The notion of creation as discovery was given its fullest expression in the aesthetic theory of Immanuel Kant (1790/1951). Nietzsche, it will be recalled, talked in general terms about the wellsprings of creation and the effects of appreciation, the psychology of creator and appreciator; his own rhapsodies concerned the successful art product but did little to enlighten the critical mind on how the two principles he discovered in Greek art applied to the actual case of contemporaneous art. If apprised of this shortcoming, he could have answered, as would be proper, that only a perception of the value of the given work would supply the knowledge sought. It is common sense to suppose that only an experience of a work itself can produce the basis of a judgment; all else is words, as empty in fact as cacophonous in sound.

Moreover, if we were to continue in the Nietzschean vein, our attention would be drawn off the primary subject of interest—the expressive quality of the work—and exhausted on the subjects of a purely psychological interest. A genius, to prove himself, must create works of genius; and a man of taste, to do likewise, must first have the experience he claims to be of aesthetic worth and then analyze its structures and communicate his findings to an audience who may check his report against their own experiences of the same object. And if this is the case, we have come full circle, back to our old description of philosophy as experience, reflection, and criticism.

The philosophy of art begins with art experiences. They are had or not, as the case may be. The second level of the philosophical discipline is precisely the one so eminently exploited by Kant. Upon reflection, art experiences are found to be "aesthetic" rather than logical; that is, the imagination functions first to form a series of impressions of sense, which are then related by judgment to a concept not given to the understanding, because prior to the formation of the object the concept does not exist. In logical, or cognitive, judgments, on the other hand, this relationship is reversed: the understanding is possessed of concepts, and the judgment determines that a given manifold of sense impressions is one of the kind fittingly described by the known concept. From all this philosophical jargon it follows that works of art are not of known or knowable kinds; they are individual, and whatever significance they have must be determined on the basis of their "wholeness" and "harmony," as Stephen Daedalus put it; or as we hear more often in the reputable criticism of our own day, in the structure of the individual work. In practice this means that the significance of any work of art must remain outside the ken of one incapable of grasping the relatedness of its internal forms.

In a word, the aesthetic significance of a work of art is the form of the work when the form is considered as unabstractable from the elements entering into relationship in a given circumscribed context. The significant form of the work is its content as it is deployed in context. *Content* and *form*, then, are not antithetical terms; as if the artist first possessed the form and then poured the content of his own experiences into it as a mould giving form to those experiences—or as if the artist first possessed the content to be expressed before discovering a form fitting for its expression. Both these approaches seem to be in error. In subsequent essays in this volume, I shall replace these critical concepts with the aesthetic categories of surface and depth.

Consider the matter more closely: discovering the form constitutes a new experience that may provide new content, as it did for Joyce in *Portrait of the Artist as a Young Man,* and this in turn would require new forms for further expression. The only hope for avoiding the futility of this endless circle lies in considering content and form to be one and the same object, the artwork, viewed from different perspectives: the form is the wholeness; the content is the harmonically related elements whose consonance taken together form the whole. Their significance or clarity is the consonance of the parts felt in an integral and integrating perception.

At this point, if we are to fly out of this labyrinth of our own construction, we should proceed to an exemplification of the findings in an actual case of criticism. But this is to fly too close to the sun. As a first step on our flight from incarceration, we must learn to use our wings, and this means to apply aesthetic categories to significant expressions.

Our experience of them shows that all arts contain some kind of sensuous surface; some contain in addition an intellectual depth. Music, nonobjective painting, and architecture are usually considered the "pure" arts; that is, their expressiveness is controlled completely by the organization of the sense impressions of the medium in question. Literature, figurative painting, sculpture, and drama all contain beyond their sensuous surfaces various elements of depth structures: represented objects, images, and ideas, depending upon the artist's vision and purpose. The expressiveness of the surface arts is given in the tensions of the organized sense impressions and for this reason is usually more immediate than that of the depth arts, whose expressiveness is controlled by the relation of the surface tension to the structural cohesiveness of the depth "message." This is the lesson to be learned in bracketing together poetry and music. Poetry is a depth art; and music is all surface. Together, united as if by love, they may produce a new medium in the art-song. The significance of each of these kinds of objects is, however, the tension of their forms. And these forms are concrete, rather than abstract, significant in their inner relatedness rather than in their separation.

Critical ineptitude begins when one glosses over something that forms an integral part of a work or when one looks for something that does not inhere within the work. A good poetic analysis will relate the music of the words of the poem to their meanings and will allow the recreation of the original expressive act. Too often we tend to forget that literature is not made with profound ideas or lofty sentiments, but with words, one of whose properties is to be sounded in speech. For this reason I call poetry a performing art, like music. A good musical analysis will avoid associating irrelevant ideas and images and feelings with the tensions felt in the musical patterns played. With these categories held fast in mind, we may proceed, as the recent German philosopher Edmund Husserl was wont to say, back to the things themselves (*zu den Sachen selbst*), have an experience, and then begin the process of criticism.

2

THE EDUCATIONAL FUNCTION
OF THE FINE ARTS

This essay appeared in one of the opening issues of Arts-in Society, *a journal published by the Exension Division of the University of Wisconsin. The task was to give a justification for the inclusion of the arts in a program of adult education. The topic of the difference between surface and depth arts recurs but is here broadened to include a list of the elements found in works of art in different media, and therewith a first account of the "deepening" of an aesthetic experience. For the list of elements found in aesthetic expressions I am indebted to the late DeWitt H. Parker (1920/1945, ch. IV).*

Given Parker's list of elements, the aesthetician may pose the problem of determining what is expressed in particular works of art: the intention of the artist or the response of the appreciators. As this disjunction is refused, an alternative is considered. Works of art "express" nothing beyond themselves, and the value of their expressiveness is the experience some viewer— whether it be the man or woman of genius or of taste—has of the elements contending for observation.

In every case, the controls on the responses to the work are defined as the internal structures of the work's own intentional context. As a result of being trained to have such experiences, a viewer's consciousness is said to undergo a change one might call "defanaticization." It will be argued later that producing citizens possessing the properly defanaticized states of consciousness is the social goql of aesthetic education.

For a special application of the aesthetic principles herein espoused for adult education, interested readers may compare the award-winning dissertation of Anne Lindsey (1982).

I

There was a time, in the annual meetings of the National Association for Art Education, when the announced subject of discussion was "the art in art education." Outside the apparent interest in defining and evaluating art objects, the aim of the participants seems to have been to emphasize the need for producing artists, that is, students capable of producing effective works of art at a fitting level of readiness, as well as future teachers of the arts capable of criticizing such works. The irony of this emphasis is that a closer look at the supposed dichotomy between artist and teacher of art will show that there are no grounds for any dispute over the matter in the first place.

It is not supposed here that there is no difference between an artist and an art teacher. It is sometimes too painfully obvious that the professional artist who is teaching in a recognized school of art is no educator and just as obvious and painful to see that some of the teachers engaged in art education are not competent artists. Nor am I suggesting that an artist is born (or inspired) and not made (or taught). Techniques, which may be taught, and inspiration, which most probably cannot, go hand in hand in the creation of expressive contexts. What is being argued is that artists are artists only because they produce works of art and that teachers of art are teachers only when they produce students who in turn either produce works of art or have their appreciation of the arts enhanced. The emphasis in this interpretation of the problem has thus shifted to the work of art as made or appreciated; and it makes little difference whether the work has been made by an artist who was self-taught or by one who learned his or her craft at the hand of another master—or even at the hand of someone something less than a master. It is imperative, then, that we return to the work; once again, back to the thing itself.

What do we find there?

One answer to this query may be of extreme importance to contemporary art educators. Any impartial analysis of works of art and of our experiences of them should yield reasons to support certain art educator prejudices and to reject others; and by appealing to experiences that are common, I hope to convince even the least endowed of the teachers or students engaged in adult education. We can, of course, hope for no more objectivity in this matter than that afforded by the communality of an experience, nor espouse a more worthy aim. It is a common assumption, for example, that education for adults must be cast on a level that only a layman can understand. And a layman is by definition one not conversant with the subtleties of a given field of inquiry. Good enough.

Viewed in this light, the assumption is not so much false as misleading. To educate anyone to anything, one must begin with the level of that student's development at the start of his or her education. But this is equally true of resident university and adolescent students, as well as of students enrolled in adult-education classes. The suggestion that adolescents may be introduced into the techniques of an intellectual discipline and be expected to read a sentence with more than one qualifying clause and still understand what is being said, should be equally applicable to an adult student with all the more reason. One might expect a greater degree of motivation, if not of sophistication, on the part of adults who show up for courses in continuing education long after completing the years of their formal education. Whatever the terminology teachers must use, however complex the thought patterns they must employ to meet the minds of their students, there must be the added pedagogical assumption that the speakers or writers know whereof they speak, because what is said or written refers to some characteristic of their own experience that they hope to communicate to an audience. It is clear enough that critics and commentators must meet this demand of objectivity; their job is to explain what they already understand, and they must use words to do so. The question is, to what extent must artist-teachers meet the same demand? To what extent, indeed, can they? Do artworks communicate? And if so, what?

If these questions can be answered, adult educators may find reasons to justify the inclusion of original works of art in a "journal of the arts in adult education." If, for example, it could be shown that the fine arts in and of themselves tend to educate their "appreciators," the case would have been made, and some doubt by that very fact would have been cast upon the propriety of the term *appreciation* as descriptive of the effect of the work upon its audience. What is involved in art appreciation? And how does that phenomenon affect subsequent human behavior? In order to make the case, I shall address myself to a prior question: What is expressed in a work of art?

Too many critics have attempted to answer this question without reflecting upon the nature of the thing assumed to be the vehicle of expression. Is a nonobjective painting a work of art? If we take "modern" art as our criterion of identification, and apply it to the traditional, we shall be led to doubt that anything before the work of the French impressionists was in fact a work of art. But the same would be true if we reverse the procedure and compare the moderns to the traditionalists. Obviously they are different. What makes each a work of art?

There is a danger here, of course, in using the term *art* in its two senses at the same time. Sometimes we say, "that is a work of art," and mean that the work is good or excellent; if we do, we are using the term normatively. We have applied some norm or standard to the work in question and have judged its worth. If posed in this normative sense, the earlier questions put to a modern and a traditional work can only produce confusion. Quite clearly, if the modern is the standard of excellence, the traditional must suffer in comparison and vice versa.

The second sense of the term *art* is a purely descriptive one. In asking the question above with reference to either the modern or the traditional style of painting, it is quite clear that both are works of art in this sense. Both are samples of paintings that are conventionally considered art. Both are expressions of a thought, feeling, desire, or value in a sensuous medium. Yet they differ. As a matter of fact, from a psychological viewpoint the experience of a modern painting has as much in common with music or the dance as it does with traditional representational painting. And no one property seems to be common to all media or modes of expression. What does the person do who adopts the task of describing works of art?

One way of starting the inquiry is to point out the various kinds of things to be investigated. As aestheticians, we are interested in musical compositions, paintings, architecture, sculpture, dances, novels, poems, theatrical performances, and the like. Now, although it is true that no one art medium is in any way like any other on the face of it, deeper analysis will show that different media may be categorized meaningfully into groups—as spatial or temporal, literary or performing arts, and so on; but even more, they do possess a common property: each is an expression in some kind of sensuous material. Thus, if we are to describe the vehicle of artistic expression, it is not out of the question to assemble a catalogue of the elements, beginning with the sensuous, that may go together to make up a work of art—in a purely descriptive sense. The problem of normative judgment is not here in question. That is a longer argument, perhaps more difficult to understand.

II

Descriptively, the vehicle of artistic expression may be considered primarily in terms of its "sensuous surface." The term *surface* here refers to all the values of the medium used in the expression as they are organized in the perception of individuals contemplating the work. It includes the play of colors and attitudes of lines in painting; the melody, harmony, and rhythm of music; the style, tone, and rhythm of prose. In certain arts, such as nonobjective painting and the so-called absolute music, the experience of the art object is exhausted by the experience of the sensuous surface and its attendant mood. Now, since all art forms present a sensuous surface of the kind described, and the measure of the artist's ability as a technician is the deftness with which he may construct a surface for the expression of his "idea," it has been assumed by some thinkers that aesthetic value is limited to this single element of an aesthetic object. Such a position, when consciously maintained as an aesthetic theory, is called a "thin" doctrine of aesthetics. It is thin because it purposely excludes any element of representation in the consideration of the value of the piece. Let us examine a judgment on a statue. An ultrapurist, one espousing the thin doctrine of aesthetics, would maintain that the representative quality of the statue is irrelevant; if the statue represents the Virgin, the likeness of the statue to the image or ideal concept we may entertain of a woman as the Mother of God is beside the point; the only requirement for a possible aesthetic judgment would be that the statue—not the woman— be well-built. In defense of this position, certain of its adherents appeal to the well-known distinction between a blueprint or a workaday photograph and a "shimmering aesthetic surface" vibrant with a life of its own.

It may be clear from this description that any nonobjective artwork is nothing more than such a surface. Although the artist may make some claim to "representing a city," he must know that he is not interested in presenting a literal visual impression of the object, the city in question. He "abstracts" from the city until he has achieved a surface that yields a mood, taken by him to be the mood of the city. Such was *Broadway Boogie Woogie* (by Piet Mondrian, 1942–43). Since no one viewing of a city can give an adequate representation of the whole geographical surface, the artist abstracts from the whole to present his "artistic" impression; and in this case the abstraction is complete: no object is seen within the confines of his composition, and his painting is therefore "nonobjective."

Does the viewer have to relate the mood of the sensuous surface to the mood of the city in order to understand the painting? If so, the painting would be considered a visual metaphor. Rather than pursue the question here, I shall delay the answer until the third section of this article. Suffice it to note here that some art objects are purely surface expressions and ordinarily do not represent anything beyond their surfaces. It should be clear, if this description is adequate, that a viewer who looks for some representational depth in a painting that contains none is bound to be disappointed. Much of the dissatisfaction with modern art stems from ignorance of the nature of nonobjective art—a

fact that is all the more astounding since music has always made a virtue of its nonobjectivity, along with much of the dance and most of our
architecture. It is clear, then, that some arts are surface arts and that this
shared property is another principle of categorization for the arts.

But whether we look at the piece under discussion as a nonobjective work or as a representational picture depends, to be sure, upon the
work itself. To exclude any representative, or depth, elements on principle is a highly arbitrary procedure. Let us consider the example of the
sculpted Virgin. We may agree with the purists that a great deal of the
aesthetic value of the statue derives from the artist's manner of depicting the subject; but we may still disagree with the concept of a
technique of depicting that is entirely divorced from the subject depicted. If the artist distorts the ideal image, this distortion is visible on
the surface of the sculpture. But any distortion is only a means for ab-
stracting from what is taken to be the real object depicted. In order to
judge the effect of a partial abstraction, it therefore becomes necessary
to conceive the idea of what the nonabstracted object would be. In other
words, some element of depth (representation) enters into the structure of the object. What are these elements? (See Parker, 1920/1945, ch.
IV.)

The first element of "depth" that enters into the artifact is a represented object; and with objects, any associated feeling or emotion
connected with them. The Virgin may call out feelings of reverence or
disgust, depending upon one's attitude toward the person alleged to
be the Mother of God. Which of these associated feelings is the correct
one? Obviously, there is no way of answering this question outside the
context of the work itself. If the figure is distorted, the distortion may
reinforce the depth feeling, whatever that may be, with the mood of
the surface; or some other object may be depicted in such a way that
the relation between the two objects would allow a clearer conception
of an idea to be associated with the first. If, for example, the Virgin is
depicted with her foot on the back of a writhing serpent, we may be
authorized in conceiving the relationship of the Virgin to the temptor,
symbolized in the serpent: Mary, the symbol of purity, takes venge-
ance on the Evil One for his victory over Eve, the mother of us all; and
womanhood is vindicated. Much of the energy spent in art history has
been of this nature; and it is certainly a part of a complete aesthetic
analysis of any work of art that does in fact contain iconic or symbolic
content.

The question to pose at this juncture is the extent to which the
iconic meanings can be considered to constitute "the meaning" of the

work. Already we have enough framework to sketch out an answer. If iconic meanings are only one of the series of elements in a work of art, starting with the sensuous surface, it is no more valid to select them from the total context than it is to select the surface itself as exhausting the meaning or the "message" of the artwork in question. The work of art is the total context of relations obtaining among all the elements. And, it may be noted in passing, it is for this reason that many works of art rejected as "obscene," "sacrilegious," "counterrevolutionary," "communistic," and the like have been rejected for nonaesthetic reasons. These epithets are moral, religious, political, socioeconomic, but not aesthetic. The aesthetic judgment states a relation between the depth and its surface or between a surface and its mood; and when we perceive a work of art, we perceive the tension holding these two factors together into a single context. Theories maintaining this necessity of relating surface to depth in aesthetic judgment of "realistic" works are called "thick," as opposed to the thin described above.

But objects and ideas do not exhaust aesthetic depth. It is clear that in moving from the perception of represented objects and their associated depth feelings to the conception of an idea, there has been a motion away from the mood of the surface. Is there any element that serves to bring our attention back to the surface in order for the experience to be a single or unified perception? Ideas are abstract, and they engage the intellect. To that extent, whenever they occur in the perception of a work of art, they tend to destroy the sense of "presentational immediacy," the sense of a feeling we attribute to the object as if it were one of its qualities rather than one of our own affective states. One of the values of perceiving a work of art is precisely this feeling. How is it retrieved in the so-called intellectual arts?

The answer to this question is readily available by a further consideration of a particular art form, literature. A poem has a surface, which is primarily auditory. But in a poem we are never merely presented with rhythmic sounds; we are presented with meaningful rhythmic sounds—words intoned in part for the communication of their meanings. We perceive the words and almost immediately conceive these meanings. And the entertainment of the meanings, the formation of ideas or concepts, tends to divert our attention from the pressing immediacy of the surface, thereby bringing it into contact with the intellectual content of the depth or content of the piece. What brings us back to the focal interest of the surface is, of course, the set of images we put into play to make the ideas more concrete. But images are vicarious, or substitute, sensations; thus literature that is composed on the surface of auditory perceptions may be buttressed in depth by a simulated sensuosity stemming from a substitute stimulation of all possible sense organs. Poetic images may be visual, auditory, tactile, olfactory, kinesthetic, even directly visceral. The richness is in the depth, not on the surface, which, however, still maintains some claim upon our attention.

In order to summarize our account of the elements of artworks, we may compose the following list. Some works of art are entirely surface: namely, the nonobjective arts in which there is no representation of recognizable objects. These are constructed uniquely out of sensuous elements and their attendant moods. They may contain forms, but they are necessarily "free forms," representative of nothing in nature. To appreciate this kind of art object one must let the senses operate in the way they are capable of operating on any perceptual field. Any attempt to impose depth upon them is to falsify the experience. In this sense they are the most immediate, and the feeling they arouse is the subjective registering of the affect of the piece, which results from a perception of the objective ordering of its sensuous elements.

The nonobjective visual arts are primarily spatial, and the "objective ordering of the visual elements" is called a design. The nonobjective aural arts are primarily temporal; a melody exists in time and is punctuated by the accents of rhythm. We say "primarily" because of the relative importance of the one mode of sensation. It is obvious that there is rhythm in painting, but it is a secondary phenomenon and appears only when the total design is broken up into individual parts and a repetition of like elements is perceived within the whole design. Likewise, there is a secondary perception of space in music: merely imagine the difference between an open-air concert and the same pieces performed within a vaulted cathedral, and you will have imagined the way in which our perceptions confined in space influence the temporal forms of music. Chamber music played outdoors tends to get lost in the surrounding space of nature.

When, on the other hand, we proceed to depth, we find there "objects," "ideas," and "images," but not necessarily all of these in any one work. Each of these sets of elements may be accompanied by associated feelings or emotions that may either reinforce or tend to modify the immediate mood of the surface. The extent to which they do so will be the "total effect" of the piece.

To put the matter more succinctly, a work of art is constructed out of these five kinds of elements. Some works will contain only the first two: surface and mood; others contain these, plus the representation of objects, ideas, or images and their associated feelings. And the whole work of art is a relational construct formed by the artist for our perception.

III

I have traced out the list of elements that make up the vehicle of artistic expression. My purpose was to arm myself for answering the question, What is expressed in a work of art? I had assumed that an answer to this last question was necessary before any speculation concerning the educational function of the fine arts would be fruitful. I now proceed to the specific task of considering the question.

Since artistic expression takes place via the art object as the vehicle of expression, some critics have assumed that the work expresses whatever the artist intended it to express in the act of creation. They argue that the artist is the dominant personality in the creation of the object and thus is free to choose what to express. But it does not follow from these statements that the work expresses a conscious intention. And because it does not follow, critics who attempt to determine the artist's intention in order to adjudge what is expressed in the work are said to have committed the "intentional fallacy." We should consider the reasons that have led other critics to deny that a work of art expresses objectively the subjective intention of an artist.

The first such reason is the rather obvious statement that some artists might not themselves know precisely what they intend to express. At the outset, such artists merely wish to make a work of art. Recent psychoanalytic literature is replete with examples to substantiate this claim. But we need not retreat to the position of the unconscious in order to ground our denial of the relevance of the artist's intention. Let us assume for the moment that the artist had a conscious intention and was successful in carrying it out in the particular work under consideration. If we ask what the work expresses, it would follow immediately that the work expresses the artist's intention; but the intention is the work, so that in the long run the work actually expresses itself. The expression is odd, but its oddity is of no consequence here. To discover the answer to our question all we would have to do is to experience the work as created—that, by supposition, is its intent. Instead, therefore, of looking to artists for clarification of their intentions, we should merely look at the works. The artist as a person disappears from the context of the judgment.

Clear enough. But what, one might ask, is the case if the artist is unsuccessful in expressing the original intention? What indeed? In this case, we would be presented with a very peculiar phenomenon—a work of art that by hypothesis is a failure. Should we go searching through the artist's wastebasket in an effort to determine what was intended, the best we could find would be a verbal description of the intention, since it was not expressed in the work. Furthermore, if our description of the work of art above is acceptable, there are no grounds for making a comparison between a verbal description, paraphrase, or gloss of the original work and the concrete expressiveness of the elements in their individual relations. The "meaning" of the original work can only be perceived or pointed to, not described. Thus, even should the artist be able to describe what was wanted in the creation, that description could not be assumed adequate to the expressiveness of the work itself. If it could, after all, there would be no purpose in constructing the object in the original form.

Aesthetic judgment consequently has nothing to do with determining an artist's intention. To put it ironically, the assumption that a work of art expresses the intent of an artist is tantamount to assuming that the work expresses nothing at all, since when successful the work is the intention and when not, the intention is not expressed, that is, objectively considered, nonexistent. For these reasons, finally, the viewer is freed from the tyranny of the artist's subjective intentions. But this freedom involves not so much the leveling of the artist as it does the elevation of works of art. In other words, "genius" is what genius does; it need not be considered subjectively as the peculiar faculty, power, or ability of the artist to do superior deeds but must eventually be considered objectively as the work produced. Shakespeare's genius was not a structure of his mental powers; it is no more and no less than the collection of his works. And Picasso's genius is quite literally hanging on the walls of houses the world over.

Having rid ourselves of genius and the overbearing attitude its assumption has produced in many of our creative artists, we are faced with another problem. If it cannot be fruitfully said that a work of art expresses the intention of an artist, perhaps it should be said that the work of art expresses whatever a viewer finds there. And there is some evidence that may be adduced to support this contention. Consider once more the nature of the expressive vehicle. The recognition of represented objects, the conception of ideas, the formation of images—in a word, the whole of the depth of a representational work—depends for fulfillment on the activity of the viewer, who must perform these functions for a work of art to exist. One critic calls this act "the performance of the work," intimating by this description that the work is per-*formed* in the appreciative act. Likewise, in arguing against the first

position, the viewer-centered theory points out that the artist's intention is purely private to the artist, while artistic expression is public and
communicable. Therefore, in order for the artist to communicate at all,
it is necessary for the artist to be the first viewer of his work. When the
two viewings are similar, communication has taken place. Thus, when
the artist associates the same kind of objects, feelings, ideas, and images with the surface of the work as any other viewer, his expression
is fulfilled. What the critic must do in confronting the work, according
to this view, is merely to gauge the effect of the work upon himself. Can
this position be maintained in the light of our aesthetic experiences?

I think it is clear that it cannot, for the following reasons. First of
all, although the artist's intention is not the expressed idea of the work,
it cannot be claimed that the artist is reduced to the level of any viewer
of the work produced. When we reduced artistic genius to the works
of an artist in their objective structures, we did not eliminate the effect
of personality on these same structures: we merely objectified whatever of the artist's personality is relevant to the given work. Picasso's
one-time connection with communism and his communist sympathies
took objective form in at least one instance, in the frightening picture
of destruction contained in the *Guernica* painting. The effect of his activity is to have embodied the destructiveness of fascism in the bro-
ken-lined forms we actually perceive. And, iconographically, the
symbols of destroyer and destroyed, the unseen planes and the whole
human scene, reinforce the mood of the line-character perceptible on
the surface of the work. Propaganda it may be, but oh! so expressive;
it is so expressive that the critic is almost forced to make a moral reference in the aesthetic judgment on the work. The critic's judgment is
presumably the same sort of judgment the artist himself made when
he decided to sign, and therefore to mark as his, whatever he discovered himself as having expressed—in this case, the universal horror of
war.

Secondly, since the depth elements come into play in aesthetic experiences by the mechanism of association, any objective work of art
may be taken to mean anything else; any two objects can be associated
by any given viewer: the association of this red with fire engines or fire
itself or roses or blood or catsup. If this is an acceptable explanation of
the experience, the result, ironically, may be that, from the viewer's
point of view, the work may express the entire universe, the entire
gamut of possible feelings. And this is the case, since there is no control on the process of association by which different objects, ideas, and
images may be brought to bear on the art object within the experience

of any one viewer—no control, that is, if not the structures of the work itself.

We may therefore agree with the viewer-centered position on the expressiveness of works of art, with the following provisory considerations: (1) that the credit for the creation of the work be placed with the artist and not with the viewer; and (2) that the viewer bring to the work only those associations that are controlled by the formal structures of the concrete object we call "the work of art." From this it would follow that a given artwork may be thought to express anything consistent with the structures of the work; and it is to this extent that a work of art may be said to express more than one thing for the author and for different viewers.

We need only remember that the author is the first viewer. The purport of our proviso is to allow for the correction of false judgments on the object: creative artists can be mistaken about the structures of their own artworks as long as these works are objective, and in the same way as any other viewers may misjudge any artist's works. Since it is the structures of the object about which disputants are in disagreement, however, there is always a way of mediating the dispute. In matters aesthetic, there are no experts, no unquestionable authorities. But anyone may become a more or less qualified viewer. The evidence that such a person is a qualified viewer is readily available in the amount of sense he or she can bring to the judgment of what constitutes the aesthetic object being observed. As some critics have insisted, the work does not mean; it is. And this is precisely what is meant by saying that a work of art expresses itself, and itself alone.

IV

In the light of the foregoing I may now pose my final question. What is the educational function subserved by producing students— and teachers—qualified to make aesthetic judgments? For the teachers engaged in the teaching of the arts, the answer seems obvious. Since their very competence is to some extent measured by their ability to substantiate personal and social judgments of the worth of a given work of art, training in aesthetic judgment is a necessary part of their development. And it is this training that has generally been lacking in the education of the average art educator. Thus the interest of their association in our subject.

But what about the students themselves? What do they gain from being introduced into the mechanics of aesthetic judgment? Some writers have had recourse to a rather weasel-like term, *culture*, to explain this educational value. But, objectively considered, this word refers to all forms of human behavior that produce objects tending to develop the potentialities of men, women, and society. Here, too, it was DeWitt H. Parker (1920/1945) who gave an early push toward the inclusion of social psychology within the realm of aesthetic inquiry. As he put it, "Since . . . art is a social phenomenon, we shall have to draw upon our knowledge of social psychology to illumine our analysis of the individual's experience" (p. 7). The only trick we have to perform is to conceive of the educational setting as a *de facto* institution in which both student and teacher behavior undergoes legitimate modification. Such behavioral modification is the purpose of all our institutions, whether they be scientific, artistic, religious, political, and the like.

Now, if this interpretation is given to the situation, the person appealing to it as descriptive of the value inculcated by instruction in aesthetic judgment is saying that making intelligent and informed judgments on art objects is valuable because it makes one cultured; but this is the same as saying that engaging in cultural enterprises makes one cultured, or, still more tautologously, that culture makes culture. We all know without even having to consider the matter that growth is growth; the question of first order remains. What, in the perception of the elements and structures of aesthetic objects, tends to produce an acculturating influence upon students in such a way as to enrich not only their own lives, but that of their society as well?

It is in answer to this question that the educational function of the fine arts becomes clear. Consider.

If it may be safely assumed that the work of art is and does not mean, then the work of art expresses only itself. It places a demand upon the perceptive and cognitive faculties of the individuals who would judge the effectiveness of the work. Even in a completely nonobjective piece, viewers' perceptivity is undergoing development as they place their perceptual apparatus under the discipline of the structures of the work. From the same element of control gained by insisting upon the intersubjectivity and communicability of feelings, students learn to control their feelings: only those feelings are relevant to the work that are consistent with the organization of the sensuous surface. We may call this the advantage of perceiving "beauty," if you like, but nothing is gained by adding this name to the experience described. The value to the perceiver in the perception of interesting surfaces is therefore double: to increase discrimination in perceptions and to control our vaguer moods. This is perhaps the oldest of known values ascribed to music, a nonobjective art. The mad king Saul was rid of his melancholic humors by the pleasant harmonies of the boy David's harp. And as "music hath charms to soothe the savage breast," so have any other art objects that yield nothing but a sensuous surface to our perception. Such is the value, in particular, of the so-called modern art—no matter what the degree of abstraction from represented reality it may achieve.

Beyond the maximum of sensitivity and perceptivity demanded in the experience of nonobjective artworks, there is the further development of the cognitive and imaginative faculties in "realistic" art. To perceive a represented object as just this object and not another, it is necessary for the viewer to conceive the nature of such objects; to understand the idea imparted by the relations between concepts, it is necessary to conceive these relations; to concretize any ideas in specific illustrating images, it is necessary to exercise the imagination. These are the further advantages of including the arts in an educational curriculum, owing in particular to the perception and judgment of realistic works of art. To be trained in constructing or reconstructing the depth of artworks is to have one's intellect developed through exercise. Thus surface and depth of an aesthetic experience demand intellectual exercise, and this exercise may produce habits of awareness that become integral parts of the personalities being trained.

But there is a further consideration, that of taste. Since, in the judgment of works of art, it is necessary to relate the expressiveness of the surface to that of the depth, when there is a depth, the exercise of aesthetic judgment serves to develop what might be called a "style of life." Ideas have only as much aesthetic value as their physical expression, and the physical expression of an idea is its embodiment in a sensuous surface. The aesthetic personality is never a fanatic; such a person is never carried away with the value of the idea itself but rather finds the worth of its expression in the tension between what is expressed and the sensuous vehicle of the expression. Such personalities as these are men and women of taste, and the production of this kind of individual is certainly a legitimate aim for educators, even those preparing individuals for their entrance into the structures and institutions of a bland society. We must only add that taste, like genius, is not primarily a reference to the taster's faculties. Men and women of taste, like those of genius, are known through their works: the former, by what they appreciate; the latter, by what they create.

3

ISNESS AND OUGHTNESS

REASONING ABOUT VALUES

Education is like art criticism in that both disciplines entail a descriptive and a normative use of discourse. A particular problem arises when we try to draw a normative conclusion from strictly descriptive premises. How does one justify the norms used in educational decisions?

In this essay (1968), first published in Art Education, *I examined the issue·as it was introduced into the discipline of art education by Elliot W. Eisner and David W. Ecker in their then-influential book of readings,* Readings in Art Education *(1966). The problem persists in the field and is another example of an educator's use of philosophy to define the discipline of art education.*

Perhaps the most obvious conclusion to draw from the discussion is that since the theoretical language of education is, like that of criticism itself, both descriptive and normative, then there must be a metaeducational discipline, with respect to educational theory, just as the normative language of art criticism demands justification in a workable metacriticism. I argue that in both cases philosophy supplies the second level discipline.

In the eighteenth century when David Hume (1738/1911) propounded the famous dictum that reason is, and of right ought only be, the slave of the passions, he was merely entering the lists in an age-old dispute concerning the virtue of self-control through reasoning. Since, in his opinion, it was the function of reason to trace the relations between ideas or to establish probabilistic judgments about matters of fact, reason could not be thought of as affecting our conduct unless the idea or matter of fact it led to was itself capable of creating a countervailing force to that of impulsive behavior. In such an eventuality, it was acting in the service of the passions. Matters of fact and

28

the relations between our ideas were disputable, but matters of taste were not: and today we still say, one man's meat is another man's poison. For some reason, the conventional wisdom does not say the same thing of women.

Hume, of course, had no way of knowing that in the twentieth century his pronouncements were to become institutionalized within the structure of professionalized art education. Eisner and Ecker (1966) summarize the predicament in the following way:

> We cannot look to scientific research to determine what we ought to do because science cannot presently tell us what kind of an education children ought to have. More generally, science cannot presently deal with normative problems. Knowing what is or what can be does not tell us what ought to be. *Science can help us attain the desired end but cannot help us determine the desirable.* (p. 16)

Reasoning further, they conclude that any major value premise governing the practical inferences of pedagogical imperatives must derive from some source other than reason itself. For example, if it is assumed that a teacher ought to maximize those conditions that lead to creativity, then it follows logically that teachers ought to maximize conditions x, y, and z, precisely those that empirical research has established to produce the desired results.

Yet everyone knows that the assumption contained in the major premise above is disputable, and it has been disputed under certain circumstances: the development of the "whole child," or the child's adaptation to a democratic society may be adopted as the ultimate educational value of art by the administrators of any given school system; and if this is true, then the conclusion of the syllogism certainly does not follow. It all depends on what the general society wishes to gain from an education in arts; and there, what is one society's meat is another society's poison.

Given the relativity of the social justification for education in the arts, any imperative that can be taken to govern educators' behavior must be interpreted as hypothetical; that is, they ought to do whatever it is claimed they should do only when a limited set of conditions exist. A minimal such set of conditions would be:

1. That their conduct be undertaken to achieve a given end, prescribed by the major value premise supplied by society or the school as an institution of society;

    2. That they possess reliable information that procedures x, y and
      z have a strong probability of achieving the prevised end.

No one doubts the force of such reasoning. Given the premises, the conclusion follows. Yet in the total situation something strikes the curious contemporary philosopher as peculiar. Why the current disagreement concerning the ultimate value of education in the arts? Why should the development of the whole child or the child's adaptation to the institutions of a democratic society take precedence over the development of an autonomous institution of art in our contemporary society?

Surely if students are to learn art, they must learn to create or appreciate it, not something else. If our education in the arts is to be true to its subject, then we should allow artists to teach art. Whenever it suffers from the strictures of extraneous controls, art itself can only be false to its subject; it, too, is an institution of our society. For the educator, then, the only question of importance seems to be one of aesthetics: what constitutes the "facts" of creation and appreciation? It should be clear to the most reluctant of our art educators that the inherent confusions and conflicts of their discipline are reflected in their disputes with artists, critics, and art appreciators—to call these latter "lovers" might be a bit misleading. Why should intellectual confusion produce conflicts in educational theory? Why other than the fact that reason is the slave of our passions? Perhaps the artists and the critics of our society can give reasons for their attitudes toward professional education in the arts; perhaps they may be able to convince us that education in aesthetic activities should be concerned with aesthetic values, not with the external aims of psychological development of social harmony.

Moreover, from the proper aesthetic viewpoint, the argument could be made that both these aims, although not on the face of it intrinsic to the aesthetic institution, are still attainable, perhaps more efficiently so, within the aesthetic institution, if educators of art did restrict their professional aims to a more strictly defined aesthetic purpose.

Be that as it may, the teacher's problem is further compounded when one considers that art educators as practitioners of a discipline are doubly concerned with value considerations: not only those social ones justifying the ends to be subserved by education in the arts, but also those of justifying the evaluations placed upon particular works of art themselves. And on this last question Hume (1777/1951) himself abandoned the doctrine of the total relativity of taste:

> Some species of beauty, especially the natural kinds, on their first
> appearance, command our affection and approbation; and where they

fail of the affect, it is impossible for any reasoning to redress their influence, or adapt them better to our taste and sentiment. But in many orders of beauty, particularly those of the finer arts, it is requisite to employ such reasoning, in order to feel the proper sentiment; and a false relish may frequently be corrected by argument and reflection. (p. 173)

Here, of course, one man's meat is no longer another's poison, provided the other is capable of having his taste educated through reason. And that has always been one of the ends subserved by aesthetics as a branch of philosophy itself.

Although these two arguments seem to lead to contradictory conclusions, the reason for such seeming lies in us, not in Hume's writing. He has often been quoted out of context and interpreted to be arguing for and against the relativity of taste. The fact of the matter is that he was always a relativist. In the first instance, he was arguing that reason *alone* is not *sufficient* to determine one's taste; and, in the second, that reason, along with both the disposition to follow it and the actual experiences of works of art, may be a *necessary* condition to having one's taste educated.

The disposition to follow reasoning about aesthetic matters certainly is not wanting. Aesthetics, as a quasi-scientific discipline dedicated to the interpretation of the facts of taste, has been in existence since the time of Plato at least; and criticism is perhaps older, since the Homeric epics contain judgments on the quality of handcrafted objects.

Moreover, the independent writings of Ecker and Eisner give further testimony that the issue has not been lost in current art educational theory. We understand, of course, that one of these men believes that a theory of art education is possible and the other not. But surely this is a question that must wait upon an adequate determination of what constitutes valid reasoning in matters aesthetic. Not any old reasoning will do. Eisner (1965), for example, is concerned with the basic information about art he found lacking in students—"even those with a college 'education'" (p. 10). It could be that his information inventory contains a few irrelevancies. How much, for example, of the available information about art terms, about art media and processes, about artists and their work, and about art history more generally is relevant to the enjoyment of a particular work under critical discussion? No answer is given this haunting question.

The assumption seems to be that the more we know in general, the more we know in particular; but this is a delusion. Descartes, in the first rule for the direction of the mind, cautions against the error of mistaking the sciences for the arts—the realm of facts for the realm of values, or, as he put it, the scope of the universal versus the definition of the particular. The methodology proper for one is not applicable to the other. The proper object of science is general (concepts); of art, individual (expressions). Benedetto Croce made the same distinction and but for his idealistic metaphysics might have succeeded in his task of integrating aesthetics into a general theory of linguistics (Kaelin, 1964b.)

Following the tendency of contemporary philosophy to consider itself a language having as its task the investigation of lower-level uses of language—this is why it is called "analytical philosophy"—Eisner (1965) suggests that we carefully distinguish between three types of statement usually made concerning the arts: the descriptive, the interpretive, and the evaluative. His own metalanguage is simple and direct:

> It's one thing to say that a painting has blue in the upper right hand corner, it's another thing to say that a painting is turbulent, and it's still a third thing to say a painting is good. (p. 11)

What could be more obvious, and yet what more misleading? It all depends upon the interpretation we lend to the statements, and to his own our author gives an adequate clue: description is about "visual 'facts'," and interpretation, about a reaction to the things described; evaluation, on the other hand, expresses a value judgment made on the work earlier described and interpreted (p. 11).

Let it be understood: I am not denying that "description, interpretation, and evaluation differ and [that] it would be useful for students to know when they are doing each" (Eisner, 1965, p. 11), only that a meaningful frame of reference has been given for us to understand the precise differences in the indicated uses of discourse. In a later essay, I shall attempt to show how the "deepening" of an aesthetic experience, from surface perception to imaginative understanding, is a continuous conscious process and as such amenable to phenomenological analysis.

Why, for example, is "blue in the upper right hand corner" a reference to a physical fact? Our perception of blue anywhere is as much a fact of interpretation as is the "turbulence" of a painting, if by interpretation we mean the gauging of an effect upon our psychic systems. From a strictly phenomenological point of view, blue is a quality and is felt; and so is an aesthetically relevant turbulence. Wherein lies the difference? We could call the experience of blue a quality felt in isolation—of the other counters of the painting's context—and the experience of a painting's turbulence one of a qualitative relationship among such isolated qualities; but then we should be distinguishing between "local" and "regional" properties of a formal system of artistic qualities (Beardsley, 1958, pp. 82–85), both of which are merely descriptive aesthetic categories, not guides to an interpretation.

To his credit, it should be noted that Eisner does not refer to interpretation as the deciphering of a "meaning" to be found in a representational painting. Meanings may be found in some paintings, in any that contain the requisite number of depth counters, but we are all familiar with the mischief created by the lovers of interpretation who condemned all so-called modern art only because they could find no meaning in a nonfigurative painting. But it can be noted that what made this mischief possible in the first place was a pseudodistinction between "description" and "interpretation" as essentially different kinds of aesthetic discourse.

Whether we are describing the sensuous features of the surface of a painting, or describing the various levels of its experiential depth, our language is descriptive of some feature of the public work of art that may be referred to with the proper phenomenologically grounded terminology. This point is already admitted by those who refer to public works of art as phenomenally objective.

It is tempting to present here a realistic position on the goodness of aesthetic objects and reduce the third level of aesthetic discourse to pure description in the same vein. But since my full argument is presented in Chapter 9, I shall consider it here only in outline. It runs like this: if goodness is a property of paintings, then it, too, may be experienced, and the phenomenon described. This does not mean, of course, that all good paintings are good for the same reason; only that some reason may be elicited for our judgment that the work is good. And here is where the logic of the judgment must be found.

This is the tack taken by Ecker (1967) in following the procedures of the so-called good-reasons school for the determination of aesthetic value. He rightly points out that an appeal to good reasons is the first step toward distinguishing personal likings from objective evaluations. It *is* odd to give any kind of reason at all for our personal likings and dislikings: on our basic reactions we can give only a psychological report. It is another matter when we are asked to justify our aesthetic judgments. Here we readily give reasons, one of which is that the structure of the piece and the feeling it controls are masterfully contrived.

The only obstacle to a clear understanding of this distinction is the continued refusal to analyze the structures of aesthetic experience; that is, the refusal to adopt or construct an adequate methodology for dealing with artworks as controlling aesthetic response. And this is the task of aesthetic theory, not of statistical inventories. On this point, Ecker's meat is Eisner's poison.

If one were to assume a scientific pose and construct a causal explanation for the confusion of aesthetic preferences for aesthetic judgments, it could be pointed out that the human organism is capable of responding to anything it can perceive, conceive, or merely imagine; it can respond to anything seen or thought of; it can even respond to its own responses and does so by creating elaborate symbolic systems that may or may not correspond to anything in reality. When a given subject reports his liking of a painting his reason tells him to be no good, or his dislike for a painting his reason tells him to be good (Ecker, 1967), he is neither confused nor in error. And the same is true for women subjects as well. Barring bad faith in their pronouncements, we cannot assume they are lying or even ignorant of their own responses; but they may be in error of what, precisely, controls those responses. For this reason aesthetic disputes are not about personal likes or dislikes but about the clearness of aesthetic perception. If someone's mind is changed about the goodness of an aesthetic object, that person has ample grounds for understanding that he or she *ought to* have responded otherwise to the phenomenally objective structures of the artwork in question. The indicated pedagogical technique to reduce such differences in "taste" is not to ask "Do you like *x*? And if so, why?", but rather, "What is it precisely that you like or dislike?" In order to answer this question, the student will be forced to analyze structures, which then may be stipulated as reasons any fair-minded judge should name for aesthetic approval.

Such is the solution of the curious paradox of Hume's peculiar evaluation of the place of reason in the determination of aesthetic worth. Ecker's argument, carried out in terms of ordinary language logic, is likewise an expression of this solution. An unqualified liking-statement is not an aesthetic judgment; a qualified liking-statement, such as preferences of trained artists and critics, may be. He does not make sufficiently clear, however, that the greater authority of a trained perceiver stems from knowing by past acquaintance what constitutes the authentic controls of aesthetic response. I should suggest, therefore, that we continue to add qualifications to the response and insist that only that person is a qualified judge who reacts to the specific structure of the particular art object. Since the language of aesthetic analysis is descriptive, there is always a possible means of reducing conflicts among judges adducing different reasons for their aesthetic judgments.

That this third step of qualification is necessary should be clear, since artists and critics, too, have irrational prejudices for one kind of expression over another. How else can one explain that a bad painting often wins the prize? If it is true, as Ecker argues, that the ultimate justification of aesthetic judgments is nonlinguistic, only the person having had the experience is a truly qualified judge; and only that person is capable of knowing what it means to use language to describe aesthetic facts with any degree of referential adequacy.

"Referential adequacy" is indeed a useful methodological concept. All we need now is a demonstration of successful criticism, especially of its ability "to make in some way more adequate one's perception of what is there" (Ecker, 1967, p. 7). In Dewey's terms, we have already judged the work when we have perceived it clearly. The linguistic expression of approval can do no more than to express after the fact that the experience of the work was felt to be good.

Ecker's final point, that the context of judgment varies in scope from the particular object to historically defined classificatory schemata, is likewise a useful pedagogical distinction. It serves to separate the primary from the secondary, the essential from the derivative. He does not go on to indicate, however, that the substitution of the wider context for the narrower in the instruction of art appreciation has so far had a deleterious effect on art education. If the explanatory language of history is used to replace the descriptive language of aesthetics, then we should have replaced the essential with the derivative, directly felt aesthetic quality with a vague "knowledge about" art and its institutions. No amount of historical facts can tell us what there is to like in an aesthetic experience if for any reason we have failed to have that experience.

We shall be excused, in conclusion, if we continue to insist that any information inventory scaled to measure, in general, knowledge about art terms, art media and processes, artists and their work, as well as about art history as a disciplinary methodology, poses the agonizing question of relevancy. There is no successful pedagogical alternative to the simple aesthetic questions: How is this artwork structured? What experience does it afford, structured as it is?

In this rather devious way, Eisner's poison has been turned into Ecker's meat. But the meat has yet to be digested into an understanding of a simple fact: what an artwork is determines the way in which one ought to respond.

I turn to the question of relevancy in aesthetic responses in the second section of this book, especially in Chapter 7.

4

AESTHETICS
AND THE TEACHING OF ART

This essay was first published in Studies in Art Education *(1964b) and was later reprinted in Eisner and Ecker, eds.,* Readings in Art Education *(1966). In it, the theme of this part changes to the possibility of teaching the art-making process. Can it be done?*

Once again we seek answers in formal aesthetic theory, and we find two answers to the question. Idealists, basing themselves on a theory of the imagination, and linguistic philosophers, pointing out the open-textured nature of aesthetic terms, claim the negative—the first on theoretical and the second on metatheoretical grounds; pragmatists and neo-pragmatists, interpreting the creative process as a sometimes successful attempt at "qualitative problem solving," defend the affirmative.

I side with the latter, but indicate a direction to be taken for making the claim stick. One might have thought the negative side of the argument would have been defeated by any obvious case of an art student who actually learned how to make art under the supervision of a teacher—as in the past apprentices learnt from masters. The use of a theory to prove the impossibility of a commonly observed phenomenon hardly needs refutation. But it is interesting to note why some theorists and metatheorists have been so pessimistic about teaching the creative process. The ordinary individual has no problem here; such a person merely accepts the old saw that an artist is born, not made. And who are we to argue with the wisdom of the streets?

I

The precarious position of the creative arts in the educational curriculum is a well-attested fact. Government, foundation, and university support is slow to come; and when it does, the persons who are most likely to benefit from such institutional largesse are the already established artists, who more and more are playing the role of the artist-teacher. The assumption seems to be that only the proven artist is capable of teaching other artists. And the facts of history give good reasons for making the assumption: the greatest teachers of art have been those masters whose pedagogical interest was dictated by the need for the cheap labor apprentices have always afforded. Since the subject of commissioned works was usually determined by the patron or purchaser, the master could lay out the composition of the piece and turn over the tedious task of filling in the detail to the eager student who had already mastered the techniques of his enterprising master. What was taught under these circumstances was a technique, and what was learned was formulable in a series of rules for the craft.

That this noble tradition of craftsmanlike preparation has been discredited in theory—although a quick walk through any gallery displaying a student art show is sufficient to demonstrate that it has not been discredited in fact—indicates that history has witnessed a changing conception of the role of the creative artist. Nor is this change in conception a recent phenomenon: like French politics, the more the situation changes, the more it remains the same.

The English language is full of aphorisms that indicate the intellectual bases for the changing conception. All the while enrollments in our art schools are on the increase, there is heard the reverberating echo of the anonymous cliché: artists are born, not made. And if the wisdom of the ages does not suffice to indicate the art educator's difficulty, the wit of G.B. Shaw is more mordant still: his "those who can do, and those who can't, teach," may be read as adding nothing more to the foregoing commonplace than his evaluation of those teachers who had never heard of it and who, as teachers of art, must be caught in a doubly compromising pose if the old adage is correct. Within the realm of philosophy itself, the same belief has had widespread acceptance. Plato and Kant were but two of its practitioners.

It will be remembered how Plato has Socrates con the young Ion into accepting the fact that he (Ion) interprets Homer so successfully only because he has been inspired, as the poet himself had been inspired by the muse. Ion's original claim, that he interprets the poet by rule and knowledge, is reduced to absurdity. And Kant's famous dictum, couched in his definition of genius as "the talent (or natural gift) which gives the rule to art" (1790/1951, p. 150), allows very little room for the teachability of the aesthetic sensibility. "Since talent, as the innate productive faculty of the artist, belongs itself to nature, we may express the matter thus: Genius is the innate mental disposition (*Ingenium*) through which nature gives the rule to art" (p. 150). Kant's predecessor, Baumgarten, suggested to would-be artists looking for inspiration to ride on horseback, to drink wine in moderation, or, providing they remain chaste, to contemplate beautiful women (Croce, 1909/1972, p. 103).

Multiplication of such examples would not be difficult. There seems to be a deeply felt conviction that art is a discipline that cannot be taught, even though the conviction is belied by many examples of successful artists who have learned at least the rudiments of their craft from some kind of teacher. Thus there results a problem, defined by the inconsistency between belief and action, which it is the province of philosophical analysis to clarify and of educational institutions to solve.

I shall attempt the clarification of the issues involved by examining some of the current philosophical theories concerning the nature of art that continue to militate against a consistent theoretical approach to art education—the idealistic and the linguistic, or analytic, approaches to the problem; then, after having shown the shortcomings of these views, I shall consider the claim of neo-pragmatism for having solved the noted deficiencies. My own claim is that the thesis of "qualitative problem solving" deriving from the aesthetic theory of John Dewey needs further amplification in an existential, phenomenological concept of an aesthetic object for a complete, workable theory of education in art. The remainder of this essay, then, will be devoted to these three tasks.

II

Idealism in aesthetics has as its distinctive mark a separation of the artifact—a physical thing—from "the work of art" or original idea of the artist, which is communicated to some audience via the artifact. As likely as not, an idealistic aesthetics will find the value of works of art to be expression or embodiment of feelings in a sensuous construct. The Croce–Collingwood theory of expression is perhaps the most influential of its kind.

For Croce, artists express feelings in the form of intuitions by giving form to the multitudes of impressions playing upon their psychic processes; until formed, however, the impressions remain unknown matter, a limiting concept postulated to fulfill the theoretical requirements of Croce's general philosophy of spirit. The essence of the human spirit is its activity: theoretical, in forming intuitions and concepts; and practical, in achieving ends of a particular sort (the realization of an end following its conception by a single individual) or of the general good (the working out of a moral life by the general community). The four divisions of the philosophy of the spirit are, in consequence, dedicated to aesthetics, logic, "economics," and morality. Any consideration of Croce's aesthetics that ignores the relatedness of the spheres of human activity is likely to miss the necessary connection between art and "economics," between the intuitions of an artist and his "externalization" of them, that has been the bane of professional art educators. Finally, the relation between aesthetics and logic is not without some import for the concept of education in art.

If an artist is passive before the impressions that play upon his psyche, his mind is active in giving form to them. The feelings of the impressions undergone are transmuted into feelings expressed in the intuition of individual forms. As individual, these intuited forms are not previsible, nor are they translatable into other terms; the artist, in this scheme, creates, finding "himself big with his theme, he knows not how; he feels the moment of birth drawing near, but he cannot will or not will it" (Croce, 1909/1972, p. 51). And not only can he not will his creation, whatever he does to incorporate his idea into a physical means is no longer art:

> The aesthetic fact is altogether completed in the expressive elabora-
> tion of impressions. When we have achieved the word within us,
> conceived definitely and vividly a figure or a statue, or found a mu-
> sical motive, expression is born and is complete; there is no need for
> anything else. . . . It is usual to distinguish the internal from the ex-
> ternal work of art: the terminology seems to us infelicitous, for the
> work of art (the aesthetic work of art) is always *internal*; and what is
> called *external* is no longer a work of art. (Croce, 1909/1972, pp. 50–51)

Technique considered as a means for achieving in external form the content of an internal artistic intuition represents the incursion of "economic" activity in the realm of the aesthetic. In Croce's technical terms, technique is "knowledge at the service of the practical activity directed to producing stimuli to aesthetic reproduction" (p. 111).

The complete artistic process, then, may be divided in Crocean terms into the following steps: (1) impressions, (2) expression (the spiritual aesthetic synthesis), (3) hedonistic accompaniment (pleasure of the beautiful), (4) translation of the aesthetic fact into physical phe-nomena, such as sounds, tones, movements, combinations of lines and colors, and so on. The resultant physical object then becomes a stim-ulus to the reproduction of the original expression and may be desig-nated as (5). At this point, a viewer may reverse the process by perceiving the physical phenomena, which are "together the aesthetic synthesis already produced," the resynthesis of which will produce the original hedonistic accompaniment (p. 97).

A moment's reflection on Croce's system will show both its ap-pealing and its nonappealing features. As theoretical activity, aesthetic intuitions are considered a kind of knowledge, the basis for all further knowledge given in conceptual awareness; as objects of logic, further-more, concepts are nothing more than relations between intuitions. Moreover, aesthetics is the beginning of language (the formulation and communication of an intellectual content), and as such the basis for a general science of linguistics. If all these claims are true, art is at least *worthy of* being taught. The difficulty of Croce's point of view is that his conceptual analysis of the artistic process makes it *impossible* to teach: his account leaves the relation between the internal synthesis of impressions and the construction of the physical artifact in mid air. The least we should be led to suppose is that some relationship obtains; presumably the artifact may be read as a sign or symbol of the internal spiritual act. Unfortunately, however, since the internal fact remains internal, there is actually no ground for understanding the relationship between the vision of the artist and what he or she constructs as a translation, or symbol, of it.

Collingwood takes up the theory at this point. Although admitting that art is a language having no technique, he doubts in fact that Croce's description of technique in the process of painting, which was borrowed from Kant's aesthetics, is adequate to the facts of the matter. First, Croce's (1909/1972) stand:

> It might be objected to the explanation of the physically beautiful as a simple aid to the reproduction of the internally beautiful, or expressions, that the artist creates his expressions by painting or by sculpturing, by writing or by composing, and that therefore the physically beautiful, instead of following, sometimes precedes the aesthetically beautiful. This would be a somewhat superficial mode of understanding the procedure of the artist, who never in reality makes a stroke with his brush without having previously seen it with his imagination. (p. 103)

Collingwood's (1958) transformation of this thesis may be accomplished in a series of steps. First of all, the artist expresses emotion that he has experienced without knowing what it is; in expressing the emotion, he "gets it clear." "A person expressing emotion . . . is treating himself and his audience in the same kind of way; he is making his emotions clear to his audience, and that is what he is doing to himself" (pp. 110–111). But this process is not guided by a technical analysis of the problem:

> The means-and-end, or technique terminology . . . is inapplicable. Until a man has expressed his emotion, he does not yet know what emotion it is. The act of expressing it is therefore an exploration of his own emotions. He is trying to find out what these emotions are. There is certainly here a directed process: an effort, that is, directed upon a certain end; but the end is not something foreseen and preconceived, to which appropriate means can be thought out in the light of our knowledge of its special character. Expression is an activity of which there can be no technique. (p. 111)

So far, so much agreement with Croce. The second step, where their differences begin to emerge, is Collingwood's attempt to show that in drawing a line, juxtaposing colors, and so on, painters are in fact making their emotions clear, and will not succeed in doing so unless they actually produce the lines and colors that "express" these emotions. A est for aesthetic goodness, then, is possible.

> Any theory of art should be required to show, if it wishes to be taken seriously, how an artist, in pursuing his artistic labour, is able to tell whether he is pursuing it successfully or unsuccessfully: how, for example, it is possible for him to say, 'I am not satisfied with that line; let us try it this way. . . . ' A theory which pushes the artistic experience too far down the scale, to a point below the region where experience has the character of knowledge, is unable to meet this demand. (p. 281)

Croce, it may be assumed, came too close to the line, having failed to observe, according to Collingwood, that for a painter

> the watching of his own work with a vigilant and discriminating eye, which decides at every moment of the process whether it is being successful or not, is not a critical activity subsequent to, and reflective upon, the artistic work, it is an integral part of the work itself. A person who can doubt this, if he has any grounds at all for his doubt, is presumably confusing the way an artist works with the way an incompetent student in an art-school works. (p. 281)

In short, following the suggestion of one of the interpreters of the Croce–Collingwood theory, an artist thinks with some consequence as an artist when he thinks in terms of the symbols of his medium (Hospers, 1956), and he knows that he has succeeded in his expression when his "statement" is clear.

Surely no other test is made for the teaching of the simple skills of verbal expression at whatever level of rhetorical instruction. The only difference would seem to be that, using language almost since birth, we are all most apt to perceive clarity in the use of linguistic symbols, whereas recognition of artistic clarity is learned late, if at all. What is needed, then, for an adequate curriculum in the education of art, is a well-founded theory of aesthetic judgment that would enable both teacher and student to perceive the clarity of a successful aesthetic expression.

The artist's work ends when the artist judges that the work is good and there is no reason to assume that the viewer judges it any differently: the guarantee that this judgment is the same would be the fact that both artist and viewer consider the artistic object in terms of the symbols of the medium used to make the expression and the clarity of the statement made. What a philosopher of art has to contribute to the curriculum of art students is a way of justifying the validity of artistic expressions. Whether or not technique can be learned, and whether or not technique is relevant to the activity of the artist, only that part of an artist's technique that has produced the object of judgment will have an effect upon the judgment of the object.

In sum, idealist aesthetics has failed art educators in that it has situated the work of art in an artist's head, where it can never be judged; has declared irrelevant any artistic techniques for the construction of physical analogues to the "work of art," which might be judged; and has, even in Collingwood, produced no clear-cut statement of the manner in which artist and audience do in fact judge the success or nonsuccess of aesthetic expressions. A corrective to the idealist separation of artifact and work of art would be possible only if it could be shown that technique is not irrelevant to art, but necessary, and so closely correlated with the forming activity of the artist that no distinction may be drawn between technique and form. This is the position maintained in the experimentalist aesthetics of John Dewey; but before considering the manner in which Dewey's theory is being treated by contemporary art educators, it behooves us to examine the case of the linguistic philosophers against the teachability of art.

III

Morris Weitz is one of the philosophers in our own time who tried to establish the conditions necessary for judging the excellence of expressions. His early answer to the problem was couched in terms of an aesthetic theory of "organicism," a theory for judging the excellence of expression on the basis of the maximal relatedness of the elements contributing to an integral experience (Weitz, 1950). Following a study of the logic of discourse about art, however, he disavowed his prior work, along with all other traditional attempts at aesthetic theory. His second point of view was most forcefully presented in his Matchette Prize–winning essay, "The Rôle of Theory in Aesthetics" (1956). There he claims that all theory about art, whether it be his own or that of others—"formalism, voluntarism, emotionalism, intellectualism, intuitionism, organicism"(p. 27)—is based upon a mistake, upon the attempt to list a set of conditions both necessary and sufficient for defining the concept "art." His own denial of such a possibility is as strongly put as one dare:

> Aesthetic theory—all of it—is wrong in principle in thinking that a
> correct theory is possible because it radically misconstrues the logic

of the concept of art. Its main contention that "art" is amenable to real or any kind of true definition is false. Its attempts to discover the necessary and sufficient properties of art is logically misbegotten for the very simple reason that such a set and, consequently, such a formula about it, is never forthcoming. Art, as the logic of the concept shows, has no set of necessary and sufficient properties, hence a theory of it is logically impossible and not merely factually difficult. Aesthetic theory tries to define what cannot be defined in the requisite sense. (pp. 27–28)

Hence, instead of a fixed, "closed" concept capable of precise application to all works of art, empirical observation of the matter suggests an open concept applicable to many different sorts of objects that may resemble each other is some ways and yet contain significantly different aspects one from the other and each from the class. There is no essence, or nature, of art, but only a "family resemblance" of many things alike enough to be compared and different enough to be seriously contrasted. In conclusion, "to understand the role of aesthetic theory is not to conceive it as definition, logically doomed to failure, but to read it as summaries of seriously made recommendations to attend in certain ways to certain features of art" (p. 35). Thus, if a certain concept cannot be precisely defined, if its nature cannot be stipulated, then it cannot be taught in the most strict interpretation of conveying knowledge concerning objects of our inquiry; all one need do is point to outstanding cases in which the term is used properly—either descriptively or normatively—to cover "paradigm" cases in order to discover what is meant when we use the term.

So far, so good; but the student would feel extremely ill at ease, if not flattered beyond all bounds, if the instructor were to point to one of the student's works as a paradigm case for the application of the term *art* in its normative sense. The logic of the concept of "paradigm" precludes this possibility—unless the instructor were capable of justifying that evaluation in terms of an experience of the work's excellence; and note, please, that the instructor is likewise precluded from comparing the student's work with some other paradigm case, for in such an instance two difficulties would arise: (1) if the student's work is comparable to the paradigm case, then the student work is derivative; and (2) unless the instructor is capable of establishing the validity of the chosen paradigm case, nothing is learned for the comparison. I conclude, therefore, that Weitz's prize essay is a mistake; and its basic mistake is the assumption that we can learn anything about the concept of art merely by inquiring into the manner in which people actually use the term. But this would seem to suggest only that linguistic analysis must be based upon something more primitive if it is to be deemed an alternative to an aesthetic theory: if linguistic analysis is to be useful within the context of art education, it must be grounded in a method of aesthetic analysis—that is to say, the analysis of the language of aesthetic discourse needs fulfillment in the analysis of the referents of such discourse.

Discourse about discourse is futile unless there is good ground for assuming that we are capable of recognizing when discourse is being used properly in the first instance. And the only way to judge whether a term is being used correctly is to examine the nature of the experience the term is intended to designate. Instead, therefore, of replacing aesthetics of the traditional kind, Weitz's second thoughts on the matter merely serve to point out the importance of finding an adequate aesthetic terminology applicable in the first instance. It is ironical that someone should be awarded a prize for discovering what Immanuel Kant had already written in 1790, that aesthetic judgment is reflective, not determinant. In contemplating a work of art, we are presented with an object for which no concept is adequate (Kant, 1790/1951).

Still, analytic philosophers are fond of pointing out the fact that real or true definitions are impossible to find. According to their preferred manner of proceeding, only family resemblances can be found for the application of terms, not essences of things capable of definition according to the strictly logical requirements set down in a list of necessary and sufficient conditions. It is perhaps appropriate to point out that Croce (1909/1972), idealist and definer that he was, was convinced of the same fact. Heeding the distinction of Kant between logical and reflective judgments, he wrote:

> Resemblances exist, and by means of them, works of art can be arranged in this or that group. But they are likenesses such as are observed among individuals, and can never be rendered with abstract determinations. That is to say, it would be incorrect to apply identification, subordination, co-ordination and the other relations of concepts to these resemblances, which consist wholly of what is called a *family likeness*, derived from the historical conditions in which the various works have appeared and from relationships of soul among artists. (p. 73)

The same kind of family resemblances, it might be noted, are to be found among the sciences. That is, the logic of the concept of science admits of no more certainty in individual applications of the term than does that of art; and no one has as yet stepped forward as a defender of the proposition that, for this reason, the philosophy of science rests upon a mistake. Yet the philosophy of science and the philosophy of art are strictly analogous as intellectual disciplines. If one is impossible, then so is the other. I conclude that "philosophical analysis" has yet to refute the claims of Croce's aesthetics, or for that matter, of his logic. The point is simply that there is much work to be done on the concept "work of art"; and, if one may dare say so, equally as much work on the "object of scientific investigation"—as much on what constitutes an acceptable scientific theory as on what constitutes an acceptable theory of art. The fiction that the way people ordinarily use aesthetic terms, or learn how to use the terms, is a solution of the problems involved is a bald deception.

Consider the case of scientific objects. The concepts we use to designate them are no less open textured than is the concept of "art," even in the evaluative sense of the two terms involved. It is apparent that, descriptively, astronomy is a science, and so are physics and biology. But not all critics are agreed on the propriety of the concept for covering such fledgling sciences as anthropology, sociology, and economics. There are family resemblances among all the sciences, as there are among the arts, but no essence anyone would call "science" unequivocally. What corresponds to the normative terms of aesthetics within the discipline of scientific behavior, on the other hand, is the notion of truth, or perhaps verified law. Both "truth" and "law" are equally open-textured concepts; no less so than "beauty" and "successful expression."

The nature of truth varies with the frame of discursive reference—in Humean terms, with whether statements relate our ideas or record our observations of matters of fact; and even within the area of facts alone, some hypotheses are considered "laws" if they summarize different areas of observation and predict wider ranges of future observations. One can only infer that if scientific discipline is thought to be more teachable than the artistic, one is misusing a term: if not *artistic*, then *scientific*, as the case may be.

The discovered laws of traditional science are, of course, teachable; and they can be used to make utilitarian objects, as the law for the conservation of energy or, variously, the conversion of matter into energy could be and was used in the construction of the atomic bomb. But this kind of scientific teaching reads the word *scientific* to mean "technological." If my analogy is correct, some artistic styles can be taught in the same manner; but if they are, this kind of artistic teaching reads the word *artistic* to mean "industry," as Kant (1790/1951) so correctly put the matter so long ago.

The result of this analogous reasoning, of course, is not to indicate that Weitz is wrong in his central contention: "art" is an open-textured concept. His ultimate mistake is based upon the faulty conclusions he draws from this banal fact. The first was to demand a logical rigor—the stipulation of the necessary and sufficient conditions for the application of a term; stating such conditions for the definition of an entity is perhaps possible only in the formal disciplines of mathematics and logic, where the notion of a "real" or "true" definition may be interpreted as making some sense in that they would be limited to those entities created by the relations of our ideas. The second fallacy was in supposing that if such definition is impossible, the instruction of art, and *mutatis mutandis* of science itself, is therefore impossible.

When a concept is open-textured the only conclusion to be drawn is that each individual case must be considered in terms of the experience it affords and how the human subject behaves in controlling the experience. It is true, for example, that theoretical controls are relatively more fixed in scientific behavior than in artistic; but no one yet has given a logical explanation of the formation of a workable hypothesis. At rock bottom, they may be nothing more than hunches or lucky guesses, not to say complete accidents of an experimental situation. Whatever they are, they are discoveries of the ongoing inquiry; just as in the Croce–Collingwood theory, works of art are the discoveries of the artistic expression.

An idealist like Croce would interpret the concurrence of these two phenomena as an indication of the fact that the imagination must function even in the controlled experiments of basic scientists. The only difference from the behavior of the "lucky" artist (or pregnant one, as one prefers), is that the model which comes to form in the scientist's mind is capable, if successful, of being applied to many repeatable instances, whereas the intuition of an artist is of a unique, unrepeatable object, which lesser critics may then take as a "paradigm case" or touchstone by which to judge other such expressions.

IV

The most influential of the recent American thinkers to give a great deal of thought to both the scientific and the artistic process of human creativity is John Dewey. His model of a five-step process of human behavior in problem solving indicates that an individual observes a situation, discovers and refines a problem, considers and compares alternative, hypothetical solutions, and tests them in thought and in action (1910). "Inquiry," which is Dewey's name for the process of problem solving, is obviously an open concept; the situation determines what the inquirer is to observe and what he *must do* if his hypotheses are to be verified. But in each case, it is the experience of the problem, and of the observed predictions, made on the basis of the hypothesis, which determines the particular character of the solution: its workability or nonworkability; hence its "truth" or "falsity."

At this point it may be of some import to indicate the obvious comparisons with the preceding approaches to aesthetics. If the analogy between "science" and "art" is maintained, as Dewey insists that it must, there is no longer any basis for the distinction between "theory" and "practice" as Croce draws it. Scientists must do something to their situations in order to gain knowledge. Any solution to a problem that is merely anticipated is only tentative; it must work out in experience in order to be accepted. As Collingwood put it, artists, in order to get their emotions straight, must think with the counters of their media by manipulating them in context.

The most explicit statement of the analogy I have been suggesting between the work of the scientist and that of the artist has already been elaborated to some extent by Francis Villemain, Nathaniel Champlin, and David Ecker. The latter's essay "The Artistic Process as Qualitative Problem Solving" (1963) puts in succinct compass the theoretical problem of conceiving the manner in which an artist solves qualitative problems. In short, it contains a philosophical presentation of the *process* of art. Now since talk about the artistic process is truly a theoretical affair, if the talk is an accurate description of what happens in general when an artist works, the case will have been made for the possibility of education in the art-creative process. The only question remaining, then, is whether Ecker's essay appropriately covers the situation involved.

The crux of Ecker's problem was to find an analogue within "the artistic process as qualitative problem solving" for the role played in the theoretical problem solving of the basic scientist by the successful hypothesis: a workable means of summarizing and predicting observed or observable data. Dewey had already indicated in the essay referred to above that a "pervasive quality" permeates every situation recognizable as such; just as the laws of logic by which inferences are drawn from the supposed truth of an hypothesis may be said to "control" our theoretical analyses of scientific problem solving, so, says Ecker, the controls of qualitative problem solving derive from the relatedness between component qualities and the pervasive quality defining the artistic situation (1963).

In the completed analogy, Ecker finds six steps are needed to capture the essence of Dewey's five-step process of "reflective thought." (1) An artist is said to begin with a *presented relationship* between the counters of the medium being worked with (line to line, line to color, color to line, color to color, and so on). In this phase, thinking with his materials, the artist may only be "playing around with" the symbols of his craft. (2) Next is *substantive mediation*, in which certain emerging relations tend to dominate; certain choices are destroyed, others opened up. (3) In the *determination of pervasive control*, a single dominant qualitative relationship emerges: "'Components' of a unique end-in-view gain identity as such by virtue of the envisioned total quality now emerging" (p. 289). And this quality may be either a traditionally definable style, or "it may be unique as a total which itself becomes a pervasive or control quality for future orderings, i.e. the appearance of a new style . . ." (p. 289). The hypothesis (of the analogy) is now present. There follow the steps of (4) *qualitative prescription:* from here on, only those components consistent with the envisioned pervasive quality are acceptable choices; through (5) *experimental exploration*, while one continues to work the medium in exploration of the possibilities of the pervasive quality; to (6) the conclusion, *the total quality*, or finished work of art.

Ecker's lucubrations on the process of artistic thought constitute a clear-cut gain over the two theoretical approaches evaluated above. In showing how what the artist does is necessary to what an artist thinks in making a work of art, he obviates some (but not all) of the difficulties attending the distinction between technique and inspiration, thus vitiating the idealist's aesthetic as a tool for educational theory. Likewise, since he is not averse to making some general prescriptions for the achievement of controls in artistic thought, he has more to offer art educators than an idea of "what to look for" as indicated by the more traditional aesthetic theories of representation (imitation), form, emotion, and the like. Any further evaluation of his description of artistic problem solving must come from an inquiry into the adequacy of his six-step process to cover our notions of what an expressive, or successful, artistic object is and does: we must cast further light on the function of the object itself as it controls our vision. It will come as no surprise, then, that the nub of the new problem is to weigh the relative importance of steps (3) "determination of pervasive control" and (6) "the total quality" of the work of art.

Ecker's statement that pervasive control is formally determined and recognizable as a "style"—either of the tradition or of a new mannerism that may be further elaborated into a tradition of its own—is the first questionable point. He illustrates his thesis with examples of work by Henry Moore, Pablo Picasso, Paul Cézanne, Piet Mondrian, and Saul Horowitz. In the work of the first four artists, we are presented with the total quality (photographically abstracted into value discriminations only), while the work of the latter is presented so as to make the pervasive quality visible in various stages of the work's completion.

Why is the pervasive style, or quality, that is already established easier to achieve than the invention of a new? And why are there good and bad paintings achieved in the various styles, whether old or new? The grounds for the second of these questions seem fairly well attested in the history of art; the grounds for the first, in the paucity of artists who might truly be said to have initiated new and significant developments in the arts. *Prima facie*, then, the questions appear meaningful for our inquiry.

In giving an answer to them, as consistently as possible with Ecker's schema of creation in the painterly arts, one could say that the pervasive quality, although effective as a means for ordering relations of (component) qualities toward an end-in-view, has failed in the case of unsuccessful paintings to yield an end-in-view (the total quality) worth the ordering. Thus it is the total quality of the piece that guides or controls the decision of the artist to cease "experimental exploration," not the pervasive quality, which, from the point of view of the total expressive object, is only another of the components currently existing; this quality constantly changes throughout the experimental exploration until finally, when the artist decides the work is done, the total quality becomes the final pervasive quality of the piece. This is the case I shall try to make in interpreting the series of stages in the development of Horowitz's painting (see Figure 4.1).

As a parenthesis, it may now be stated that Ecker has not so much solved the problem of the idealists as indicated where in the process of painting it really occurs; for in distinguishing technique from inspiration the idealists were only making the point that before a work is achieved (in the mind, for Croce; on the canvas, for Collingwood) there is no way of ordering physical means for the attainment of an end, even if we call that end an "end-in-view." To claim that it exists only "in-view" is to admit with the idealists that it exists only in the creative imagination. This process of envisaging, imagining, or perceiving an end remains as mysterious in the neo-pragmatic scheme as it appeared in the idealistic theories examined above. And, surely, it is for this reason that it is easier to recognize and to judge (the token with respect to the type) an existing style than to explain the expressiveness of an entirely new and different work of art.

V

For the clue to our interpretation, let us start with the analogy being pursued. In Dewey's scheme, thinking arises in an unsettled and

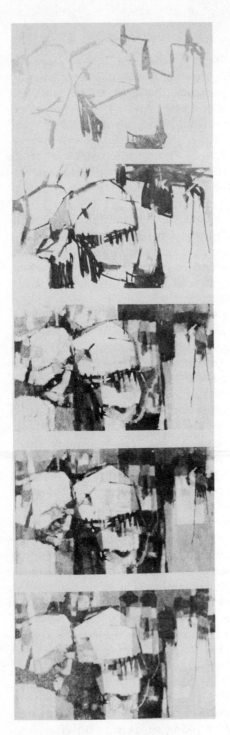

FIGURE 4.1
Five stages of a painting
by Saul Horowitz.

Reprinted from *The Journal of Aesthetics
and Art Criticism,* vol. 21, no. 3 (Spring,
1963). Used by permission of the American Society for Aesthetics.

ends in a settled situation. To be accurate in our rendering of his thought within an artistic frame of reference, the perception of the finished status of the art object must correspond to the settledness of the problematic situation; the final perception must in some sense satisfy the inquirer that his or her initial problem is solved. Thus the workability of the hypothesis and the success of the expression are the correlates standing in analogous relation. Since the success of the scientific hypothesis is to be judged in action, there is no reason to suppose that the success of the total expressiveness of the artwork is to be judged in any other way. In other words, both kinds of situations must be lived, or experienced, if the problem is first to be felt and if the hypothesis or final pervasive quality of both kinds of situation is then to succeed in settling the respective kinds of problem. Judgment, then, must begin with the experience of the finished quality of every problematic situation; and to be able to judge we can do no better than follow the phenomenologist's prescription to go back to the things themselves as they appear to our vision, that is, the phenomena of the problematic situation.

Accordingly, let us look at the series of steps in the development of Saul Horowitz's painting (refer to Figure 4.1). Ecker (1963) is firm in his statement: "Here is a sequence of photographs of a painting by Saul Horowitz. All of the stages of the painting are not shown. However, the qualities of the final painting *are* present in the beginning sketch" (p. 288; italics in original). But what appears to our vision? What is the case? Are all the qualities of the final painting present in the beginning sketch? Not to my vision; nor, I would wager, to the vision of the artist at this stage of the painting's development. The final painting, of course, contains the "total quality," but at what stage is the pervasive quality of the whole first apparent? One might be forgiven for assuming that the pervasive quality is present in the first exposure, since the qualities of the last are supposed to be in the first. But that would be an error of visual judgment. The first stage is at most an experience of three planes: the greyish background, the blackish lines and forms appearing on the ground, and the space tensional plane between. Although in the last stage the first two of these planes are still *generally* visible, a great deal has been done to them, as well as to the interstitial space tensional plane.

In the final stage, the background no longer serves as ground; it is no longer a single plane. It has been modified by the addition of other forms on the various receding planes (the variety of the planes being determined by the relative value discriminations in the variety of forms placed between the initial fore- and backgrounds), so that it appears as if it were a light perceived from behind the picture-plane. What one perceives of it is now controlled by the action of the interposed solid black or deeper grey forms. The point is that the ground now functions in a way different from the way it did in the first exposure. There, it appeared as a deep space against which the action of the lines is set. And, to bring this analysis to some kind of end, these original lines have been lost as lines acting against the inert grey of the original ground, and even for the most part as interacting with each other as tensional forces on the same plane, since they now serve to create space as outlines of solid forms where they are visible to all.

My suspicion is that Ecker has judged the painting as a "flat" design rather than for what it is and does to our creative vision. And if this is true, it would be more proper to say that some of the linear action taking place on the first plane as it is constituted in the first stage of the painting has been retained in the last, but what has been lost is more significant for the total quality of the work than what is retained. Since the work is nonobjective, no "depth" or representational elements appear. The sensuous surface of the painting has, however, undergone a complete transformation from the beginning to the last stage.

The pervasive quality and the total quality of the *painting* (in its finished state) are the same; and neither is apparent until the work has been achieved. Dewey, it will be recalled, maintained that *every* situation is known by virtue of its pervasive quality—the moodal sense of wholeness within which we are capable of making distinctions and marking associations. Only when the painting has been achieved could it be imitated or copied in many variations and thus become a "pervasive or control quality for future orderings" (Ecker, 1963, p. 289). But then, future orderings will produce other pervasive (or final) qualities. An idealist, in interpreting these scribblings, would be tempted to say that the pervasive (total) quality of the painting is *implicit* in the first stage and *explicit* only in the last. Furthermore, we judge that a quality is implicit in a situation only by grasping an *imaginary* modification of the given situation; and all explicit qualities are immediately visible to our *perceptive* faculties.

The trick, of course, is to be able to grasp imaginatively those modifications of a given situation that will enable a painter to perceive that a total satisfying situation has been achieved. What takes place between the first strokes on a virgin canvas and the final perception is precisely the essence of painting. Many mistakes will be made, and some of them will be erased; but which strokes are mistaken and how they are to be erased is still a matter of aesthetic judgment. If, there-

fore, the aesthetician has anything to offer an art educator in this matter, it will be a procedure for judging an object of art—no matter at
which stage of development that object happens to be. The only requirement for being able to judge a visual object is that it be visible.
And it is for this reason that a painter must know what constitutes the
visibility of things seen (Kaelin, 1965).

In sum, the neo-pragmatic description of the *artistic process* demands completion by a phenomenological account of visibility. It is the
appearance of structures within a visual field—the description of which
is missing in Ecker's account—that is the *product* of art to be judged: if
not by the painter, then at least by critics, who may not be so kind, but
who are most assuredly informed enough to know that the process and
the products of art are not totally independent phenomena.

5

WHY TEACH ART
IN THE PUBLIC SCHOOLS?

Where the previous essays were written to justify the instruction in the arts on the basis of the institutional effects of creation and criticism, on the basis, that is, of the internal functioning of aesthetic communications media, this essay takes the tack of following out the by-products of creative communication. It was composed to answer the question, What benefit may accrue to the society that permits the free functioning of its aesthetic institutions? In a nutshell, our educational system should be expected to produce the kind of citizens the society needs to function as it must. Depending upon the carry-over effect of public instruction, this sort of consequence may be called an "external" social benefit, since although it is produced by the exercise of the processes of creative communication, it is felt within the other behavioral patterns institutionalized within the general society.

The essay was originally published in the twentieth-anniversary issue of The Journal of Aesthetic Education *(1986). Its argument may be compared to my earlier "The Educational Function of the Fine Arts," Chapter 2 in this collection. The similarities in these last two essays could be attributed to the profession's propensity for reinventing the wheel. However that may be, this essay is more concisely expressed than the former, which appeared in 1960; and reconsidering the argument of the older essay has allowed me to relate it to the newer "institutional theory of art."*

I

When it comes to answering questions, art educators have always been better at their staples—What should we teach? To whom? In what sequence?—than with finding some kind of answer to the question superintendents of schools find still more basic, Why teach art at all?

In the grip of any imaginable budget crunch, no one charged with making the decision would continue to face his or her constituency with no better answer to this one than the supposition that artworks and the arts are nice to have, like flowers on a lady's Easter bonnet or the lights on a Christmas tree. We think we know why, in every move back to the basics of education, we strengthen our instruction in reading, writing, and basic mathematics. These core studies are necessary for entrance into the study of the sciences, where the knowledge produced has that rare capacity of exhibiting on its face the very social utility it is the business of public instruction to promulgate. Why should we not argue that teaching art in the public schools is good for enhancing our society's culture? Indeed, we might, as I did in the previous essay; but we could not let it stand at that. For either we are engaging in tautologies, which give us no new information, or we continue to assume that culture is some kind of good in itself, concerning which there is no point in posing question of utility.

Do we mean by "culture" only the making and appreciating of works of art in the various media? If so, we have the tautology. If culture is a good in itself, questioning its utility deserves the same kind of response Louis Armstrong is reported to have given the aficionado who asked, What is jazz?—If you have to ask, you will never know. Puritans ask because they fear the "immorality" of art; so do Philistines, who find it useless in an economy of personal power, as do our proletarian folk, who see in it only a personal luxury, good only for the idle rich (Parker, 1920/1945).

In what follows, I shall argue the paradoxical case that what is good about the arts is the aesthetic experiences they provide—the case of art for the sake of art—in an attempt to show that society stands to gain most by allowing its institutions to function freely, as they are designed to function, for the purpose of liberating the human impulse to masterful self-expression.

Perhaps a little bit more quickly than it should have been, my hand has been played. Art does have a function, and more than one at that; just as sex has a function, and more than one at that. When George Bernard Shaw referred to marriage as the most licentious of our institutions, he had in mind the power of the institution to liberate the libidinal energies of the people who enter into it by contract for that specific purpose; and no one who understands the arrangements permitted by the contract is shocked by the comedian's insinuations. His barb is comic only because it states an ultimate truth concerning our society and the place of individuals seeking fulfillment within its institutions, that these have been established for the purpose of permitting the achievement of deeply felt personal values—sexual gratification in this case—at the same time society stands to gain from the regulation of the behavior that, outside of the institutionally permitted framework, may have disastrous effects on that society, such as an increasing teenage pregnancy rate and the corresponding increase in

abortions, foundlings in need of homes, or young women tied as single parents to the nurture of their offspring.

These consequences, like some others mostly medical, such as the
increase in uncontrollable sexually transmitted diseases, call for social
control in other institutions: in the courts, where women's rights to
control their own bodies may someday be settled; in the procedures for
adoption; in improved day-care centers; and, finally, in the profession
of medicine in all its functions: in the healing and the prevention of
disease and in the basic research that makes the other two possible.

Can there be an "institutional definition of 'art' "? And what would
be its consequence for art education? For the second time in this essay, I shall cite the aesthetics of DeWitt H. Parker (1920/1945): "Since
. . . art is a social phenomenon, we shall have to draw upon our
knowledge of social psychology to illumine our analysis of the individual's [aesthetic] experience" (p. 7). The question comes down ultimately to the relations between an individual's impulse to action (of a
certain type) and a set of institutions within our society that give form
to this impulse.

II

It may come as a surprise to some students of aesthetics to be re-
minded that Parker's suggestion was made as early as 1920, the year of
the first edition of his *Principles of Aesthetics* (1920/1945). He, of course,
was intent upon describing the necessary psychological component
within the study of aesthetics, and he sensed that the "mental facts" of
the aesthetic discipline were influenced by the habits and customs of
groups to respond in correlatively similar ways to apparently similar
stimuli. I mention the fact almost in passing; for the irony of the matter is that it fell to a student of Parker, the late Morris Weitz, to produce the impetus for the current drive toward an "institutional
definition of 'art.' "

The move was curious in that Parker's initial essentialism was reflected in Weitz's early *Philosophy of the Arts* (1950), in which the author argued for an "organic theory of aesthetic expression." In spite of
the success of that treatise, Weitz later fell under the influence of Wittgenstein, following a tour to England, and published the essay that was
to determine a new direction of aesthetic inquiry in American letters.
He argued, in "The Rôle of Theory in Aesthetics" (1956), that art was
an open concept and hence could not be defined by a set of necessary
and sufficient conditions that would govern its use in a theoretical context; consequently, all attempts at aesthetic theorizing, including his

own prior attempt, should be interpreted as so many suggestions of what might be found in our cursory examinations of works of art, which, like "games," would exhibit a nest of characteristics possessing "family resemblances" between one another but never an essential characteristic shared by everything so-called.

It was Maurice Mandelbaum (1965), responding in general to the Wittgensteinian confusion of "exhibited" and merely "relational" characteristics of works of art, who examined the various forms the notion of the open concept of art had taken in recent analytic aesthetics. He criticized the work of Paul Ziff, imputing to him an implicit theory of art in his identification of Poussin's *Rape of the Sabine Women* as an obviously good work of art; of Weitz, for confusing the issue of defining works of art with foreclosure on the use of a concept; and of P.O. Kristeller, for his confusion of the issue of a possible classification of the arts with the possibility of a viable aesthetic theory. Of all these criticisms, it was the distinction between "exhibited" and "nonexhibited," or relational characteristics, that produced the theoretical consequences of note.

Two primary examples of these consequences are so similar that they have become interpreted as a single theory. I am referring, of course, to the so-called "Danto–Dickie institutional theory" of art (Danto, 1964, 1973; Dickie, 1979, 1984).

Danto had appealed to the "relational" characteristics of artworks as differentiating between impostures and fakes on the one hand, and copies on the other, and between both of these and original works of art. He reasoned that if there were no necessary and sufficient conditions for the correct employment of an aesthetic concept, there seemed to be at least two "defeasible conditions" for attributing or ascribing the condition of art to certain artifacts. For example, if the artifact is a fake painting, it is essentially not a work of art; it does not deserve the name, since it "makes no artistic statement." Likewise, if the artifact is not the product of an artist—but of a child, a chimpanzee, or a copyist—it should not be considered a work of art. What makes art of an artifact is its entrance into the "artworld," the institutional complex within which *bona fide* works of art receive the ascription of art much in the same way a child becomes a "Christian" at baptism. That an artifact be considered a work of art, even in the classificatory sense of the term, means only that someone has conferred upon it by the outward sign of permitting its entrance into the artworld the inner grace that stems from the work's making an artistic statement (Dickie, 1979).

Accepting the fact that the status of being a work of art may be conferred by the relational properties of certain artifacts to enter into socially determined relationships, George Dickie propounded his own "institutional definition" of a work of art (1984). Although he at first thought that even artifactuality could be conferred upon a work of art, since some *objets trouvés* were admitted by the artworld to be authentic works of art without having been specifically fashioned into the form in which they were exhibited as such, Dickie later insisted that the classificatory genus of artworks was indeed their artifactuality (since any change in the context within which such works are exhibited changes the very nature of the object viewed in the newer context), and in consequence, only the special status attributed to some artifacts by members of the artworld can be socially conferred upon works of art— just as the baptized infant changes from a state of original sin to a state of acquired grace through the passage of the cleansing waters.

The point here, as at the baptismal font, is only that someone authorized to make the conferral has indeed conferred the proper status upon the subject or object in question. For artifacts, what is conferred is the status of being a "candidate for appreciation." Three additional determinants of the "conferral" are required for artifacts to be recognized as works of art: that it be performed by someone speaking in the name of the artworld; that the work be declared worthy of aesthetic appreciation; and that others accede to the judgment of the artworld representative that the work is indeed worthy of contemplation. Together, these relational properties of artworks constitute the specific difference needed to complete the canonic form of an Aristotelian definition.

I do not wish to confute the claims made by the Danto–Dickie theory of art, nor to question why our theoretical definitions need take an Aristotelian form. I merely wish to point out that no one has as yet attempted, to my knowledge, to reap full benefits of an institutional account of artworks. The new approach, as indicated above, grew out of the frustrations felt by aestheticians in failing to come up some viable definition of any sort for works of art. What Dickie found in Danto was, as he called it, the beginning of the third phase of the problem of defining "art," a change from the "dreary and superficial definitions" of the pre-Wittgensteinian aesthetic theorizing (phase I) through the absolute denial of the possibility of a theoretical definition, as in Ziff and Weitz (phase II). The gambit opened here is phase III, and it was established by Mandelbaum's criticism of phase II of this historical development within traditional aesthetic theory.

Perhaps Dickie's greatest obstacle was the opposition of his colleagues to accepting the term *institution* in the way he insisted it should be employed, that is, as an established practice, law, or custom. If he is right, what makes a work of art a work of art is the network of behavioral patterns by which its status as an artwork has been conferred upon it, beginning with criticism and (sometimes) ending in exhibition in a public place, where an audience may repair to appreciate it, even to judge whether a mistake had been made by the initial conferral of status. But such a judgment is obviously only another example of artistic criticism, as informed or uninformed as it might be.

We may generalize Dickie's definition, it seems to me, by postulating the existence of an aesthetic institution, as I have been doing in these essays, whether we call it "the artworld" or not, that is similar in structure to religious, educational, legal, medical, and similar institutions, which have as their purpose both to permit and to regulate the behavioral patterns constituting the formal practices of producing, criticizing, exhibiting, and appreciating works of art. In this way, the work of art is viewed as the vehicle by which the aesthetic motivations of individuals come to be expressed in a social context. Making the work constitutes a gesture (of establishing its artifactuality); responding to it gives it its aesthetic significance, as recorded in the conferral of the status. When, moreover, the person making the gesture and the person perceiving it respond in similar ways, we may say that communication has taken place.

Danto, we recall, thought it was necessary for a work of art "to make a statement"; his analysis of the "artworld" indicates that making an artistic statement is no simple matter but rather requires a series of roles, each defining the other in their relationship, that allow individuals to enter into the social fabric of human institutions where their behavior becomes mutually communicative and significant. Indeed, what we call a "society" is from one point of view—the social interactionist— a nexus of such institutions making overlapping and sometimes conflicting claims on the behavior of individuals pursuing the values embodied within the practices permitted and regulated by the institutions. George Bernard Shaw may have been right, but we had already learned all the theoretical background to his jibe by reading G.H. Mead's *Mind, Self and Society from the Standpoint of a Social Behaviorist* (1934).

III

It is at this point that art educators may pick up the thread. In one sense, of course, we must educate both teachers and students of the arts to perform according to their various rôles in the schools, themselves institutions of our society. What I am proposing is that we allow students to play the role of artists, to make something of interest to them that may be of interest to someone else. The aesthetic institution exists for the purpose of creating the maximum of aesthetic value. But "making an artistic statement," or making a gesture that is to become a candidate for aesthetic appreciation, necessitates the complementary role of critic. That is the role proper to the teacher, whose appreciation must be informed with a set of workable aesthetic categories, not only out of fairness to the student artist but also as a guarantee for the effectiveness of his or her own participation in the communicative process.

By way of illustration, consider the range one might find in student works. It is certainly to be expected that this range will already have been exhibited in the history of the art under consideration—from totally nonobjective works, exhibiting only the Gestalt properties of sensuous elements; to superrealistic works that attempt to represent natural objects such as they appear to our natural perception; to abstract works, in which natural objects are represented in such a way as to emphasize the sensuous values of the medium used to make the representations. All these may be candidates for our aesthetic appreciation, but it seems nothing but fair, on the part of our teachers, that they be able to explain the categories they have used to make their critical judgments. Aesthetics, as the criticism of criticism, and art history make their formal entry into the aesthetic education process at this point.

For those readers already familiar with the movement, it should be clear that my institutional account gives some credence to the new "discipline-based art education program" now being developed by the Getty Foundation. That program considers four arts-related disciplines to constitute the domain of art education: art production, art history, aesthetics, and criticism. A "discipline" is given the contextual definition as being constituted by three component elements: (1) a corps of expert practitioners, (2) a body of knowledge and concepts, and (3) a formulizable set of principles for making an inquiry into the domain of art.

But it seems clear upon reflection that the four disciplines mentioned exemplify these three components in uneven and different ways. We can avoid the charge of making art production look too much like the other arts-related disciplines—especially with respect to their rule-governed behavior—if we merely agree to take the institutional point of view that the producers of art participate in the aesthetic institution by playing a distinctive role and that this role finds its complement in those of the critic, aesthetician, and historian.

One simple change is being requested—that we stop envisaging ourselves as "experts" whose educational practice is to teach a subject discipline. What we actually do is to teach students, either children or adults, with the aid of a complementary set of knowledge bases, each of which has been established by a history of codifiable behavioral practices. That is what makes it possible for them to become functioning rôles within the aesthetic institution.

IV

What then would be the purpose of promulgating the aims of the aesthetic institution in the public schools?

If social interactionism may be introduced as the theory by which our educational practices are to be justified, the answer now seems clearer, if not totally perspicuous. Promoting the conditions for the creation and appreciation of novel significance within the aesthetic institution will have educational benefits no other "discipline" can provide so well. Let us only agree that we learn by doing something and that doing something in repeated patterns produces a habit. We conclude that the good of aesthetic education is to be found in the habits it inculcates. And what are these?

For an answer to this question, consider only two further characteristics of the creative communicative process.

The first is that aesthetic activity engages our sensibility, not for its own sake, but for its connection with the vague feelings controlled by the subtle tonal differences perceptible by our senses; that it engages our imaginations to view objects and ideas under the guise of the manner in which they have been represented in successful works of art, and, so, to control our depth feelings associated with the objects of our natural environment. But whether the artwork be nonobjective, representational, or to some degree abstract, the value of experiencing such objects is the enjoyment of the feelings, either of a vague or a depth nature, *only as these feelings are controlled by the vehicle of expression.*

Doubtlessly, there is a whole theory of aesthetics embedded in these assertions (already discussed in my "The Educational Function of the Fine Arts," Chapter 2 of this volume). But what that theory allows us to perceive is that the ultimate social product of the aesthetic institution is not more works of art, even as candidates for aesthetic appreciation, but the type of person capable of appreciating works of art with the appropriate critical attitude. For want of a better term, I call such persons "defanaticized." The value of a defanaticized consciousness to the general society, when that society is democratic, seems as patent to me as that of the research scientist whose work allows us to solve the problems of our everyday living by making clear what results can be expected to follow upon sets of given conditions.

My second consideration is merely to point out that pursuing art for art's sake is the same as to allow the free function of the aesthetic institution within our society. Like all the other institutions, it is both permissive and regulatory: it permits the maximal pursuit of novel significance, and it regulates the way in which such significance comes to be appreciated, through informed criticism.

V

At this stage I hope I have made my case that teaching art in the public school makes perfectly good sense, if only we view it as an institution by which complementary social roles guide individual conduct. Because the habits promulgated within this institution are nowhere else so readily attainable, to exclude the arts from the curricula of our schools is to deprive ourselves of an obvious social good— a wider range of citizens capable of whatever kind of behavior is permitted by heightened sensitivity, imagination, and the depths of feeling experienced under the conditions of perceptual control. Why Plato should have wished to make philosophers kings after having banished the poets from his ideal republic I could never understand. Was it a bad theory of art, as representation of real objects? A bad theory of criticism? Or merely a bad theory of justice? In my estimation, it was a little bit of all three.

Thus an institutional view of aesthetic behavior not only gives an answer to the question of why we should promote it in our public schools but also goes a long way toward showing the best way for how this is to be done. In a word, we shall have to begin—and to end—by teaching our students how to play the aesthetic education game, how to enter into their rôles, and what expectation it is rational to bring to their performances. We must stop teaching the subject matters of our disciplines as if they were already bodies of codified knowledge and start teaching students to behave in the ways prescribed for the aesthetic institution by the matters of our disciplines, be they art history, art criticism, or aesthetics.

The creative process itself is a discipline only in the sense that its limits are prescribed by both subjective and objective conditions: by the force of an artist's imagination, on the one hand; and, on the other, by the qualities of some medium of art to be transformed by the artist's skill to present a novel significance to someone's critical appreciation. The pedagogical program that first succeeds in introducing the social dynamics of the artworld to the classroom teaching of art will have been the first to show the relevance of aesthetic theory to both the matters and the techniques of aesthetic instruction.

PART II

THE PHENOMENOLOGICAL METHOD IN ART EDUCATION

Up to now, the aesthetic analyses were given from the point of view of an eclectic method, partly linguistic analytical, partly phenomenological, and partly more traditional in constitution.

In this section, an attempt will be made to formalize an aesthetics for art educators from the unique point of view that goes by the ungodly name of *existential phenomenology*. The difficulty in pronouncing the vocables, or even in remembering the name, should not be interpreted as an argument against trying to get clear on the significance of the methodology.

We continue to follow the "pragmatic maxim" that the significance of an idea is measured by its success in solving problematic situations. That the methodology in question actually works in the area of art education must be taken on faith until art educators have mastered the discipline.

6

AESTHETIC EDUCATION

A ROLE FOR AESTHETICS PROPER

This essay attempts a definition for the discipline of aesthetic education. It was originally developed as a keynote address for the April 1967 conference of the Arizona Art Education Association and first published in The Journal of Aesthetic Education *(1968c).*

I had defined aesthetics proper *in my* An Existentialist Aesthetic *(1962). In that book, I introduced the formal notions of the phenomenological* epochē *as a conscious act of limiting one's attention to the appearance of an object in an act of perception, and the resulting "context of significance" for the determination of aesthetic value within the experience of a perceiver, as useful notions to clarify at least some of the functions to be fulfilled by a program in aesthetic education. The notion of "aesthetic education" as a unique discipline for the general education of young schoolchildren seems to have fewer proponents some twenty years after the essay's first appearance. But the claims made for aesthetic education as a discipline of inquiry apply equally well to art or music education, both of which had predated the aesthetic education movement.*

The current furor for a disciplined-based art education program of instruction was already in the air—as may be seen in the following essays.

I

The appearance of a new journal (*The Journal of Aesthetic Education*) dedicated to the issues of aesthetic education provides a challenge to several recognized professional disciplines. Is there ground for assuming that "aesthetic education" rightfully constitutes a division of the society of professional educators? And, if so, can its program best be developed by encouraging men and women working in the several art-related disciplines to form a cooperative, interdisciplinary concern? Or can a newer single discipline be created to handle its problems?

One still feels the temptation to apologize for the barbarism of such terms as *educationist*; but since educators are either teachers or administrators in institutions of higher learning, some other term must be used to refer to specialists working within the field of education as the subject of inquiry. Such specialists teach the teachers of our public schools and quite often look to philosophy for a justification of their profession and to empirical scientific theory and practice to validate their proposals. For these reasons usage must accommodate itself to barbarity.

The term *educator* is much less barbarous; but it is unfortunately already ambiguous in current usage. Sometimes those educators who are teachers object to being classified with others who only administer an educational institution; and sometimes there is ample grounds to substantiate this dislike. Those of us who have become accustomed to the term *educationist* have been forced to learn to whom it is correctly applied. It is not uncommon, currently, to have departments of education within schools of education, the latter themselves being a division of the American university.

Europeans are less squeamish. Their educationists teach *pedagogy*, and that term might have sufficed for us, too, except for the fact that neither educators nor educationists seem to care for the name *pedagogue*. And for good reason: a pedagogue is all too often only a pedant. Surely it is one of the aims of educational theory to rid our schools of unconscionable pedantry, and should it succeed in thus improving educational practice, it will have gone far to justify its own (second-level) practice.

As anyone who is interested can easily find out, pedantry is the particular bane of instruction in the arts, music and letters. Developing a specific antidote to this poison may very well justify the existence of a special discipline in aesthetic education; along with art education, and music education, and science education, and all the rest, "aesthetic education" may be considered a special theory of inquiry within general educational theory. Its scope would be defined by a delimitation of the aesthetic character of certain behavioral patterns, including the creation and appreciation of artworks in the various art media, and eventually, I shall argue, by the causes and effects of such behavior in our general society. Where to begin?

And how is the end to be achieved? Does the achievement of a single pragmatic end suffice for the satisfaction of all interests that may be taken in aesthetic experiences considered as the subject matter of education? To rid the educational world of pedantry would not of itself eliminate all the sources of incompetence, nor would it establish criteria for the recognition of competence. This, too, must be an aim of our inquiry. To shuck off incompetency and incompetents may be only the first step toward producing competency and competents; but whether or not, our decisions must be based upon sound criteria for distinguishing the two modes of educational practice.

The first step to be taken in this attempt is the clear delineation of the aims and resources of our public educational institutions, with particular reference here to the aesthetic domain of human behavior.

Current practice is of some help in laying out the division of labor. Aesthetics is an established philosophical discipline concerned with the description and evaluation of aesthetic experiences. Whether or not this is done by constructing a general theory whose purpose is to explain our everyday aesthetic preferences and judgments, the field of inquiry is adequately, if not clearly, delineated as one in which some kind of reason is given for our aesthetic judgments. And the discipline may be considered as metatheoretical insofar as it stipulates the conditions under which some of those reasons may be considered "good," that is, well founded.

If it be admitted, then, that a primary use of language is the expression of aesthetic judgments, and such judgments are taken on experiences of a certain specifiable kind, aesthetics as a philosophical discipline will concern itself with both the description of these experiences and the evaluation of reasons given for the judgments made upon them. In a word, aesthetics as a normative science must clearly distinguish between the aesthetic and the nonaesthetic (descriptive analysis) on the one hand, and the aesthetic and the unaesthetic (normative prescription) on the other. That the latter depends upon the former should be obvious: any disagreement in judgment must be reduced, if at all, by an examination of the conditions under which a given object is experienced. As I have argued before, the question here is not, Do you like x, and if so, why? but rather, What precisely is it that you like about x? Only upon finding an answer to this question is the more crucial question possible: Is your reason for liking this object aesthetically relevant? Not any old preference will do. Anyone who would become a specialist in aesthetic education, or in the aesthetic education of children in general, must familiarize him- or herself with the methods and results of philosophical aesthetics, which is dedicated to finding answers to just such questions as these.

The second established discipline is education itself, the realm of our formidable educationists, whose task is the instruction of teaching methods, the design of curricula, and a justification, philosophical or otherwise, for the dispersal of public funds in carrying out specific programs of public instruction. It is at this level of professional interest that questions of the following sort can, and should, be asked: Why teach art, rather than mathematics, science, or the communications skills? If art is to be thought of as a necessary element of the child's curriculum, at what age should its instruction begin? To what lengths should it be pushed? Are our methods to be based upon a model of scientific communication? Or is teaching itself more like an art than a science? Educational questions have a way of proliferating almost to infinity. What makes a good teacher? How can we assure ourselves that our educational training produces good teachers?

Answers to these questions must be found by research. But what kind of research? If John Dewey was right that philosophy, properly conceived, is already a general theory of education, then our research must be philosophical, in the best, most comprehensive, sense of this term. But no way of doing philosophy is proper which ignores the results of the sciences that have established the facts of a problematic situation, and none is proper which imports its standards of evaluation from a realm of experience extraneous to the one standing in judgment. Thus if teaching is a science, it must be judged by scientific standards even if the subject being taught is art; and if it is an art, it must be judged by standards applicable to art, even if the subject being taught is a science.

In the following I shall argue that aesthetic education is a proper subdivision of educational theory in general; that its theory is conceivable in terms of an "aesthetics proper" (in which the value of the aesthetic experiences to individuals is continuous with that accruing to a society that encourages such experiences); that a single method—phenomenology—may be applied to show this continuity; that the value of aesthetic experiences to individuals and to society constitutes a sufficient justification for instruction in the arts; and, finally, that the same method used to establish the foregoing may be developed into a general educational research tool.

II

Consider the first two of the aforementioned theses. Professors of both philosophy and education have been known to be guilty of assuming that knowledge of the general implies that of a specific skill. Thus if philosophy is a general technique for the analysis of linguistic puzzles, the person who is skilled in resolving such puzzles—either by semantical clarification or logical derivation—without further training in the specific subject matter of a specific discipline may go to work on the language of scientists, art critics, moral agents, or what have you, with equal facility. A prospective teacher who has been taught the psychology of learning (and what, pray tell, about that of teaching?)

should be able to teach anything at all. Armed with this marvelous tool, the high school coach may double as instructor of art appreciation; and when the need arises, said coach may even fill in for the ailing teacher of the physical sciences.

Those of us who have been trained primarily in a subject-matter discipline, on the other hand, have been just as guilty of assuming that knowledge of the discipline suffices for our qualifications as teacher. The day comes, however, when we are dismissed for being something less than an inspiring teacher, and we are faced with the shortcomings of our own assumption; knowledge of motivation and knowledge of the basic teaching skills are both necessary tools for the competent performance of our professional tasks.

Perhaps it was the philosophers' awareness that a knowledge of the rules for semantical and logical analysis is prerequisite to an efficient performance of the philosophy of science, history, art, and conduct that led to the current philosophical preoccupation with linguistic expertise. But by no stretch of the logical imagination can a necessary condition be raised to the status of sufficiency. All our logical technicians need to perceive the limitations of their practice is to engage in a conversation with scientists, historians, artists, and ordinary human beings faced with the problem of moral decision. Tools alone do not a teacher or a philosopher make.

But the possession of the tools and the knowledge of the phenomena of a first-order human activity may succeed in the tasks for which each alone has been observed to fail. Not motivation in general, but motivation in, through, and toward a specific subject discipline is the mark of a successful teacher; not logic as the clarifications of meanings in general, but logic as clarifying the meanings within a particular frame of reference defines the practice of the philosopher who would leave a mark on the institutions of society. Our educationists who are looking for a workable philosophy of education have already indicated their interest in achieving, not expertise, but a competent degree of expertness in education.

If specialists in "aesthetic education" have failed heretofore, they must learn to ground their theory of education and their personal research in a thoroughgoing understanding of the facts of aesthetics, where once again philosophy may be of some consequence, if only to guarantee that the aesthetic component of their discipline be adequately conceived.

We move, in a step, to the second of our theses. Whether, in oldfashioned terms, aesthetics is considered the science of beauty or of beautiful objects or, in more recent terms, it is thought of as "the science of expression considered as a general theory of linguistic," the practitioners of the discipline have a choice: to narrow the field to a limited set of objects or judgments, or to broaden it to include the full range of consequences such objects and judgments have on the lives of individuals and their society. I have chosen the latter alternative, and have referred to the proposed discipline as *aesthetics proper*.

As the science of the beautiful, aesthetics concerned itself with the appreciation of natural objects or artifacts expressive of an ideal Beauty. Plato so conceived it. But Plato was a complete philosopher. He likewise observed that poets produced objects that tended to disturb the passions of the populace, and so he proposed a law restricting the freedom of the makers of rhymes whose products produced social disharmony (Jowett, 1937b). Thus at the very beginnings of aesthetics considered as a philosophical discipline, two observations were clear: (1) if we observe the practice of artists, we find that they pursue a value other than the representation of an ideal Beauty, and (2) the consequences of this pursuit may be such as to warrant some measure of social control.

Modern fascist and contemporary communist states have faced the same problem. They could maintain their notion of an ideal society and incorporate the works and activity of creative artists within it only by limiting creativity: by stipulating what goal is to be pursued by the working artist.

Contemporary Soviet society is one of the few which has succeeded in professionalizing its artists, thereby incorporating the profession of art into the institutional structure of society, but not without some loss in potential value of truly creative expression. For the Soviets, Socialist Realism is useful, as is their nationalistic music; the rest is "decadent Westernism," "empty formalism," or—these all seem to be the same—"reactionary bourgeois expressionism." Only since the late 1980s has there been some glimmering of an openness in Soviet society, owing to the influence of Chairman Gorbachev's policy of *glasnost*, that has allowed various forms of artistic expression previously kept under wraps there to be unearthed.

When the question of the federal subsidization of the arts is opened in our own society, many of our artists express an open fear of the kind of controls governmental subsidization had produced in Soviet Russia during the thirties and forties, controls that *glasnost* has far from eradicated: whoever pays the piper calls the tune. The federal arts projects of our own government during the thirties sponsored art that was as socially realistic as anything produced in Russia following the revolution; and if these schemes did allow artists to meet some of their economic obligations, the price of this socialization of the artists was indeed allowing the piper to call the tune. The free artists of both countries have preferred to remain underground.

It is not being argued that an "aesthetics proper" is to be developed which would enable the administrators of a given society to adjudicate the dispute arising out of the conflict of values in society. That is still the task of sound philosophical thinking and of the functioning of interrelated institutions, each of which is the embodiment of a value in our societies. What is being urged is that aesthetics proper should concern itself with making clear the claims of artists that they have something to contribute to society that no one else can contribute and that the aesthetic institution works best only under the conditions of freedom of expression. If an aesthetic idea is a discovery of an artist manipulating the materials of his or her craft, then for there to be any such discovery, artists must be allowed the freedom to experiment. They will have succeeded in communicating with their fellows if others are capable of rediscovering the idea as it has been embodied in their works.

Aesthetics proper, then, may be thought of as the discipline concerning itself with artistic communication—with the description of creativity, of works of art, and of artistic appreciation. The consummation of this activity, submitted to the discipline of material embodiment, allows for the institutionalization of art as a basic human impulse: that toward excellence in creative expression. And this may or may not have anything to do with our love of or appetition toward beautiful things. But all this is only to say that aesthetics proper is a philosophy of art, where art is considered an institution of the general society. Lest this last term create a fear of creeping sociologism, it should be noted that "society" means here only the nexus of communicating individuals interacting via institutional means. Therein lies an appropriate means for the "social control" of individual artists.

If such a discipline can be developed, it would be obvious how the two senses of the word *culture* tend to flow back into one. In the anthropological sense, *culture* is nothing more than the fixation of basic human activities that in the first instance were appreciated as works or expressions of "fine" culture. If we approve of an anthropologist's studying the artifacts of a lost civilization in an effort to determine the culture of its people, the reason is supplied by the fact that art has always been an institution of society, more or less free, more or less controlled as are the other institutions of a society, yet always serving to unite people into a single appreciative audience. Art by its very nature produces community, uniting people in the appreciation of a common value.

And to perform their tasks, and to justify funds therefor, aesthetic

educators must study the intricacies of these socioartistic relationships. Otherwise, they are likely to continue to make an appearance
before the authorities, hat in hand, mouthing such platitudes as "after
all, it is good to have some cultured people around." But the questions
may always be asked, Is it? How do you know? And what makes you
think you can produce a cultured person?

III

The confusion of traditional aesthetics is as pronounced in its
supposed results as in its methods. The Plato of the *Symposium* spoke
of a single, all-encompassing science of the beautiful, to be based ultimately upon an intuition of Beauty itself. But in the other writings of
Plato one can find descriptions of art objects as imitations, as pleasing
form, and even as expression insofar as they are capable of evoking
strong states of passion or of soothing the soul wracked by disquieting
humors. His method was simple: ordinary description of single events,
and dialectical reasoning for the determination of an essence. Through
centuries of speculation by artists, critics, historians, and philosophers, aesthetic interest in the single event slipped out of the picture
in favor of essential descriptions: aestheticians became theoreticians,
and "the aesthetic object" and "the aesthetic experience" took promi-
nence over our everyday concerns with aesthetic objects and aesthetic
experiences. When we return to this concern we find that not all objects of art represent something; that anything one can think of has
some kind of form; and that all human experience is accompanied by
some kind of emotional state. For *anaesthesis* is unconsciousness, as all
aisthesis is consciousness.

Careful philosophers drew the necessary conclusions. Imitation is
neither necessary nor sufficient for the success or failure of a work of
art; and although form is necessary, it is not sufficient to differentiate
an aesthetic form from a nonaesthetic awareness. Expression, when
carefully analyzed, may qualify as both necessary and sufficient for a
complete description of a work of art, provided that the expressiveness
of the work is considered in the total context of the experience it affords. As long, that is, as the expressiveness is felt by some subject,
whether artist or audience, a context of experience is established that
enables a reflective individual to determine the reason or reasons for
making an aesthetic judgment.

Today two methods of aesthetic analysis dominate the philosophical scene. The first is the "good-reasons" school, employing the logic

of ordinary language to judgments of aesthetic worth; and the second is phenomenological, likewise employing ordinary language in application of the method, even though at the methodological level of discourse the neologisms of its founders are legendary. What phenomenological analysts analyze is the structures of conscious aesthetic experiences. Although the one form of analysis is interested primarily in "aesthetic concepts," and the other in "aesthetic categories," the claim to success made for each must be measured in terms of "referential" or empirical, adequacy (Ecker, 1967). After all, if I cite as a reason for my aesthetic judgment the presence of something which is not to be found within the structures of an experience, no one will be convinced of the goodness of my reason. It seems obvious, then, that some kind of awareness of the expressiveness of aesthetic contexts in general is a prerequisite—not for having aesthetic experiences, but for knowing what to look for as reasons for approval in a specific case. The concepts or categories may be as general as you please; their application must always be specific, as well as testable within the given context of experience upon which the judgment rests.

In what follows the context of experience will be considered as a locus of interaction between the object being judged and the critical judge. It opens with the percipient's contact with the work and comes to closure in a critical appraisal of its intrinsic worth.

The first condition necessary for having experiences of the kind being referred to is—for the want of a better term— openness. Martin Heidegger (1927/1962) refers to existential openness (*Erschlossenheit*) as a constitutive state of human existence (*Dasein*), divisible into three "equiprimordial" moments: affectivity, understanding, and expression (*Rede*). To treat openness as if it were a constitutive state of the being of humans is to claim, at least, that everyone is capable of verifying their existence; and to call them "equiprimordial" is to state, at least, that no temporal precedence may be attributed to the one or the other of these states. They all bespeak a single existential condition of a human being, determined by its relationship to its world. We may feel, then come to an understanding of the object of our feeling, and finally express what we have already understood by having the feeling in the first place; or the expression and the understanding may be simultaneous—as would appear to be the case when an artist has discovered an idea in the very act of expressing it. In each case, the existential condition is defined as the modification of a subject living in the midst of an individually significant "world."

Since the publication of *Being and Time*, in 1927, the philosophical world has feigned to misunderstand what the ponderous German said.

But artists have not, nor have perceptive psychoanalysts. They know that an individual subject is capable of living in a unique universe, that this universe is expressible, and that what is expressed is capable of being understood by the person who cares enough to respond to the expression with his or her own openness. I have elsewhere explained the usefulness of Heidegger's *existentials*, that is, his ontological categories, as pedagogical tools for instruction in the creative aspect of aesthetic communication (Kaelin, 1966). Here I shall limit my own discourse to the manner in which aesthetic experiences come to closure in aesthetic judgment.

To do so, it is necessary only to show what categories of human experience are relevant to an interpretation of a specific aesthetic context; or, what is the same thing, to show the limits of relevance to aesthetic responses. We know, for example, that any human subject may react in any direction and with any intensity to any stimulus and may even compound the difficulty by reacting to his or her own prior reactions. The question is always, What kind of response is relevant to the given object? The answer to this question is formulable in terms of the categories that describe a "context of significance."

In order to insure relevance from the outset, we may start with effectuating the phenomenological *epoché*, that is, with limiting our attention to the object as it conditions our present experience. Edmund Husserl (1913/1962) referred to this practice as "putting the world into brackets." For an aesthetician's purposes, however, it would be more adequate to interpret the metaphorical placement of brackets around the consciousness intending the object (of art) and that object as fulfilling that conscious intention. For that reason I say we bracket out of relevance all our past knowledge, all theories supposedly true of the objects of perception as merely natural objects, and attend only to the way natural or art objects appear to the scrutiny of the responding consciousness. What gets bracketed out are the properties of an object that do not appear to consciousness; what gets bracketed in are those properties that do "show themselves as they are in themselves." Ordinary language calls this bracketing procedure a conscious change of attitude—or a change of conscious attitude: it is one in which we consider the experience of the object for what it is, rather than as a sign of an occurrent phenomenon of nature. That is another attitude, one we call "scientific" or "natural," in which our responses are interpreted in terms of natural or physical laws. To bracket out the significance of the world, of course, would be ruinous for any project having as its aim the understanding of natural laws; it is not ruinous, however, and indeed may be the only practicable means available to the person who would come to an understanding of the data of an immediate perceptual experience. And only in those can intrinsic value be found.

As the initial stage of our method, then, we should begin our critical descriptions of aesthetic objects by placing brackets around an immediate consciousness and its intentional object (the artifact as it appears to us). As a result of this procedure we have an intuition, or direct awareness of the quality of the object, and our analysis may begin. In the next step, any workable set of aesthetic concepts may be applied: matter and form, subject and treatment, or local and regional properties. The test of their success is the ability to make our perception clearer. If they fail to do this, we reject them; just as we reject them if, semantically considered, they fail to point out unique referents within the context of experience. I prefer the notions of "surface" and "depth."

Both of these categories are experiential terms; both are analytical, and neither are to be thought of as affording a rule for creating or appreciating works of art. They merely characterize what might be found in a given work of art, and both are not always found in every work of art. If a work is nonobjective, for example, there is no depth as I define it; and if it were possible to experience the relations between ideas and images of objects without tying such an experience to physical or sensuous counters or markers, there could be surfaceless expressions as well. A response to mathematical or logical relations would be a case in point; and the so-called conceptual artists of our own time exploit this same phenomenon.

Following D.W. Prall (1929/1967a), whose work is still the best available on the subject, an aesthetic surface is the felt quality of any organized sensuous field. For example, the structures of music exist in sound (and silence); of architecture, in masses (and empty space); of nonobjective painting, in space made visual by line, color, and free forms. Indeed, ultrapurists look for nothing but these medial values and their moodal accompaniment.

But some surfaces thicken. And on this point Prall's explanatory apparatus breaks down. It seems completely arbitrary to insist that a shape has value only as creating a space within a painting if indeed that space is recognizable as the representation of a bull or a horse. When we respond to the shape as a representation of bull or horse, our experience deepens: more of the world can now be included within our brackets. If we look more closely, we can identify other objects: a broken statue of a warrior, frozen in rigor mortis, its severed arm clutching a broken sword; a mother in agony over the death of her child; a woman falling through the shattered timbers of a burning building; a flickering light; a wounded dove, its peace gone astray; a lamp-bearer rubber-necking into the carnage, with one arm grotesquely projecting into the center of the piece, and the other gripping protectively at her exposed breasts; and so forth. Let the mind play over these images and an idea grips the understanding: the wages of war, as it is currently waged, is death and destruction.

This is no game fought between man on horse and an irritated bull in a blistering Spanish afternoon. The attack occurred at night as the light's last flicker attests. Man, woman, child, and horse are all dead or dying, suffering or fleeing along with the dove of peace. The bull almost impassively contemplates the scene. Salvation, when things come to such a pass, must be found in his persistence and courage. The virtue of the brave bull is to resist to the end the torments of his persecutors.

So interpreted, our experience of Picasso's *Guernica* deepens, and it comes to closure in a single act of expressive response in which we perceive the fittingness of this surface—all broken planes and jagged edges in the stark contrast of black and white—to represent this depth, the equally stark contrast between the living and the dead, the flickering of the light repetitive of the condition of those flitting in between—like all viewers of the painting.

If this theory concerning the deepening of a surface aesthetic experience is correct, depth paintings always pose the problem of relevant interpretation. Whose interpretation is acceptable? The one that gives maximal significance to all the counters—both surface and depth—as their relations create the expressive context? Or the one that exaggerates the significance of one counter within the experiential context? An idea not traceable to images, an image not controlled by the organization of the surface is irrelevant. If such an image or such an idea occurs to you, merely bracket it out of the experience; it is no part of the intentional work of art.

I have elsewhere (1964a) constructed a list of postulates for the interpretation of an artwork's significance and have since reformulated that list to include four, rather than the original three, postulates, which were intended to indicate what may be found in aesthetic expressions and how these same expressions are experienced in their immediate qualitative determinations. The "context" referred to in the postulates is neither purely subjective—the intent of an artist or the reactions of a viewer—nor strictly objective, as if we were considering the artwork as a natural, purely physical object. The aesthetic context is a positive experiential interaction between a percipient (perceiving subject) and the artist's arrangement of the medium's counters.

The following is the revised list of my postulates:

Postulate 1.   All aesthetic expressions are context-bound; that is, whatever expressiveness is generated by an art object is to be found within the realm of human experience as the interaction between a perceiver and the intentional object of perception—within the brackets of our "phenomenological reduction."

Postulate 2.   The aesthetic context is constructed by the network of relations set up between the counters of a given medium: either surface to surface, surface to depth, depth to depth, or overall surface to overall depth.

Postulate 3.   No single counter of an aesthetic context possesses an absolute (nonrelative) significance. Expressed affirmatively: every counter of an aesthetic context has only that significance within context as accrues to it by virtue of a relationship with another counter. This postulate is perhaps the most useful for the purpose of the evaluation of first-order criticisms: any preference for a given work based upon an absolute value attributed to a single counter or set of counters of the context is an example of the "reductionist fallacy." Psychologically interpreted, the postulate could be called the Gestalt principle that governs our perceptions of significant objects. Aesthetic wholes are always more than a mere sum of their parts.

Postulate 4.   The significance of the total context (not its signification, which no work of art has, considered as a whole, although it is in part composed of significations organized into the depth structures of a work) is the felt expressiveness of all the funding counters; that is, the experience of the relations between surface counters (where apposite) and their representations out of which the total context was constructed by the artist.

What is the significance of these postulates? As always when looking for an answer to a practical problem, significance is measured in use: what they permit us to do.

Other aestheticians have referred to a bracketed aesthetic context of experience as "the object of criticism" (Pepper, 1949, pp. 169ff). "Object of appreciation" would do just as well, as long as we do not forget that the context is defined as an activity of a perceiving subject; that indeed is the object of our critical reflections on works of art. Such things come to exist only in the experience of persons who have opened themselves to the expressiveness of a sensuous surface and allowed their understandings and imaginations to be guided by controlled responses set up thereon. This is not to claim that an actual aesthetic experience begins with an awareness of the surface and then proceeds to closure in an idea; nor that there is only one interpretation of the given work; but only that the system of postulates devised to interpret the meaning of aesthetic categories affords a method of critical procedure, according to which any image or idea that is not traceable to the organization of sensuous counters is patently irrelevant.

The same Gestalt principle that validates Postulate 3 makes it impossible for us to attribute any temporal priority to the surface of the work. What we include within the brackets of our phenomenological reduction of the physical work of art is a *system* of relevant counters. We begin with an experience and end, if the work is good, with a clarified and intensified experience. If, on the other hand, our second experience (the postanalytic) is more confused or less intense, our judgment can only be that the work is not good: it does not survive analysis.

IV

If the value of an aesthetic object is the experience it affords, the value of adopting a given method for instruction in artistic appreciation should be the guarantee of relevancy in response. A work of art is not an invitation to respond in any way whatsoever. It is, however, a call to the sharing of human values as these are expressed within the artistic communicative process. As was claimed in the prior sections of this article, the value protected by our aesthetic institutions is the initiation of significance into the corporate structure of society. The test that such communications are authentic can be constructed only if the viewer is led to adopt the same criteria of judgment as the sincere artist who is constantly checking on the clarity of his or her own expression. Aesthetic judgment is central for the development of the institution we seek to describe, and training in aesthetic judgment is necessary for a greater participation by the several members of the social body in the effectiveness of its institutions. If this can be achieved in the aesthetic institution, finally, the social worth of both creation and appreciation may be taken as established.

We began by bracketing out irrelevancies, the better to comprehend the significance of aesthetic experiences and their intrinsic worth to the members of society capable of enjoying them. As a result, everything extrinsic to a consummatory aesthetic experience is declared irrelevant even to these widened brackets, which include the results of having such experiences. All didacticism, all moralism, all propaganda falls without the enclosing grasp of our newly set brackets. And if this is the case, the value of art is not in the truths it may propagate. But this is only to say that the function of art is not to teach, preach, or incite to political action. Viewed in this light, the institutionalization of art around one of these extrinsic or ancillary functions is readily seen as a misunderstanding; and the professionalization of artists within such a social structure, a violation of artistic freedom following upon the prior violation of the autonomy of art.

No wonder, then, that creative artists have always stubbornly refused the blandishments of federal governments, whether Soviet or American. What remains to be constructed is a social system in which freedom to experiment and to create, the autonomy of aesthetic objects, and the responses of informed audiences are all protected and allowed to be regulated by the sole relevant aesthetic criterion, the aesthetic judgment of perceptive individuals. Enlightened criticism is the institutional control on the license of artistic freedom. And this is what no society has yet succeeded in achieving on a massive scale. It cannot be done, moreover, unless aesthetic judgment becomes a universal requirement for graduation from institutions of public instruction.

The sooner the training is begun, the better; it can be started in the child's first drawing class. Waiting for a class in aesthetics, which is usually not taught until the upper classes of college, is a waste of human resources. For this reason, it seems to make greater sense to instruct the teachers of our public schools in the art of making aesthetic judgments and to allow them to pass on this technique to their students. Such is the task of the profession of aesthetic education.

But the case is not completely established. We have as yet to make clear the values of aesthetic education to the students and to society as a whole.

First, for the students. Successful artists, submitting their imaginations to the discipline of the materials of a given art medium, learn the skills no other endeavor can afford: to make a sensuous construct of immediate significance to themselves. We call such things works of art. Aided by a properly trained teacher, other students may be brought to an understanding of this significance and, thus, have their own imaginations or understandings controlled by the perceptual structures of the student-artist's construct. For verbally handicapped or autistic children this may be the only way to permit communication and, hence, participation in the greater social scheme. Does the value of aesthetic education stop here?

Obviously not. But to make this clear we must now widen the scope of our restricting brackets. No truly human activity can remain thus restricted too long. Having aesthetic experiences and making aesthetic judgments can have tremendous social consequences. Here once again training in aesthetic judgment contributes what no other academic discipline can do so well: it imposes a natural limitation upon the license of self-expression. Such, indeed, is the function of criticism as an aesthetic institution.

It will be recalled that one of the rules for the determination of aesthetic significance prohibited assigning an absolute value to any single counter of an aesthetic context. Any idea discriminable within the context has only that value which stems from a relationship to some other counter as determined by a perception of the artist's manner of portrayal. The habit of judging images or ideas so expressed, and of determining their significance within the ranges of feeling actually felt, produces a type of personality no society can afford to be without. We can place the value of an expression on an image or idea considered out of context; but if we do, we are producing a scientific or a religious personality. We can place values on ideas and images for their use in propagandizing one political program; but if we do, we are producing a political fanatic. Who needs them? Certainly a truly open society does not. Is that what *glasnost* is all about? We may hope so.

Disciplined judgment may be admitted as a corrective to bigotry and fanaticism, but in what sense does the scientific endeavor stand in need of the kind of restriction, or correction, we find desirable? This case is not as easy as the others.

It seems obvious at the outset that contextual judgments are necessary for the correct development of science itself. The significance of a successful hypothesis is its workability, that is, its explanatory and predictive power. One must consult the context of available data and the existing state of knowledge merely to come to a workable hypothesis, and there must be a further return to the data of experience to test whether or not it actually works as supposed. Surely nothing could be more careful or disciplined. So much is certain.

The question becomes more complicated, however, when we realize that not even the scientific impulse is immune to fanaticization. This happens every time scientific discoveries are applied toward the construction of needless gadgets, whether simple infernal machines or monstrous institutions. And when infernal machines are placed in the hands of monstrous institutions, ordinary people become quickly aware of the fact that an unmentionable substance has just hit the fan. The crash program to construct an atomic bomb was a perfect case in point:

in itself, applied science at its best. Unfortunately, however, there were no clearly definable scientific principles for guiding the decisions to use the bombs; that is a moral or aesthetic question. To make a decision such as this one must be able to imagine the quality of life in the world once the bombs have been dropped—the aesthetic—and then to weigh this quality against that projected upon the world if they are not to be dropped—the moral.

Moreover, since technocracy is the trend of today's warring ideologies, the problem becomes much broader than a simple decision to use or not to use a bomb. The social sciences, from which one might seek some guidance for solving this kind of social problem, are themselves contributory to the dangers of the fanaticized technological consciousness. With only a little more progress in genetics, we could be only a step away from the *Brave New World*, the prototype of contemporary horror tales. But that novel, like such others as *On the Beach*, *1984*, and *Fahrenheit 451*, gives ample testimony that an aesthetic consciousness has its role in determining human motives.

Science, then, needs fulfillment as a tool for making social decisions; and it can find such fulfillment only in the further development of moral and aesthetic consciousness. Science for science's sake, without any application to the problems of mankind, is as empty as the catchphrase *art for art's sake*. Both activities are meaningful to the degree they enrich the lives of men and women. This they can do only by remaining true to their intrinsic purposes: science to uncover the truth, and art to present the quality of a lived experience in a perceptual context.

In the proposed discipline of an "aesthetics proper" we widen the brackets originally placed around a consciousness and its immediate objects of perception to include the effects of having aesthetic experiences on individuals and their societies; we thus arrive at a hypothesis that may be empirically verified by using the techniques of the social sciences. Take two groups, one for control, and measure the differences resulting from having the one submitted to the discipline of aesthetic judgment. It would be surprising indeed if the aestheticized group would not respond differently from another group randomly selected from the overall population. If one were adequately trained to the experience of aesthetic quality and the process of applying an aesthetic criterion to the problem of its judgment, and the results were significantly positive, we should have made the case for institutionalizing the aesthetic impulse. Aesthetic education would then be a necessary part in the instruction of every child in a democratic community, and not merely something "'nice" to be allowed if the other, more pressing, conditions of life permit. Art is not a leisure-time activity but a necessary condition for the goodness of life.

V

One thesis remains. Can phenomenology, or a revised form thereof, be applied as the method of educational inquiry? The answer would seem to be affirmative if a model for educational practice could be erected that is consistent with that constructed above for aesthetic communication. And as of 1965, research had already begun.

Suspecting that the explanatory model of science had been defective for the prediction of desirable educational results, Eisner and Ecker (1966) indicated two sources of difficulty: first of all, current research was largely statistical in character, concerned with groups or classes of individuals, not with the specific manner in which given individuals react to their own classifications or to their own situations within the educational setting. We should all remember the "black is beautiful" movement, in which the slogan was used to promote self-esteem in our black students. And, of course, teachers, too, though they may have thought that their procedures were rationally constructed upon scientifically observable data, faced the same necessity of individual decision within the operative classroom situations.

For this reason, Eisner and Ecker (1966) wrote:

> Findings from statistical research must be treated with the utmost care in making teaching decisions designed to affect particular cases. The usefulness of such findings is realized only if artfully transformed. This kind of transformation is difficult because some of the actions the teacher employs in the teaching act may be only tenuously influenced by the findings he may want to use in the classroom. That is, his own behavior as a teacher may not be controlled, in the main, by a rational consciousness logically guiding his day-to-day, personal interactions with students. (pp. 15–16)

And they went on to speculate that

> it may not be too far-fetched to entertain the thought that some of the preconscious aspects of teacher behavior may be among the most artful and beneficial of the teaching act. (p. 16)

Here we found the beginnings of a new approach. Teaching itself may be considered an art, and not in the merely technical sense of the word.

A teacher manages a complex system of qualities. What she does at any given moment must depend upon what she sees developing between the students and herself. Her aim is always increased communication, that is, participation in the social process of acculturation. The process of aesthetic education merely illustrates the process of the interaction between the institutions of our society: the aesthetic, which governs the formal behavior patterns of aesthetic communication, and the educative, which allows for maximal self-expansion (Kaelin, 1966).

If the second of the limitations Ecker and Eisner have found for the use of a totally scientific method in teaching—the ethical question of which value the teaching and learning is to be thought of as accomplishing—is understood to be solved by the decision to learn and teach art, rather than good citizenship or what have you, then the total picture becomes somewhat clearer. The teacher in her classroom is an artist communicating the values of her subject discipline; and there is nothing wrong with this aim as long as we refuse to limit her behavior to the communication of subject matter, as opposed to the many and diverse skills of other disciplines related to the primary institution of art communication. What gets communicated in this educative system is a number of skills for participating in the primary process of aesthetic creation and appreciation.

If our model worked once before, it may work once more. All we need to do is to learn to put the brackets of our conscious inquiry around the autonomously significant context. They would include ourselves as observant educational researchers and a successful teacher manipulating the complex counters of her medium. To be sure, this will give us no rules for producing successful teaching, just as aesthetics gives us no rules for the production or appreciation of artworks; but it should go far toward enabling us to create the educational categories for determining the relevance of our educational practices and for controlling further observations.

Do we dare construct these aesthetic educational categories? If we do, and if we succeed, our criteria of judgment of specific cases will always be found in the interpretation of a given context, since each context found to be significant bears within its own structure the criterion of its significance.

7

EPOCHĒ AND RELEVANCE
IN AESTHETIC DISCOURSE

The categories are still three; the postulates for interpreting their use in context, four. The problem treated in this essay is that of establishing the relevance of our descriptive statements about works of art. It stems from the derivation of the interpretive postulates as a means of running through the horns of a dilemma: that what is expressed in works of art is either the intention of an artist or the response of some viewer. We remember the consequences of these assumptions. The first leads to the "intentional fallacy," while the second leads to the "affective fallacy." In order to avoid the null hypothesis of the first and the infinity hypothesis of the second, we assume that an artwork expresses something rather than nothing and one thing rather than another. The trick is to be able to state, within the bounds of possible interpretive reason, what is expressed. Where our eidetic description of artworks permits the inclusion of ideas and images, as well as of their associated depth feelings, some principle of relevance must be applied to our interpretive language.

Relevance in critical discourse is not the same as relevance in pedagogical methodology. The issues are related but not the same. Anyone interested in the possible confusion should consult the next essay. The subject of this essay is the relevance, read "fittingness," of language used to describe, interpret, or evaluate art. If a name were to be given to this subject, it would be "critical relevance," which would form a part of what is in the next essay called the "pedagogical principle of completeness."

My argument is simple. Practicing the phenomenological epochē*—or disconnecting oneself from the relationship one must have with one's own lived, practical world—enables the aesthetic percipient to concentrate on the qualities of objects given to perception. In effect, we "bracket out of relevance" whatever is not consistent with the appearance of objects and restrict our attention to what appears to the attentive consciousness. In this way, we "bracket into relevance" whatever attaches to perceptual objects in the qualitative apprehensions we have of them.*

As a consequence, the debate arises as to whether there is a difference between the physical objects that serve as bearers of aesthetic properties and those aesthetic objects that are constituted by the properties so borne. An associated debate centers on the apparent "psychologism" that has accompanied much of recent philosophical discussion.

In the following, I try to give answers to these disputed questions; and, at the same time, to show the connections between a phenomenological and a pragmatic aesthetics. To achieve this latter end, I reopen discussion of David W. Ecker's theory of artistic creation, considered in Chapter 4.

The article first appeared in R.A. Smith, ed., Aesthetic Concepts and Education *(Kaelin, 1970b).*

I

Thinking about artworks or our experiences of them is not a prerogative of philosophers, even when they are specialists in aesthetic theory or in the analysis of aesthetic discourse. Some art historians, for example, have been known to think about the primary subject of their discipline using concepts other than those of chronology and stylistics; and, as the cases of Berenson and Panofsky attest, some actually succeeded in providing useful conceptual tools for the analyses of philosophical aestheticians. Critics, too, sometimes succeed in making sense, at least in describing, if less often in evaluating, works of art. Thus, when he coined the expression *action painting*, Harold Rosenberg bequeathed to art historians a name for a whole school of American painters. His description was both apt and useful. And, along with museum habitués, artists themselves commonly talk to one another about their experiences of works of art and quite naturally expect to be understood. As long as there is a public object whose features may be pointed to or isolated by analysis and referred to within the context of intersubjective experience, communication is assured.

For ordinary purposes of communication, moreover, ordinary discourse suffices: experiences of artworks are either had or not; and for those who care to do so, these experiences may be analyzed and described in terms of what we see, hear, understand, or feel. Indeed, so common is this habit and so widespread the interest in the valid use of aesthetic discourse that verbal communication of our first-order aesthetic experiences has itself become the object of a second-order, reflective concern. In essence this happens every time critics or historians become critical of their own observations and principles.

Whether critics are merely describing what they have seen or are engaged in a lengthy explanation of its supposed significance, questions about the adequacy of their results lead them out of one attitude or function into another: question their results and they are likely to appeal to the workability of their method; question their methods, and they should be willing to consider the methodological inquiry that led them to adopt it in the first place. Aesthetic educators face the same situation.

But here there is a difference. Although critics or historians may proceed without regard to reflective, philosophical justification of their respective methods, the seriousness of pedagogical instruction necessitates an immediate appeal to methodological grounds (Kaelin, 1964b). For, if teachers of teachers are to impart anything to their wards, it should be a workable method for instruction in the first-order discipline; and unless this is done in an authoritarian fashion, some justification for the proposed method must be given. Thus aesthetics, which is considered as a method of humanistic research, and meta-aesthetics, as its methodology, constitute an essential part of the pedagogical inquiry that has come to be called "aesthetic education."

My contention is that aesthetic theory must comprise sufficient justifying grounds for the employment of specific educational procedures dedicated to instruction in the arts. Such principles as pedagogical autonomy, relevance, and completeness are, in particular, extensions of aesthetic theorizing to the realm of educational theory and practice. I should like in what follows to clarify the expression *aesthetic relevance* of discourse about the arts in terms of a strictly phenomenological methodology. The need for such a clarification will be established by a review of the art teacher's daily predicament—serving either as a practicing critic of a student's work or as a metacritic of a student's criticism.

II

Teachers of art are inevitably called upon to justify the statements they make about works of art and criticisms of works of art. Whether these are being created by the teacher or a student or merely being shown for the appreciation of a class of students, some minimal requirements are to be met before one would admit that education is in fact taking place in the situation: the interpreter's remarks must first make sense, and secondly they must in some sense be true. But these dual criteria of all intellectual inquiry are not always as clear and distinct as some philosophers would have us believe. I shall argue, as usual, that making sense is the primary concern of thinkers and that the question of truth or falsity can arise only in a context in which sense has already been determined. But the case to be made is not so simple.

An example from the history of philosophy will serve as introduction to the argument. Applying the "hyperbolic doubt" as a methodical means of establishing certain truths, Descartes is led to an intuition of two distinct attributes: extension and thought, which, being totally unlike, are conceived as essential properties of distinct substances. The move from attribute to substance is taken as axiomatic in that nothing can come from nothing. Now human beings display both sorts of attributes. Their bodies are extended, and their souls or minds are capable of thought. Moreover, it is supposed that bodies are of themselves incapable of movement, so that the locomotion of human beings betrays an influence of the soul upon the body. Interaction of the human body and mind is presumably a fact, and closer examination of the structure of the body should reveal the mechanism of interaction. Under the force of passionate disturbance it is observed that the "animal spirits" move with increased rapidity. As these converge upon the brain to leave their traces, there must be a place (since the body is spatial) in which the convergence is felt; and so, the pineal gland—which just happens to be located at the base of the brain—is the designated location for the mind-body interaction.

No student of contemporary psychology is a victim of Descartes' error, but history is full of irony. We could, for example, claim that there is no interaction between bodies and minds, as Spinoza did; but in that eventuality we should be found in the embarrassing position of admitting that it makes sense to speak of minds as somehow distinct from bodily dispositions. The pineal gland hypothesis is not false—indeed it is neither true nor false, since hypotheses are neither; it is merely senseless. The first irony I shall note is that Descrates' interest in mental-bodily interaction led to a strict physiological psychology—and ultimately to behaviorism—which allows us to claim that the term *mind* as used by Descartes refers to nothing and thus quite literally lacks a sense.

The point of this discursus is to show that outright inconsistency is not the only way of failing to make sense; it is just the most patent. Importing purely metaphysical concepts, such as "substance," into a psychological universe of discourse is another. And that was the error of Descartes. As far as I know, Descartes' account of substantial relations did not become inconsistent until he began talking of finite substances (which need nothing else in order for themselves to exist) as dependent upon infinite substance or God. Spinoza's ethics was conceived in an effort to clear up this patent inconsistency. Psychologists today, it should be noted, do suppose the existence of entities or functions that are themselves observable. Such concepts, called "intervening variables" or "hypothetical constructs," help us form or give structure to hypotheses that are tested for sense by the criterion of consistency as measured by relatedness to observations already made and other propositions already known; and the "truth" of these hypotheses are then tested against a set of predicted consequences, which again are of an order of direct observation.

Since to call an hypothesis *true* is to stretch the commonsense notion of that term as correctness or correspondence—the facts recorded in acceptable hypotheses are general and not individual and directly observable—various pragmatists have suggested other terms as epistemologically more suitable: *workability* or *success in inquiry*. Indeed, Charles Peirce (1940) generalized the patterns of thought in hypothesis formation and confirmation to express his "pragmatic maxim" as a general theory of meaning:

> Consider what effects, that might conceivably have practical bearings [as inducement to habitual action], we conceive the object of our conception to have. Then, our conception of these effects is the whole of our conception of the object. (p. 346)

The example used by Peirce to illustrate his maxim is the Catholic belief in transubstantiation, the miracle of the Eucharist; he would have made fewer enemies and yet have registered the same point by using the Cartesian belief in the existence of substance itself. This, of course, was done by David Hume; and since Hume's time, science has become a study, not of substances and their behavior, but of observable data and their relations. It is my intention to apply Peirce's maxim to the concept of method in art criticism.

Since it is difficult to argue with success, and success in inquiry is one measure of "scientific truth," pragmatic theories of meaning and truth have had wide acceptance. But the consequences of such acceptance have not been an unmixed blessing to art educators who have attempted to apply these doctrines to the strictly aesthetic concerns of their discipline.

On the one hand, they have felt the traditional demand of making sense by adopting categories of common sense or the science of psychology to interpret the process of aesthetic communication: "intention" and "execution" for the artistic component, "substance" and "form" for the vehicular, and "reaction" or "effect" (sometimes "affect") for the appreciative are prevalent examples. When critical analyses of these categories are shown to make little effective sense or to produce few practical results, art educators are tempted to agree with the dismal pronouncement that aesthetics is a dull inquiry (Passmore, 1951) and tend to seek counsel in other disciplines. In 1966, however, the attempt to incorporate aesthetics and criticism into the art educational curriculum was already well founded (see Eisner & Ecker, 1966; R.A. Smith, 1966).

But, on the other hand, some art educators, like David W. Ecker, have accepted the pragmatic challenge to develop a theory of artistic creation in methodological terms (1963). The artistic process, like any other mode of thought, is a matter of practical problem solving, the distinctive mark of the artist's thought being the qualitative nature of his or her problems. As I have explained earlier, Ecker's step-by-step analysis of the process closely parallels Dewey's often-formulated series of steps in a complete act of reflective thought. Although his account has the advantage of determining "meaning" in terms of the action and reactions of a painter to the work in progress, he was criticized by Monroe Beardsley for having produced just another "finalistic" interpretation of artistic creation (1965). Beardsley's reservations about such theories concern the sense of the means-ends categories implicit in Ecker's account, as well as the seemingly futile possibility of generalizing the description.

My own criticism of Ecker's argument (Kaelin, 1964b) suggested only that it was incomplete, that to make sense of the distinctions made (such as a presented relationship of component qualities, substantive mediation, pervasive control, qualitative prescription, experimental exploration, and total quality) it is necessary to understand the structures of immediate experience in each act of artistic decision: in effect, that we must return to the facts of perception, and to ourselves in the act of perceiving, if we are to understand the propriety of identifying any of the steps in his description of the process, but especially if the last stage, that of total quality recognition, is to be counted as the solution to an artist's original problem. Ecker leaves that a mystery, as if a successful work must necessarily be recognized as such. I suggested before that it may be profitable to heed Husserl's (1910-11/1965) admonition and return *zu den Sachen selbst* (to the phenomena as they appear). When this question of doubt arises, we can only look again to see whether our perception is as lucid as we took it to be.

I shall save comments on the problematic character of artistic creation here and shall return to the subject after the phenomenological categories necessary for its elucidation have been made apparent.

III

It has been suggested so far that art educators are in need of a workable method for justifying statements made about works of art, either in process or completed, and that the usual requirements of "consistency" and "truth" are too simple to serve even the minimal requirements of validity in verbal communications. Lack of contradiction does not suffice as a criterion of sense making; and in cases of hypothesis formation and confirmation the question of whether a construct makes sense is answered, according to the pragmatic maxim, by both "truth" and consistency taken together. Application of Dewey's pragmatic truth test to the art educator's concern with creation calls for a further method of elucidating perceptual clarity. What the student needs is a set of aesthetic categories by which to establish the meaning of empirically constituted data. Here the art educator-aesthetician has a choice of concepts: those of common sense, of practical psychology, or of traditional aesthetics. But however the choice is to be made, critical analysis of concepts is always in order; and the choice must be justified in terms of how well they fit the facts of aesthetic experience. Husserlian phenomenology claims to be *the*—I should settle for *a*—method of performing the necessary critical analysis. Other practitioners of the method are Roman Ingarden, in literature (1931/1973a); Merleau-Ponty, in the aesthetics of painting (1945/1962, 1948/1965); and Jean-Paul Sartre, in the psychology of the imagination (1940/1948).

The difficulty of expounding the Husserlian methodology is compounded by the various formulations the German master saw fit to give it. The clearest general exposition was first given in the three volumes of the *Ideen*, only the first volume of which has been translated into English (Husserl, 1913/1962). When the system became known, Husserl was criticized for "solipsism," and he reworked the substance of his Parisian lectures, which acknowledge his debt to Descartes in radicalizing thought in the *Meditations*, into his own *Cartesianische Meditationen* (1926/1963). These first made their appearance in French translation in Paris in 1931. Although both treatises attempt to construct a ground for the certainty of human knowledge (Husserl, 1910-11/1965), the first contains an exposition of the method, a description of the constitution of human experience, and a differentiation of "regional" ontologies (in which the dependency of psychology upon phenomenology is clarified), and the second seeks to correct the misinterpretation of the "constitution" thesis as a kind of transcendental solipsism.

What mattered for some of Husserl's disciples was the difference in the description of the method found in the two. *Ideas* (1913/1962) sketched out a three-phase process of critical reduction: the phenomenological, which, bracketing out the relevance of data from the natural standpoint, also "puts brackets around" a conscious intention and the object as intended; the eidetic, which reduces the intended object to a description of the meanings or meaning patterns by which it is known for what it is; and the transcendental, which limits attention to the immediate structures of the intending consciousness. In this last "reduction," the objects of inquiry are the "transcendences in immanence," that is, the essential structures implicit in any of its first-order acts of awareness. Reflection is the only method of access to these structures.

Consciousness itself is always of some object: its definition is the intending of transcendent objects (read here "other than consciousness itself") found in a conscious agent's world. In the *Cartesianische Meditationen* (1926/1963), however, the phenomenological reduction is itself called "transcendental," and eidetic description is declared to be the method of reflective self-conscious analysis. Any preference given to one or the other of these formulations is usually justified in terms of the objective of the inquiry. Since Husserl's own purpose was to explain the relationship between "transcendental phenomenology," an eidetic science of possible conscious structures, and psychology, a summation of empirical facts, he felt the need to reformulate the method; his original formulation, however, is more useful for a critical (methodological) analysis of art-critical discourse.

According to Husserl, phenomenology is the one "critical" philosophical method that has succeeded in its aims; and either way we use it, it must begin with the suspension of the dogmatic attitudes of common sense or of prior philosophies. Indeed, common sense and traditional philosophy were said to possess a common failure as explanations of our knowledge: each left unexamined the belief that our worlds contain objects which cause within us psychological effects that come to be interpreted as (secondary or tertiary) properties of the objects themselves. Unless we take up an attitude (the phenomenological) that calls into question the validity of our beliefs established in the first (or natural) attitude, these beliefs are dogmatic indeed.

Descartes is praised by Husserl (1913/1962) for being the first modern philosopher to call all his prior beliefs into question. And along with Descartes, Hume and Kant are noted to have glimpsed the import of a possible phenomenological method: Hume, for his tracing of ideas to their ultimate source in experience, including those of "substance" and "cause"; and Kant, for his transcendental deduction of the categories of mind. This historical account of the development of Husserl's method leads one to contemplate a second irony in the history of thought—one which goes far beyond a simple confusion in psychology owing to Descartes' retention of the idea of substance.

Lack of attention to the historical record has put American aestheticians in a poor position for appreciating the work of one of their
most illustrious colleagues. The fact is that the Husserlian distinction
between "intentional" and "real," or scientific, objects once had a wide
currency in American aesthetics, owing to the earlier work of D.W.
Prall. In *Aesthetic Judgment* (1967a), he describes an aesthetic object as
"purely intentional," that is, an intuition of the qualities that appear
on the surface of objects and whose organization therefore has come to
be called an "aesthetic surface." This is the source of my own category
of "sensuous surface."

Beauty, according to Prall, is a "supervenient quality" (nonnatural
perhaps) that is what it is despite the flux, and our varying conscious
experience, of the objects of nature. Thus in the following statement he
is describing the phenomenological *epoché*:

> Discriminating perception focussed upon an object as it appears di-
> rectly to sense, without ulterior interest to direct that perception in-
> ward to an understanding of the actual forces or underlying structure
> giving rise to this appearance, or forward to the purposes to which
> the object may be turned or the events its presence and movement
> may presage, or outward to its relations in the general structure and
> the moving flux—such free attentive activity may fairly be said to
> mark the situation in which beauty is felt. (p. 57)

And this lesson in the reduction of the perceivable to the effect of its
immediate presence is not lost in the second of Prall's (1967b) treatises:

> Aesthetic content is not process at all. It is quality; color and sound,
> not physical wave motions; it is attracting, exciting quality; deep, rich
> color, moving emotional sound, not nerve currents or accelerated
> breathing or pulse. (p. 11)

By thus restricting his analysis to the properties of intentional objects,
Prall meant to correct what he took to be the aberrant naturalism of
George Santayana (1896/1955).

But his own attempts to find expressiveness controlled by "the order of elements intrinsic to sound, color and spatial form" (Prall, 1967a,
pp. 71–75) betrays a lack of confidence in the immediacy of aesthetic
experiences. In spite of the separation of natural qualities from those
of immediate perception, Prall thought it useful to search out the
structural properties of sound (pitch, timbre, loudness) and color (hue,
saturation, value) as if these were the natural causes of aesthetic qual-

ity perception, an understanding of which enables us to give an explanation of our experiences of aesthetic expressiveness. Once the experience has been had, no such explanation is requisite. In phenomenological terms, Prall considered the experience of aesthetic quality from the reduced, phenomenological standpoint; but the explanation he offered is couched in terms of categories composed from the natural standpoint. Since he thus violates the reduction, there is a corresponding confusion of aesthetic categories.

Besides offering a method to avoid such confusion, phenomenology must come up with an interpretation of aesthetic experiences in which the surface qualities of objects are observed to "deepen" into a recognition of objects and ideas represented in certain works of art. And this is the source of my second category, "experiential depth."

Faced with natural or artificial objects remarkable for their aesthetic expressiveness, we are enjoined by Husserl to suspend our belief in all natural or causal explanations. If we follow the indication, we have an experience of the aesthetic (or surface) properties of the objects our consciousness intends. As art appreciators we have only to let the work happen. Failure to do so gives us some object other than that of our immediate, first-order experiences that should be elucidated in our art-critical discourse, just as Husserl claimed that failure to "disconnect the objects of consciousness" from the causal events of the world produced a corresponding failure in classical epistemology and logic. He calls the inquiry based upon this failure "psychologism."

When we consider that psychology itself is one of the empirical sciences in need of critical justification, we can understand Husserl's objections to psychologistic explanations of all human knowledge. The point has been made in recent aesthetics by George Dickie, who posed the question, "Is Psychology Relevant to Aesthetics?" (1962). Indeed, the question was rhetorical, since the obvious answer is, no. Not only was psychology not particularly relevant to aesthetic theory, but the so-called aesthetic attitude, which formed the basis of many a theory, was itself a simple "myth" (Dickie, 1964).

If Dickie is surprised to be thus associated with a phenomenological motive, the reason is simple to comprehend. His animadversions against claims of relevancy in response to artworks that are what they are because of a mysterious "aesthetic attitude" on the part of a subject are entirely sound. Moreover, Dickie's 1964 attitude itself ran parallel to the thesis of Paul Ziff, who objected to the characterization of "aesthetic objects" when anyone was speaking of works of art. Ziff (1954) maintained that there are not two different objects, which might be known by the response of some viewers, but only differing "descriptions" of the same object. But if these views are thought of as a denial of our possibility to practice the phenomenological *epochē* (the suspension of the natural attitude for the adoption of the phenomenological), then they bespeak an understanding of the methodological procedure that is merely defective. For, as in pragmatic aesthetics, so in the phenomenological, one either has or does not have an experience of the qualities of an artwork, and only subsequently is judgment upon it pronounced. The reduction occurs after our experience of the quality—to fix it for our reflection; not before, as a precondition to our having the experience. And in pointing out the differences between a "naturalistic" and a "phenomenological" description, Ziff seems to be right on the money.

Thus it is not claimed that one must first produce a certain psychological disposition or set in order to perceive the aesthetic qualities of objects; one might, as Prall (1967a) maintained, merely be struck by the obtrusive qualities of a situation. Moreover, one practices the phenomenological reduction precisely in order to avoid falling into a psychologistic interpretation of aesthetic experiences. In doing so, one merely suspends belief in the natural laws we know to have been effective at the time one had the experience in question. It was Prall's failure to carry out the consequences of the reduction that led him to seek the causal influence of the natural, intrinsic orders of sensory elements.

The result of suspending belief—or of disconnecting an aesthetic experience from the context of "natural" events—is the opening of the possibility of finding a categorial interpretation of the experience *in its own terms*. We merely describe what has happened. Ordinary language suffices to describe the objects of such experiences as long as we do not lapse into the naive realism characteristic of most ordinary people and ordinary language philosophers (Ziff, 1954); for to do so would likewise violate the reduction. Bracketing out the naturalistic significance of the world allows the phenomenological aesthetician to bracket the significance of an aesthetic context within the parameters of his or her own consciousness.

To practice the reduction means that we must attend to those properties, and to those alone, of which we are aware at the moment of our aesthetic apprehension. And to be able to do this, we need nothing more than the capacity to concentrate, that is, to focus attention and to reflect. No, the pursuit of the psychological conditions under which attention focusing and reflection take place add nothing relevant to our aesthetic knowledge; Dickie's argument is still correct. But our ability to attend and to reflect are amply verified in ordinary experience and may be formed by our decision to act in a certain way. Anyone can effectuate the phenomenological reduction, and having done so, such persons can describe the objects of their awareness.

Knowledge of the facts of aesthetic experience is gained first of all by acquaintance. Once we have reduced our attention to the aesthetic properties of natural or artificial objects, the process of interpretation may begin. Without the interpretation we should not even properly refer to it as cognitive; it is merely felt as the expressiveness of a given object or situation. Once we decided to bracket this act of becoming acquainted with aesthetic quality, however, we have constituted a "context of significance." It is this context that is analyzed and described by the art critic intent upon elucidating the content of his experience. And as long as each individual who calls into question the descriptions of a critic is willing to make the same reduction—that is, place brackets around his consciousness of the same object—there is ground for arbitrating individual differences in reaction. The context of significance so created has been called by Stephen Pepper (1949) "the object of criticism" (pp. 168–69).

When we reflect upon the content of the reduction, we find the scope of possible statements about the work of art to be strictly limited: physical descriptions of "the aesthetic object" are noted to be patently irrelevant, as, by the way, are the historical, biographical, psychological, sociological, and the like, usually made by "critics" who have adopted the one point of view or the other.

The first advantage of the phenomenological *epochē*, then, is the determination of the scope of relevant discourse about the expressiveness of artworks that are enclosed in the bracketed experience. Whatever significance we find in the experience is bound to this context (Kaelin, 1964a), and what can be discriminated within the context are the referents of the words we use to describe the work in question. Primarily to guarantee a value-free terminology, I call these contextual discriminations "counters."

If we perceive a yellow and a blue within the design of a painting, for example, it would be both meaningful and true to point out that such counters exist within the context of the painting's significance structure. Such elementary descriptive statements allow me to call attention to the "local qualities" (Beardsley, 1958, pp. 82–85) of works of art. Indeed, as I continue to attend to these qualities, I may find that each of these counters affects the other, that the yellow perceived together with the blue constitutes a "space tension" as the design begins to function as a unit in which a newly significant region of the painting comes alive. The pull of the yellow against the blue may be stable, in which case a yellow plane or figure stands out, to vision, off the picture plane, while the blue recedes. Or the arrangement of other color values may reverse the progression and recession of the colored areas. And if the tension is only relatively stable, the painter may use this phenomenon for the representation of motion in the design. Cubist painters often used the stable type of spatial tension, while futurists tended to exploit the unstable relations for the purpose of depicting rhythmic or frenetic movement. In either case, the relations between perceptual counters themselves become counters of the significant context.

The question about the significance of the counters now becomes possible, and what is more, answerable. No individual counter bears an absolute significance; so runs the third postulate. Blue does not mean "purity" or "repose," and yellow does not mean "gaiety" or "excitement." Since to attribute such absolute meanings to an individual counter is to violate the reduction—or the context, if you will—one would be guilty of importing meanings from a source other than an experience of the work in question.

We must be careful, however, to distinguish "significance" from signification. The former is the felt quality of the presentation—of the organized surface of the painting; the latter, the representation of an object or idea, which, if discriminated within the context, may become another counter of the expressive vehicle.

The significance of surface is thus controlled by the perception of the relatedness of surface counters; and each individual counter has only that significance which its relations to other counters of a like kind create. The affective tone of the surface organization is nothing more or less than the state of the viewer's conscious-bodily states in the act of perception. And in nonobjective paintings there is no other significance.

Nonobjective paintings, then, are describable in terms of surface counters and their affective correlates; and the various kinds of sensorily discriminable counters go to make up the different media and intermedia that have become working materials for artistic exploitation: for example, visual, aural, kinesthetic, tactual, and the like.

An aesthetic surface thickens or deepens whenever depth counters make their appearance. The easiest way of imagining this process is to contemplate the motion of a line as it closes to form a figure. When the figure is that of a represented object, the context has become more complex. A simple portrait, a totally imaginary representation, or a historical commemorative work may be structured in such a way as to be ultrarealistic (as in *trompe-l'oeil*), realistic (as in Renaissance perspective painting), or in any degree of abstraction. Total abstraction, of course, is nonobjective; that is, statements about any putative depth content of such work are irrelevant, since there are no counters within the work to stand as referents for the words used in such statements. In successfully organized abstract contexts, moreover, any meaningful statement about the depth reveals an equally significant surface phenomenon, and vice versa.

Depth counters gain significance in context in the same way as any other counter: by a relation to other counters, be they surface or depth. One of the simplest cases of this phenomenon is the portrait. The significance of a portrait is not the subject who has served as model, nor even some abstract idea that may be associated with the object as depicted (posture, attitude, social position, and so forth); both of these are merely counters adding complexity to the context. The case of Van Gogh comes readily to mind. He recounts in his letters the difficulty of painting a bridge to be seen as the peasants who customarily use it see the object. The same struggle to capture the personality of his human models is apparent on the surface of his paintings. So plainly is this the case that we may conclude: the significance of a depth counter is the manner in which the surface is arranged to create the appearance of that object.

In more complicated cases, one depth counter is related to others of the same kind: between the representations of a woman and a child at the breast we are authorized to "see" a mother; but what motherhood means, as above, is determined by the qualitative feel of the surface organized to represent the idea. To use an analogy from logic, the depth of a painting is like the subject of a sentence; its predicate is expressed nonverbally through the aesthetic surface. For this reason there are as many significances to, for example, a crucifixion as there are ways of organizing a surface in order to represent one. A Gruenewald and a Rembrandt express two different things, even when painting the execution of Christ; only the subject is the same. All the results of iconology and iconography are explicable in the same way. The depth signification of the painting is readable from the relationship of represented objects, and the significance of that signification is felt as one perceives the surface through which it is expressed.

Surrealists have succeeded in increasing the surface-depth tensions by ambiguity in their depth representations. As the dream object overlaps with the natural object, the original signification of the latter becomes modified, but not confused; for the funding images suggest a third, "surreal" representation, whose significance once more is presented on a striking sensuous surface.

In summary, an expressive context is composed of counters, either surface alone or both surface and depth. The significance of the context is experienced as the counters "fund" into perceptual closure: into the intentional "object" of our aesthetic awareness. Our critical statements are descriptive either of the counters or of the way in which they fund into a uniquely significant act. Thus, having bracketed our consciousness of a single object and described the structures involved in our experience of that object, we should have effectuated the eidetic reduction for works of that kind—here, works of art.

The result of this analysis is a set of categories that may be applied to any work of art. I have been applying them in criticism of paintings since 1965 (Kaelin, 1965).

IV

Still another problem deserves further consideration, however. We have examined some of the confusions surrounding the notion of an "aesthetic attitude" and have found them to be correlative to some corresponding confusions about an essential "aesthetic object." I have suggested that, since metaphysical speculation is out of order as beyond the scope of aesthetic relevance, it is not pertinent to affirm or deny the existence of a peculiarly aesthetic object different from physical objects. The work of art is the object of our awareness, and it was constructed by an artist in the physical medium of his or her art. Nor is there a peculiarly aesthetic attitude we may be blind to in another attitude. Aesthetic perception may take place in varying degrees of intensity; and when it has taken place, we need only bracket our consciousness of the object, hold it for contemplation, and reflect upon it. The next step is description.

But descriptions, even so-called phenomenological ones, are of different kinds. The critic attempts to describe the essence of an individual object, that is, the structures of meaning implicit in the experience of that thing. The language of the critic who succeeds in this effort permits us to enter into the process of creative communication, if for some reason the work itself failed to communicate with us in the first instance. Even should the reader not boggle at the expression *an individual essence*, interpreted, as per Heidegger, as the manner in which a thing comes to be what it is and persists in that state, there is still the larger question of the relationship between such essences and the "meanings" elucidated in the eidetic descriptions of the last section of this article.

Have phenomenologists been overhasty in their conclusions that such categories may be applied to any work of art? Roman Ingarden, in *The Literary Work of Art* (1931/1973a), does not hesitate to describe the essence of all literary works as a polyphonic harmony of surface and depth significance strata within an intentional object. One counterexample would suffice to disprove his conclusion, and it is perhaps for this reason that he has left both the polyphony and the harmony unanalyzed; for to dispel their vagueness would be to invite criticism and easy refutation.

Yet the concept of a polyphonic harmony remains as open as the very concept of art (Weitz, 1956); and the specific nature of the harmony, which is determined by the actual qualities of the perceived context, does not go counter to the description of "essences" as "family resemblances," as was maintained by Ludwig Wittgenstein (1953, p. 32). In each case, one would have to look and see, listen and hear, what the expression was.

The point is that, despite their own misleading language, phenomenologists need not fall victim to the essentialist fallacy. It is a fallacy to insist that essences exist in nature or in some transcendent metaphysical realm; but if the *eidos* is not a Platonic essence subsisting for all eternity, but a unity of meanings funding into a single significance or signification (depending upon whether our knowledge is aesthetic or cognitively conceptual), no ontological claims need be made at all. A critic describes objects phenomenologically reduced—separated from their context in the causal order of natural events. In the effort to tell it like it is, the critic must merely refrain from all kinds of suppositions, be they physical or metaphysical, according to which the objects of perception *must* be what they appear to be.

There may be as many such essences as there are ways of funding significance, as there are works of art or real, natural objects. In both these kinds of objects or "essences" it is the experience which stands warrant for the description. Art-critical language, of course, describes the structures of an actual work of art. Two faculties are therefore required to succeed at art criticism: besides practicing the first stage of the phenomenological reduction, critics must be perceptive of the structures inherent in individual works of art and endowed with enough verbal ability to describe what they perceive.

The aesthetician, on the other hand, works at the second phase of the reduction. Aiming at a general description of the conscious structures or meanings implicit in many works of art, he is at liberty to vary his examples, even to the point of extrapolating beyond his own narrow acquaintance with actual works of art. He may do this by modifying his consciousness to consider purely imaginary works of art, those which have never been executed in a physical medium. His descriptions are then of possible works of art. And if it were possible to imagine all the conditions under which a work of art could appear to some consciousness, then aesthetics could become an *a priori* science (i.e. effective without regard to particular critical statements), much in the way that geometry is an *a priori* science, and as, in presenting his general methodology, Husserl always claimed phenomenology to function.

Whether the phenomenological aesthetician succeeds at describing all those structures involved in any possible work of art depends, of course, upon the aesthetician's skill at finding real examples or at conjuring imaginary cases that illustrate the possible ways human consciousness may be affected by artistic creations. It is best, no doubt, to leave "art" an open concept; as long as the context of significance governs whatever sense can be made and the contextuality of the context is open to some kind of eidetic description, there should be no insurmountable difficulties in making sense of particular works of art, however much they differ among themselves and in spite of the fact that some of them have as yet to be created.

Consciousness modification—the change from actual perceptual cases to imaginary ones—is actually used in ordinary language analysis as well as in positivistic reasoning. When considering actual cases of word use, the linguistic analyst refers the statements (or other expressions) to the conditions under which they are uttered. This is possible because it has already been established that the context of the use is indicative of the meaning. But this axiom itself has been established, as a methodological principle, by the consideration of many examples including all those in which the analyst starts out by saying, "Suppose someone were to say. . . ." What the analyst does is to call our attention to a possible use of the words in question, and elucidates their meaning by referring to the conditions under which the words were supposedly uttered—to the context of possible use. It is for this reason, no doubt, that J.L. Austin (1961) referred to the method of ordinary language analysis as "linguistic phenomenology" (p. 130). And aesthetic phenomenology shares his interest in therapeutic analysis.

On the side of logical empiricism, the technique of consciousness modification as a means of eidetic intuition is not without parallels to empirical generalization over a range of observational data (Merleau-Ponty, 1964a). In pointing out the parallels, Merleau-Ponty has shown that inductive generalizations produce the same results: the intuition of an essence—or generally applicable concept—even if the procedures differ. Thus, whether we start with a single example and describe the structures of meaning implicit in our consciousness of it, or we begin by collecting many similar examples and abstract the similarities or family resemblances for naming as universals, the objects thus noted, described, or named are purely intentional: phenomena of meaning and not of physical or metaphysical existence.

However the knowledge of these intentional meanings is arrived at, the meanings may be arranged into regions, domains, or frames of reference. As a domain they constitute a range of relevant points of reference and delimit a corresponding range of discriminable acts of sense-making. Anything falling within the range of eidetic description makes some kind of sense, but whether a particular description of an individual essence is true or false must be decided on the basis of what appears in an experience of that object. For an applied aesthetics this means only that, given a set of meaningful aesthetic categories, a student may proceed to use them in the interpretation of individual works of art. This is what Husserl meant by getting back to the things themselves. And we could do worse than follow his advice in planning programs of aesthetic education.

For this reason also, courses in aesthetics cannot be taught without first-order criticism. Although one could explain a set of aesthetic categories in terms of the levels of human experience from surface to depth—from sensory perception and affective tone to imagination or conception of real objects, ideas and emotion—one could not demonstrate the sense of the explanation without considering individual works. In every case, as above, the context of analysis is what controls the limits of actual sense; and the range of the application of a concept or category is its actual pragmatic meaning.

A course in aesthetics conceived on this pattern is a course in the criticism of criticism; but for the purpose of economy in time it may be more profitable to begin with a derivation of the categories—by presentation of actual or imaginary cases. Once the student has learned what it makes sense to say he can then be turned to the task of describing particular works of art. In the process he will have learned what kinds of statements are relevant to his analyses and thus, at the same time, the kinds of statements he must avoid if his words are to make sense. In this way telling the truth comes after learning how to make sense, at least in the pedagogical situation.

We can do neither, of course, unless we are capable of "reading" the essence of a phenomenon as it is revealed in experience. In this sense, the truth of a phenomenon lets itself be seen; and language analysis alone, unaccompanied by the revelation of phenomenal truth, can produce no aesthetic knowledge (Kaelin, 1967). A correct interpretation of the sense revealed in the phenomenal occurrence, however, not only can, but does. Again, this means only that whatever language we choose to use in the description of our aesthetic experiences must be tested for adequacy against the facts of those experiences. It is the *epochē* that holds these facts for our continual reflective observation and thereby establishes the grounds for whatever truths we may state concerning them (Kaelin, 1965).

V

It has been argued in the preceding sections that a modified form of the Husserlian *epochē* constitutes a workable method of aesthetic analysis—one called for in the work of D.W. Prall but not successfully worked out in either of his two treatises, owing to his failure to abide by the conditions of the reduction. The strictly interpreted phenomenological phase of the *epochē* serves to isolate an aesthetic significance in its context and thus helps to constitute the facts that must serve as the referents of aesthetic discourse. The phenomenological aesthetician practices the *epochē* one step further by reducing the context of significance to its constituent structures, such as "surface," "depth," and "total expressiveness." As a means for showing how these categories may be applied to expressive contexts, I have devised the four postulates of my eidetic description of works of art set forth in Chapter 6.

Aesthetic categories are given an interpretation in terms of conscious responses to an artwork as created by the "problem-solving" artist (Ecker, 1963). Those which have been isolated may be used as criteria of meaningfulness, as practical guides to "the kinds of things to look for" in the appreciation of works of art. A pragmatic test of their usefulness is available in the degree to which students who apply them begin to find meaning in the confusing scene displayed in the history of the art endeavor, as well as in the degree to which actual disagreements about the nature of particular artworks are solved.

This latter result should come as no surprise, moreover, since qualified observers of aesthetic objects tend to agree, both in their first-order descriptions and their assessments of aesthetic value, and observers become qualified to the degree they possess aesthetic knowledge. It is for this reason that panels of judges for art shows are picked from among experts—on the assumption that an expert at least knows what to look for in aesthetic expressions of a certain kind. The current concern for a methodical approach to aesthetic education bespeaks a similar motive for the production of informed teachers. To a certain extent, then, the final test must be found in these pragmatic realms. Can the method be taught to teachers, and can they produce students who are more knowledgeable than those who have been trained heretofore?

The method seems to work for appreciation. Can it be applied to those contexts in which "creation" is the subject of training? Descriptions of "the creative process" are notoriously vague, and many of them are undertaken with some kind of axe—psychological, metaphysical, or aesthetic—to grind (Ghiselin, 1955). One of them, however, the study of David W. Ecker (1963), seems to be relatively free from the dogmatic presuppositions that have colored many of the preceding analyses. His approach is both empirical and methodological.

In an effort to distinguish the part of creation pertaining to the imagination and the part belonging to perception, Ecker has devised a scheme for photographing a painting as it can be said to exist at each stage of its development (see Figure 4.1, p. 50, this volume), with the later stage being inferred as an imagined future state with respect to the prior. Each stage is then given a description in terms of the relations between qualities revealed to perception. The account, which closely parallels Dewey's description of the stages in a complete act of reflective thought, has been criticized by Beardsley (1965) and myself (1964b).

Beardsley admits the subtlety of Ecker's case but discovers an error of intentionalism. Since Ecker claims that in one stage of a painting's development a pervasive quality of the problematic context becomes clear, and that this pervasive quality then tends to serve for further decisions on the inclusion or exclusion of certain possible moves until the final quality of the work becomes apparent to perception, Beardsley's criticism has some point. For from the moment a decision has been made on the pervasive quality of the developing piece, the rest of the artistic decisions become assigned and hence are tasks, rather than problems. The same criticism is possible for Croce's doctrine of "the aesthetic object," which is said to exist whole and entire in the imaginative activity of the artist, such that whatever "externalization" of this intention is necessary to be performed consists in the task of finding the proper physical and psychological materials for the construction of the physical analogue to the purely intentional aesthetic object.

Ecker lets himself open to this charge by citing examples of teachers of art who assign classroom tasks of making, say, a cubist painting. Since this style of painting has already been known and fully developed by earlier painters, the "problem" of the student is nothing more than the fulfillment of the assigned task. In the creation of an actual work of art, the student would discover the aesthetic object by manipulating the counters of the medium. It was in this way that Collingwood modified Croce's "intentionalism" (Hospers, 1956) without rejecting the original thesis that the creation of an art object is an act of original expression and a phenomenon of basic communication.

The question then arises whether appeals to an artist's imaginative intentions are always fallacious in aesthetic discourse. And, if not, what kind of explanation can be given to the imaginative component of the artist's activity?

It seems clear that appeals to the intention of the artist—as to what the artist wanted to do—are always fallacious if putative knowledge concerning this intention is erected into a criterion for judging the value of the completed object. We may safely assume that the artist did what he wanted to do; and in this case, his purely subjective intention coincides with the structures of the perceived work, which is the physical embodiment of that intention. Yet, since the object as structured is the object to be judged, and by hypothesis the object and the intention are the same, it is obvious that the intention cannot be used as a criterion for judging the excellence of the object. As embodied, our judgment is upon the intention itself. And, alternatively, if for some reason there is a discrepancy between the subjective intention of the artist and the properties of his work, then by definition (using the intentional criterion) the work is a failure. In this case, moreover, one would have to give some sort of evidence that knowledge of an unexpressed intention was warranted. Then, if it could be explained how the creator or the appreciator came to an awareness of the subjective intention, one would be in position to show how it became aborted in the context of the unsuccessful work. But to this day no such explanation has been forthcoming.

Still, it is another thing to claim that some artists do as a matter of fact have a perfectly clear idea of what they wish to do in creating both surface and depth of their works of art. Some do, and some do not; and of those who do, not all of them formulate their intention prior to manipulating the "component qualities" placed at their disposal by the materials of the medium. Thus some artists seem perfectly capable of imagining colors as they themselves and others come to perceive them and of imagining sounds as they must be produced for anyone to hear music. To call all such appeals a fallacy of explanation is a piece of dogmatic condemnation without grounds in the empirical conditions of having the experience. What must be done is to find the explanation of these facts, when they are facts, that fails to do violence to either the demands for sense or the established relevance of the facts. How is it possible for one to imagine that which has not yet been done in the medium but which one knows must be done if a successful (read "expressive" here) work is to be produced?

Ecker devised his method of photographic reproduction to this end. The later stage before its actual execution had to be imagined, if it was indeed imagined, on the basis of the possibilities apparent in the prior stage. And to see a possibility is precisely what we usually mean by imagining the existence of the object to be created. We need not go as far as Croce and claim that the imagining is the creating; the intention must still be embodied in a physical medium. We say only that the artist sees what must be done; to use Sartrean language, the artist sees something, as it were, in absentia (Sartre, 1940/1948).

Given the step-by-step development of a painting, one merely infers from what was done that the later stage was indeed a part of the prior context as one of its possibilities. Other decisions, of course, could have been made; but the fact that they were not is sufficient proof that they were no part of the artist's effective intention. How one picks out a given stage of a painting's development as the pervasive quality of the piece (which is then erected into a prescriptive control of further decision) remains a mystery in Ecker's account, however. This is not to claim that there are no pervasive qualities in aesthetic contexts. They correspond more clearly to the total expressiveness of the context itself and thus with the "total quality of the piece," or they change from stage to stage and thus correspond to the phenomenologically reduced quality of each stage of a painting's development, there to be perceived. The problem then seems to be one of determining in just what stage the final quality of the piece becomes visible as a possibility in a preceding stage. Empirically this may happen at any stage following the first decisions, and indeed even before a single decision has been realized on canvas.

According to the testimony of some successful artists, this happens as a matter of fact. How do such phenomena come to pass? The phenomenological description of them necessitates the third and final stage of the reduction—the transcendental—which, it should be remembered, isolates the structures of consciousness—or of the intending bodily complex—immanent in the intentionality of the act itself.

To shorten a long story, within the stream of an artist's consciousness there are many acts, all intending some kind of object. The noematic correlate (the unity of eidetic meaning structures) of each noetic act (the intending) may remain constant while the object bracketed with them changes ontological character. This is the effect of consciousness modification. The artist may look at what he has done (in an act of perception), and in this case, the object is a real design on a real canvas and the noematic correlate of his act is the phenomenologically reduced qualities of that object considered as "meaningful structures"; or he may look at what he has done and see (by an act of the imagination) what it is possible to do by projecting an imaginative design on real canvas. The real canvas remains precisely what it is in both cases; but being phenomenologically reduced in aesthetic perception to the noematic correlate of an intending consciousness, that structure is modifiable by the addition or subtraction of other structures (by gobs of paint or lines, also phenomenologically reduced) in such a way that a new object has at least this kind of intentional existence. Whether this artist succeeds in changing the aesthetic character of the real canvas (as perceived in phenomenological reduction) depends upon the availability of physical materials, which, reduced to their noematic structures, yield the qualities desired. Each of these additions or subtractions may be described in terms of the categories explained in Section III of this essay.

If this account is accurate, the creative painter continually modified his consciousness from an act of perception to one of imagination, and vice versa, without our being able to say which came first, as with the chicken and the egg. In creation, consciousness is continually modified; it "flips" and it "flops"; but once more, to deny the possibility of such action is hardly consistent with the observation of creators in the act of making a work of art (Kaelin, 1966, 1968b). And to insist upon an explanation at variance with the facts of our experience is precisely what we mean by "having an axe to grind."

To carry my explanation one step further, I could appeal to the existential concept of "temporality," one of the preconditions of my projectional principle to be employed in classroom situations (see Heidegger, 1927/1962, pp. 383–423). Human beings live in their privately significant worlds, and they are capable of projecting changes in their environments in accordance with their perceptions of the possibilities offered by those environments; nothing outrageously nonempirical is being supposed here. To continue the inquiry, however, would take me beyond the limits designated by the title of this chapter, and, incidentally, change the phenomenological inspiration from the work of Husserl to that of Heidegger. Suffice it to say here, since a more complete account of the contributions of Husserl and Heidegger to aesthetic educational theory is envisaged for a future essay, that the artist, being simultaneously a past and a living project toward a significant future, not only can, but most obviously does, make decisions to create an environment consistent with his or her own creative desires (Kaelin, 1966). Thus it is in watching their work that we perceive "where the students are." And this is still a viable starting point for aesthetic education.

8

AN EXISTENTIAL-PHENOMENOLOGICAL
ACCOUNT OF
AESTHETIC EDUCATION

What follows is the longest of the essays in this collection (1968a). The reason: it was originally published as a monograph in The Penn State Papers in Art Education, *edited by Paul Edmonston of that university.*

The monograph was first delivered as a set of two lectures at Penn State in the spring of 1968. Professor William Stewart prepared the introduction. When he asked me why a philosopher should spend so much time with the problems of art education, I replied, "My conviction is that the best way for a philosopher to have an effect on the institutions of his society is to concern himself with the problems of teachers, who cannot avoid dealing with changing social conditions."

The answer might have been given by a John Dewey, but the content of the lectures was dedicated to the attempt to formalize a program of art education on the basis of the existential phenomenology introduced in the preceding essays.

As always in this new edition of the essays, I have attempted to remove superfluous repetition in their content. The central question of this essay is, how much of traditional aesthetics is relevant to the training of the teachers of art: for them to learn, and for the teachers to teach, the better to improve our instruction in the arts?

I

The purpose of this essay is methodological—to construct a conceptual model for the teaching of art. In order to avoid the ragged ends of an unprincipled eclecticism, I shall attempt the construction from a single set of postulates concerning the nature of classroom situations in which aesthetic values are created or appreciated, and I shall use a simple set of procedures displaying those properties any method should possess to be considered workable. I begin, then, with a metatheoretical concern for the rationality of aesthetic discourse. For example, besides empirical adequacy and logical consistency—the ultimate principles for governing the sense-making properties of a symbol system—one ought to elaborate methodical procedures that are decisive; whatever else they do, they must permit us to make a decision concerning the acceptability of a truth claim. They must also be fallible, rather than infallible, to allow for the correctability of our system, and universal, in the sense of being applicable by any interested investigator, in order to meet the demands of replicability. In making a decision, one must be able to make a mistake, and that mistake must be able to be corrected; and once corrected, that conclusion must be able to be tested by others using the same method.

The method in question is phenomenology, whose empirical adequacy is guaranteed by the fact that the categories it uses to describe aesthetic experiences are derived from our everyday contacts with works of art, both in and outside the classroom. It will be logically consistent if the relevant data of such experiences are formulated in descriptions, or postulates, that harbor no self-contradictions. These two methodological criteria are so well known there is little cause to expand further upon them. They are, in general, the metatheoretical principles that must be embodied in any theoretical construction.

What is less understood in educational circles, perhaps, is that the other criteria—decidability, fallibility, and universality—are directly related to adequacy in reference and consistency in sense. No method would be empirically adequate that failed to allow decision between positive and negative assessments of value in the thing or process being judged. "Truth" is such a value in the natural and behavioral sciences, as is "logical truth," or validity, in the formal sciences of logic and mathematics. My contention is merely that "success" or "failure" in the achievement of aesthetic expressiveness is judged in a way analogous to the bipolar decisions made in these sciences—if the proper method can be found.

Moreover, to be applicable to the classroom in which aesthetic activity is being "taught," the method must be adequate in two different senses, following two different sorts of consideration. Both the teacher and the student must be able to judge the success of the primary aesthetic activity, and the teacher and the administrative superiors must be able to judge the success or failure of the secondary, pedagogical activity. We do not expect our teachers to make a work of art of classroom instruction—that may be possible, and even constitute a reason for rapid promotion, but only if, in the primary instance, valid aesthetic results are obtained in student behavior.

This split between levels of activity results in two distinct, yet related, contexts of judgment. In the past, the first was relegated to practicing aestheticians or critics and the second, to educators; but the rise of the relatively new field of "aesthetic education" indicates that the separation may be untenable. So far, unfortunately, no one has come up with a single method for determining the procedures by which the aesthetic and the pedagogical concerns merge into a single discipline. It could be done, perhaps, by an aesthetician who takes the problems of education seriously, or by an educator who takes those of aesthetics seriously; but whether the one or the other, the solution must be found at the level of methodology and, hence, of philosophical metatheoretical analysis.

There have been few results to date because it has not been shown generally that teachers of the arts are in fact engaging in inquiry into the workaday experience of classroom instruction. A great many of them, perhaps the majority, do not engage in any sort of inquiry—but only because they have no idea at all about what they are doing. Others know what they are about but have not pursued their reflective concern far enough to have established the roots of their methods in sound methodology—either for fear or awe of philosophy or because of an uncritical acceptance of a method laid down by a revered teacher. Since results are important, only they seem to count. Yet some are relevant, and others are irrelevant; and of those that are indeed relevant, some are more efficiently produced than others.

There is little need to spend too much time on avowedly irrelevant results. These may be defined with respect to the objectives sought in the educational process. We may, for example, seek to "educate the whole child," or to produce social and democratic attitudes and values within the personality structures of individual students, or merely to develop the student's capacity for effective nonverbal communication. This latter aim, which is quite appropriate for students with an admitted verbal deficiency, seems on the face of it to be more relevant than the prior two, for the following reasons.

There is considerable vagueness about the concept of the "whole child," and if it is used as the aim that justifies inclusion of aesthetic materials in the public schools, it would seem to imply either that the creation and appreciation of works of art affect the personality of the student in its totality or that aesthetic activity completes what other disciplines leave untouched in human development. Either consequence is fraught with difficulties. How can it be proved that aesthetic education touches the total personality structure of individuals, while the pursuit of the social sciences, mathematics, natural science, and communications do not? And if it merely fills in what these others leave

blank, what is the evidence for our claim that it does? Either this objective, which has been espoused for aesthetic education, is a pious
platitude or it is grounded in a well-founded theory of human nature
and of aesthetic experiences. Our method—the one to be used in the
attainment of such an objective—must stem from such a base.

The reasoning is the same as for any other objective imposed upon
the general educational process. If it is claimed that the inclusion of
aesthetic materials is an effective means for attaining a given end, then
it should be shown that *some* manner of handling those materials is *best
suited* for so doing. Hit-and-miss, considered as a method for doing
something, should always be used as the last resort, since it has always produced as many misses as hits.

The choice of nonverbal communication as an aesthetic educational objective enjoys at least a measure of *a priori* plausibility: since
the majority of the arts are nonverbal, any appreciable development of
artistic skills would seem to imply that of nonverbal communications
skills. But even this choice of an objective for aesthetic education must
be made with some caution: first of all, it carries with it the stigma of
the verbally handicapped—or underprivileged, as the case may be—
such that "artistically talented" comes in our appraisals paradoxically
to mean "verbally blocked," if not "autistic"; and, secondly, as before,
the adoption of this aim must be justified in terms of an explanation of
the way in which artistic instruction can function to develop personality or intelligence in a strictly nonverbal manner.

We want, in other words, to avoid the uneasy dichotomy between
nonverbal and verbal intelligence—otherwise, having their curriculum
devoted to only one aspect of their experience, our arts students who
may score high on qualitative intelligence tests may never achieve the
intellectual mastery of that intelligence that stems from an understanding of what, after all, they are doing when creating or appreciating a
work of art. To supply this understanding is the function of traditional
categories of philosophical aesthetics.

I should like to fulfill this function, but at the same time I should
like to avoid the mere association of nonverbal or qualitative intelligence with "talent" or "taste"—otherwise, we shall easily fall prey to
the assumption that such individuals are born, not made, and that for
this reason they are uneducable. It is apparent that some students do
possess a greater facility for mathematics, the sciences, or verbal communication and equally clear that other students have a greater apti-
tude for creative expression. Education in the appropriate skills is as
possible for the one group as for the other. What has been lacking so
far is only the justification for the choice of one kind of skill over the

other—in particular, a sufficient explanation of the connection between the development of verbal and nonverbal skills and the production of a worthier individual or society by our educational institutions.
The moral question of the worth of individuals and societies cannot be
ignored if our educational posture is to be considered sound.

We may attempt to avoid the question by proceeding arbitrarily
with the assumption that any development of the individual is good
for the society, or that any development of the society is good for the
individual. But if we do that, we beg the question of the issue between democracy and totalitarianism. Whether we choose one or the
other, a further demonstration must be made: for a democracy, that
instruction in nonverbal skills does, as a matter of fact, produce a
"better" individual; and for the totalitarian choice, that the creation and
appreciation of artworks constitute distinct social values. In both cases,
we are thrown back to the necessity of grounding our educational procedures in something else: either in the appropriate sciences describing human behavior and development, such as psychology, social
psychology, or philosophical anthropology; or, in the second instance,
in a sound theory of aesthetic experiences that takes account of social
reality as the background to, and ultimate receptor of, created aesthetic values.

The case will not be easy. There is the difficult selection to be made
between the "objective" methods of the behavioral sciences, as opposed to the "subjective" techniques of a philosophical anthropology;
or at least some consideration must be given for rejecting the disjunction of these alternatives. And, on the other side of the issue, we must
face the methodological issues involved in constructing a method of
aesthetic analysis that will prove itself by producing results both in and
outside the classroom. Indeed, if it can be shown that a particular
method produces pragmatic results outside the classroom, then there
would be some ground for its adoption inside. All we should have to
do then is to train our teachers to employ the method.

My contention is simple: existential phenomenology (1) provides
a single method for establishing the ground for aesthetic education
(Kaelin, 1966); (2) as applied to creation and appreciation as a communicative process, it establishes a method to be used—or at least
tried—in classroom instruction; and (3) that when it is tried, and if it
produces the desired results of increasing communications between
social individuals, then it also provides a way to explain how individual expressions enrich the general society.

I shall proceed by stipulating a series of educational postulates,
derivable from the following definitions:

Definition 1. "Education" means the planned process of developing the distinctively human personality. It may be practiced upon individuals or groups, the latter large or small. It succeeds when the person or group being educated is led out of the condition in which the educator finds it to a newer, enriched situation in which different alternatives for human action are opened up.

Definition 2. "Aesthetic" education refers to the means by which the human individuals or groups are brought to the broader horizons of their enriched situations; specifically, through the creation or appreciation of the values embodied in works of art.

The principles, postulated upon the adoption of the stipulated definitions, are, like the earlier developed set of "aesthetic postulates" (see Chapter 6), four in number:

Principle 1. The place to start is where the individual is, but to end there is, according to Definition 1, an admission of failure. Such is my "projectional principle."

Principle 2. The educational values to be espoused are those inherent in the process of artistic communication and not imposed upon it from without; they are imaginatively projected by the student as initiator of the communication. Thus, in aesthetic education, it is not our aim to produce better citizens, informed consumers of society's products, or what have you—although this may be one of the fringe benefits of aesthetic education as a by-product of the creation of aesthetic values. We may refer to this postulate as the "autonomy principle."

Principle 3. To use any means other than the specifically aesthetic, such as metaphysics, linguistics, or history, even as these may relate to the arts, is, according to Definition 2, likewise a failure. So runs my "relevancy principle."

Principle 4. Lastly, to use only some of the means available to us in a complete act of artistic communication is, though relevant, doomed to limited success. For example, to allow students merely to "express themselves" with no concern for the value of the works they produce may have a useful therapeutic effect but will not allow the individual to participate fully in the communicative processes of the classroom or of the general society. Here, as always, the school is considered a microcosm of the general society. What carries over from classroom to general social living is the habit of participating in the communicative processes by which our social relations are governed.

For example, students must learn to "internalize", that is, respond to their creations in the same or analogous way to that of the teacher who criticizes their work and to their peers who may appreciate it. In the same way, appreciation may be cut off from the communicative process. We may look upon the work as "reflective of its time" or as "reminiscent" of the work of other artists at other times and so lose sight of the embodied intention of its creator. In short, any treatment of the art object in separation from the conscious activities of its creator or appreciators—beginning with the projection of a creative value and ending with its judgment—is a violation of what I call the "completeness principle."

To summarize this description: effective aesthetic education is effectuated by the pedagogical use of artistic, or creative, communication—autonomously, completely, relevantly, and projectively; it begins with the individual's or group's capacity to create or appreciate aesthetic value at one moment in their life's history and carries over, as a habit, into an enriched situation wherein they and others are exposed to new alternatives for individual or social action.

Our choice of *communication* rather than *expression* is no mere happenstance. If, at ground level, student artists express their natures in some sense of this term, they have undergone at least the beginning of social communication; and the teacher who must act as audience and as critic of the students' work completes what the students have initiated. In this set of relations, we have, in miniature, a model of the functioning "aesthetic institution" (Kaelin, 1962).

My plan in what follows is to schematize the general patterns of the social behavior implicit in aesthetic communication as it takes place outside the classroom in order to define the relevant roles of both student and teacher within.

II

If the justification of pedagogical means rests upon their adequation to educational objectives, then the phenomenological account of the means available to the aesthetic educator—the criteria for which are found in the nature of aesthetic communication itself—may be said at least to point in the right direction. Before moving to a consideration of these means, we should pay some attention here to the direction in which they actually point. It was mentioned above that some degree of arbitrary decision is possible in the selection of the ends to be pursued in public education. Upon serious reconsideration, however, there is nothing of the kind. What we decide to do depends upon a prior selection of the means to be used to educate our students, and these, we have stipulated above, are to be those supplied by the aesthetic institution.

The distinction between the individual and society can be maintained only by the individual or the society that has already misconceived its aims, its nature, or its functioning. The cries of "conformity" that we may hear from the one side are sure to be countered, if not dampened, by the equally vociferous shouts of "irresponsibility" stemming from the other. But the point is, no shouting match will ever settle the issue, as will no toss of a pair of dice. As the French poet, Stéphane Mallarmé, has said: *"un coup de dés jamais n'abolira le hasard"* (a toss of the dice will never abolish chance).

Next, if educational ends are to be justified, they must come out of a careful consideration of the nature of the individuals being educated, and a choice between possible ends must be made in light of the state of knowledge available in either the behavioral and social sciences or some other, perhaps more reliable, source. Since such knowledge of human behavior is subject to change, it is not unreasonable to expect that our projected goals should be continually reevaluated.

And, lastly, if there is any point to constructing an existential-phenomenological model for aesthetic education, it must assuredly be the realization that the insight and knowledge of its philosophical point of view have not yet been applied to the task. What becomes of our educational projects when it is understood that students themselves already represent a specific project of existence? Obviously, we must develop a method for handling such projects without destroying their significance.

When such a method is found, and applied to the problem at hand, we shall find no necessary contradiction between the goals of individuals and those of society; both exist for the purpose of liberating and giving form to creative impulses. In terms of existentialistic jargon, our being in the world is always a being with others, and institutions exist to permit the interaction of the individuals guided by them. Creative communication, the value served by the aesthetic institution, is therefore both the means and the end of classroom behavior; or, if you prefer Dewey's manner of expressing the idea, there is a continuity of the means and the ends of the educational institution. It is the means, not by hypothesis, but by definition, since the education we are concerned with is to be "aesthetic"; and the ends, not by arbitrary decision, but by an examination of the nature of those beings it is our purpose to educate and of the social context in which such education must take place.

In a word, the human being is, in some sense of the term, defined by its means of communication. Even if we reject Heidegger's (1927/1962) notion that existential openness expresses itself as affectivity, understanding, and expression, this is one of the conclusions to be drawn from his description of man as *transcendence*. Although the import of the term is simple, existentialistic philosophers who have used it have been charged with systematic obfuscation. It is misleading, of course, if interpreted in a Platonic or even a Kantian sense; for human beings do not transcend themselves toward a mysterious realm of essences, or of *noumena*, which is somehow beyond the pale of our everyday experience. Heidegger's term for the phenomenon is *existentiality*, by which he refers to the fact that men and women are in some fundamental sense what they are to become, that is, projections toward some as yet undetermined future; this future, moreover, can be actualized only by a free decision or commitment of the individual.

If such an ontological description of a human being is accurate—at least it should convince us that human beings are essentially educable—then some of our educational thinking must undergo a change. We must, first of all, stop looking for the determination of behavior exclusively in terms past, causal influences—economic, religious, sociological, and so on—in order to discover "where the students are." Economically deprived, socially disadvantaged, and religiously indoctrinated individuals may indeed tend to act in one way rather than another; but what it means to be any of these things is not determined once and for all, nor for all individuals so classed. Some individuals may react to their environment in such a way as to revolt, to change forcibly the conditions they find restricting; others may meekly accept them in order not to rock the boat; still others may accept their role in full cognizance of its consequences, however harmful to themselves.

This variability in individual reaction to social classification means only that individuals alone determine the meaning of their social classification and that, consequently, the days of looking for an adequate description of the "adolescent" or the "feminine" mystique, for example, should be relegated to the past. It should suffice to realize that the various "mystiques" are just that, an unwarranted belief in the mystical essence of an adolescent or feminine transcendence. Not essence, but existence, is the foundation of critical educational theory; and correlation between classes and determinable behavioral patterns is the current scientific jargon for "essence" or "essential determination."

For that reason, the question raised above as to whether the "objective" methods of the behavioral sciences are the only ones proper to determine educational aims and pedagogical procedures is found to be part of a new, and equally unfounded, "scientific mystique." Suppose that our statistical correlations were as perfect as they might be, suppose that a well-founded correlation between "being an x" and "behaving in fashion y" were established, what would the consequences be? Depending upon our evaluation of the behavior pattern, one would only have to concentrate upon the procedures necessary and sufficient for producing beings of the kind x, or for changing them in order to obviate this result. But this would be disastrous for the openness of our society. Our educators would have to become technicians for producing more refined examples of the kind of being nature already produces without educational interference. And no justification could be given for the value placed upon the behavior to be encouraged or eradicated.

The same point may be made in another way. There is a difference between training and education. We can certainly train individuals to do what we want them to do once we have determined, hypothetically and not categorically, what they ought to do; but we do not do so in the process of educating them, in the sense that we lead them to actualize one or more of their existential possibilities. We can train individuals to learn what we already know, but we cannot educate them in the process to discover what we do not yet know. Dewey (1916/1966) referred to this distinction by separating "problems" from "tasks." The latter may be imposed upon our students, but the former must stem from the students' own existential situations. Only by allowing the students to work on their own problems, or, what is the same, to discover the significance of their own lives, can we lay any claim to having educated them.

Once again, the reason is obvious. To impose a goal upon the behavior of an individual which is our own or that of the general society is to introduce a break into the continuity of ends and means distinctive of ordinary normative human behavior (Dewey, 1920/1950). The teacher breaks the continuity of the students' behavioral patterns—between their own and the socially approved role offered them—by espousing an end that is not theirs; and, quite naturally, we go on to complain of a "generation gap" between students and teachers. Once the end has been espoused, there ensues the second break, which is the imposition of the known techniques for attaining such an end. Numerous are the "teachers" of art who impose their ends upon their hapless students. A casual walk through a student art show is sufficient evidence for this conclusion. Unfortunately, however, the same phenomenon occurs in education in the sciences as well as in the arts. Instead of scientists bent upon the discovery of truths, we produce technicians who have learned the tricks of the trade, based upon the truths discovered by others; instead of artists, imitators and illustrators.

The only way I can conceive of reestablishing the continuity between ends and means is to free our educational systems from the values of the teachers—and, at the same time, our classrooms from the glibly expected, socially defined behavioral patterns already integrated into the existing institutional framework. Education must be considered a dialogue between the educator and the educatee, and the dialogue must be initiated by a gesture of the latter. When it succeeds, communication will have taken place, and society will have been necessarily enriched.

Making a work of art is such an initiating gesture, to which both student and teacher must learn to react in a relevant fashion. To this end, both must be expected to become acquainted with aesthetic categories capable of describing the manner in which the communication of aesthetic values takes place. Within the classroom, the projected existence of the artifact becomes a goal, and all the objects of the environment become, or must be made, means for achieving the goal. In this way, student artists project themselves by communicating a value to be appreciated; and the teacher, projecting in turn the students' successful transcendences, is at best a guide or helpmate in the students' initiating projects.

Our model conception of the subject of education—the students—thus nears completion. They are not things to be manipulated, nor essences to be trained for a pre-existent societal role. They are transcendences, capable of projecting their own goals, always existing already in some sort of situation, and in direct rapport with the objects of nature and other beings of their own kind. Their attempts at creation are attempts to realize their own imaginary values. In short, an existential analysis of human beings spells out the fuller interpretation of my "projectional principle" of education; and, at the same time, it suggests whatever sense it makes to say that educational procedures "start where the students are."

One serious qualification, however, has been added: students must be allowed to determine exactly where they are. Since they do this by projecting their own goals, it is not enough to investigate the conditions of their backgrounds.

Existentially considered, where one wants to go, and not where one has been in the past, determines what and where one is at any given moment of decision. But this is only to say once more that human beings define themselves by a project of existence in reaction to ontic conditions of their real-life worlds; and this, ontologically, is what is meant by calling those beings "transcendences."

III

Where my projectional principle is grounded in an existential analysis of human behavior, the other three principles—autonomy, relevance, and completeness—are more closely related to the aesthetic aims of our educational procedures and, hence, derive from aesthetic theory.

As for autonomy, we have already eliminated many of the extrinsic values one might pursue in education by restricting its objectives to the enhancement of communication between student and teacher and, through the teacher, between the student and the general society. We avoided the easier choice of conformity as the ultimate value served by this process by further restricting the rôle of the teacher to that of cooperative interlocutor in the educative dialogue, initiated in the first place by the student's efforts at self-expression. If eventually students must succeed in discovering their self-identities, the society must find a place for those identities to be expressed. In our search for the means by which this end is to be attained, we must limn still further restrictions in our attempt to delineate the exact scope of aesthetic education as an intellectual discipline.

We may begin by asking why heteronomy is illicit as an educational principle. Why exclude such things as psychology, personal biography, even art history in so far as the student's own art-making is concerned? When we answer that education is a process of developing a student's capacity for self-determination, and go on to qualify *edu-*

cation with the adjective *aesthetic*, a number of choices have been determined for us. Looking for an expansion of that term, we sought out an institutional framework—an aesthetic institution—that would permit a student's creative energies to reach fulfillment in a social context. That institution, we claimed, is constituted by all those formal behavioral patterns by which artists communicate an aesthetic value to an appreciative audience through the medium of art. In general, then, there are three areas of possible aesthetic inquiry into the workings of the aesthetic institution: the making of an artwork, the artwork itself, and some appreciator's act of appreciation. And these are precisely those areas affected by the autonomous functioning of the aesthetic institution. It should come as no surprise, then, that the educational procedures to be developed for permitting the communication of aesthetic values will be shaped by these same three areas of experience.

Following upon the projective principle, the application of a strict principle of autonomy may seem to encourage permissiveness in student behavior. Let us look more closely at this charge. To be permissive is not necessarily to be irresponsible. If any derogation is implied in the use of the term, it could only stem from an opposing system of values. It is an old debater's trick to charge one's opponent with permissiveness—as Democrats do to Republicans when Republicans are not doing the same thing to Democrats. What if the opposite of permissiveness were the denial of self-determination? To deny a person the freedom to determine oneself expresses a lack of respect for that person. We could do that only if we could be sure of our superior knowledge and authority and if we could expect our students to recognize that we actually possess such knowledge and authority. The famous "generation gap," which always seems to be more pronounced in the current generation than in all previous generations, describes the results of acting in such a manner.

When we actually deny our students the freedom to project their own values, we obviously place ourselves in opposition to their needs and desires and thereby deny the value of our projectional principle. Not only do we create obstacles to real education, we may also unconsciously serve the more reactionary tendencies of the existing society. But autonomy of the means is of the essence here. We must do nothing to foreclose on the autonomous functioning of the aesthetic institution in our schools—as in our society—because the freedom of self-expression is one of the necessary conditions for the creation of a personal value and for its communication to others. The conclusion seems imperative, then, that if we are to "teach" creativity, then we must open ourselves to the effects of our students' creative gestures.

Besides, the permissiveness of the projectional principle is not absolute. Every transcendence must grow out of facticity, or the necessary relationship between the human subject and its situation; that is, to a past, in which some significance is already at one's disposal and which it is the role of the teacher's actual authority to make perspicuous to the student. We could not be free if our behavior were not determined, at least to the extent of being bound to a situation—either traditional and typical, or idiosyncratic and personal—that offers its elements as means toward effective action. John Dewey (1920/1950) had already broached this idea as early as 1920.

We maintained above that the facticity of students' situations—studied by the behavioral sciences—is only one of the determinants of their behavior. Where the means to a desired end are lacking, we may give up the end, or look around for other ways to construct those means viewed as necessary to attain a projected end. We merely said that if our communication is to be considered creative, students must be allowed the freedom to initiate the action. It should be clear that the other postulates—from autonomy to completeness—are intended to spell out the conditions for guaranteeing the possibility of there being a social context for the creation and appreciation of an aesthetic value.

Beyond the projectional principle, therefore, our first appeal is to the principle of autonomy, which would eliminate all but the essentially aesthetic means for attaining our general educational ends. We have defined it as communication through creation and appreciation. Specifically, then, we refer to that education as aesthetic which allows one to play the rôle of artist by making works of art or that of appreciator by experiencing the expressiveness of works of art and criticizing them. All other activities fall beyond the scope of an aesthetic education.

It should be clear, then, that educational permissiveness in the realm of the aesthetic is restrained in the school the same way the permissiveness of aesthetic creation is restrained in the general society— by the effects of criticism. That is the role played by the teacher in the classroom. In that role, the teacher functions as a guide for students in understanding the true worth of their aesthetic creations.

If we decide to restrict ourselves to those facets of the aesthetic institution outlined above as creation, appreciation, and the work of art itself, we shall have laid bare the requirements for the stipulation of the means to be employed in aesthetic education, just as our discussion of existentiality helped us outline the ends of such an education.

For our current purposes, we shall investigate creativity as the basis of the autonomy principle; the work of art, as that of the relevancy principle; and appreciation and criticism, as that of the completeness principle.

IV

Discussions of the "creations" of student artists could be thought to be highly presumptive—if the same could not be said for many of the works of established artists. The confusion here is not caused so much by the admitted minimal results of student activity as by the overbearing assurance on the part of successful artists that they already understand the mechanics of their own creativity. Knowing how to do something does not imply that the person who does, knows what he is doing, nor even his knowing that what he so successfully does has the worth he may attribute to it.

Plato tried to expose this problem in that remarkable dialogue, *Ion*, in which Ion the rhapsode is convinced by Socrates that he (Ion) is wrong to maintain that he excels in interpreting Homer by rule or knowledge, and that he is, instead, inspired by the excellence of the poet, just as the poet himself had been inspired by the muse. It did not occur to Ion to point out that between performance by rule and performance by inspiration there may be a more meaningful alternative. Instead, Socrates is reported to have gained a cheap victory for the Platonic—or "speech" model of communication: first, someone has an idea; then one expresses that idea in a set of symbols; and then someone else reads the idea in the context of the expressing symbols. In short, the process runs: idea, work (artistic vehicle), and idea in that order.

What would happen if instead of first having an idea to be expressed in overt physical form, the artist communicated in a creative fashion in the act of manipulating the sensuous materials of the craft? The communication would be measured by the degree to which both artist and audience reacted in similar or analogous ways to the actual construction of the art object (Kaelin, 1959).

Existential individuals think much in the same way. By hypothesis, their creative ideas are not yet known when they begin to think; they think in the symbols of their trade and discover what they meant to say at the same time they have finished the symbolic manipulation, that is, with the judgment that their works are complete. This new— call it "creative" model, since the Platonic model could only be called "re-creative" or "reproductive" in that according to it we are judging the work with respect to a pre-existent idea—takes on a very different form. Since artists are working to clarify their vague notions and feelings stemming from their prior relations to their environmental situation, and do so by creating works that are the meaningful projection of older into newer situations, artistic communication may be schematized as

$$\text{Work} \begin{cases} \nearrow \text{Reaction}_1 \\ \searrow \text{Reaction}_2 \end{cases}$$

where the reactions are those of artist and audience, or between the artist in the imaginative mode and the same artist in the perceptive mode of experiencing the work. The successful communication between the two has introduced a new channel of social interaction and thus has enriched the culture of the society in which the communication has taken place.

The advantages of this model over the Platonic model are apparent: it can be applied to nonobjective as well as to representational works of art; it allows the inclusion of such "aberrant" artistic techniques as action painting and improvisational jazz as well as deliberative, step-by-step decision making in the development of an aesthetic idea; it explains why creation is truly a thought process, since the productive thinking is performed in terms of the sensuous medium itself; and, lastly, it goes a long way toward showing how the social function of art is intrinsic to the creative process, not grafted on from without on the basis of some economic or political or religious value's being substituted for the aesthetic.

Its chief disadvantages seem to be two: it has been espoused by existentialist thinkers as well as by our own American pragmatists (see Mead, 1934, pp. 71–72, 181, 268–269, 335). It was perhaps because of the support given the idea by the European phenomenologists, however, that it was largely misunderstood. American philosophers of the fifties and sixties were simply not given to reading European sources. But such a "disadvantage" as this is nothing more than a cultural prejudice; that it should be felt as such is nothing more than a symptom of disease in the philosophical community. That it should be misunderstood, on the other hand, poses a greater challenge, but a problem more readily solvable by philosophical analysis. We may begin by admitting that no one creates or appreciates a work by rule: there is no single standard for aesthetic excellence—a point established by Immanuel Kant when he distinguished between logical and aesthetic judgments. The former must be founded on determinate concepts, while the latter are based upon indeterminate concepts, such as "beauty," "sublimity," and the like. An aesthetic idea is therefore an intuition for which no adequate concept may be found—a pronouncement that has, in more recent times, been translated into the "open concept" theory of aesthetic predicates (Weitz, 1956).

But we need not admit for this reason that an aesthetic idea occurs only on the conditions of "inspiration." The aesthetic idea was likewise pronounced by Kant to be a discovery; we add only that the discovery is made by artists manipulating the sensuous materials of their media.

I shall attempt the further reduction of alternatives by considering a standard treatment of *inspiration* (see Ghiselin, 1955). The term is ambiguous, of course; and the ambiguity will be useful in my reduction.

Artists who claim to be inspired are reporting on a psychological fact; they claim either to have found a significant fragment of artistic materials (the Beethovian example) for continued development, or to have hit upon an entire piece in a single swoop of the creative imagination (the Mozartian example). The first example is destructive of the inspirational theory; for if inspiration is an awareness of a fragment of the artistic piece, the creative process must also contain further phases: (1) development of the expressive potential of the fragment (the elaboration phase), which may be long, laborious, and contain many erratic issues that must be eliminated from the final work; (2) conception, which contains the original inspiration along with its developmental material, minus the errors and false continuations; and, lastly, (3) the execution, in which the conceived idea is translated into a physical medium. Beethoven was a genius who worked in this way.

If we may believe the reports of Mozart's genius, on the other hand, the initial inspiration was equivalent to the conception stage of the Beethovian example; he or some enthusiast writing in the name of his genius wrote that the musical composition occurred whole and entire in a blinding flash of inspiration. Once it was had, the composition could be notated and ultimately performed. And in the performance, the composer at least would be in a position to judge the adequacy of the significance enregistered. The Mozartian example, then, would seem to support the Platonic model of artistic communication: he aesthetic idea existed prior to its commitment to the sensuous counters of the medium. That is, imagination has preceded execution.

But what occurs on the second look? The final test in both examples is the correspondence between the inspiration-conception and the performance. And such a correspondence is possible only if what the composer imagines is imagined in the same way one perceives the actual appearance of the work in question during the performance or execution. It is as possible for certain creators to "hear in the mind's ear" or to "see in the mind's eye" before the manipulation of a physical medium: the only way to "read" music is to "hear" the composition whose recipe the score contains. It matters little, however, whether one has produced the composition by manipulating physical or imaginative counters: to think at all in a productive sense, one must manipulate counters.

If one were tempted to compare the genius of Beethoven with that of Mozart, and find it more laborious, less brilliant, more demanding of time, and the like, one should be dissuaded; for the measure of genius is the production of significant results, not the relative ease of conception, nor the time it takes to come to a full inspiration that allows our judgment of artistic significance; that is a property delivered over to our hearing, be it imaginative or perceptive, in which the time created in the musical structures affects the consciousness (or temporality) of the hearer.

The same point has been made in general aesthetic theory by those who refer to an "intentional fallacy" (Wimsatt & Beardsley, 1946). It is committed by those who insist that every artist must have had some intention in making a work of art and that the effective work is good or not on the basis of the clarity in the expression of the intention. The fallacy is a fallacy of judgment, not of creation; for if the creator did have an intention before the execution of the work (through the imagination) and succeeded in expressing that intention, one should only have to examine the artwork to discover what the intention was, not to look for a purely subjective intention to discover what the work is. Moreover, it is the intention of the artist as successfully embodied that must come under judgment; so it cannot stand as a criterion for the success of the work itself. Only the work having an unsuccessfully embodied intention could be examined in the hope of finding "something," but by hypothesis that "something" is not there. And if it is not there, why look for it? And where? The work would be, by definition, a failure.

We avoid the fallacy, of course, by assuming that the artist intended to do what he or she did in fact; and we make our judgment on the basis of the way in which the perceptual object affects our consciousness. In a classroom situation, judgments of intention can be made only on the basis of explicit expression; and we can do this because the word *intention* has both a subjective and an objective import. If it is merely subjective, the only test possible for it is the fact that the intention has been objectively embodied; and when it is embodied, it is there for everyone to perceive. Thus we do not deny that an artist or a student is capable of framing a subjective "intention"; we deny only that such an intention may be known if it remains unexpressed. In this way, with the assumption that an artist has done what he or she actually intended to do, there is no difference between "inspiration" and "execution."

The creative process then becomes amenable to phenomenological analysis. In framing their intentions as purely subjective phenomena, the students or artists project a specific future. To embody that intention they must return to the initial situation from which the intention is projected and manipulate the means offered by that situation until the significance of the work is apparent in a newly established situation. In this way, the future and the past become related in a vivid present, as memory and projected images indicate what must be done in the present moment of creation. It is in such moments that individuals work out the conditions of their own self-transcendence. In the same way, the autonomy principle, which puts all the value of aesthetic education on the act of communication, leads one to consider the work of art as the project of an artist's existence—and it makes no difference if the artist is a student or an accomplished professional whose works may seem on the basis of a greater accomplishment to be much more inspired than those of struggling students.

In sum, an analysis of the term *inspiration* leads us to understand its prevailing mystique: it is so ambiguous as to refer to each of the stages of the so-called "creative process." It may mean the moment of awareness in which one has hit upon a pregnant idea to be developed; or it may refer to the manner in which even an insipid idea has been developed, either imaginatively, without the support of a physical medium, or in the perceptual field of the artist's consciousness. In the first of these senses, the artist may be said to be inspired, but only in the latter does he elicit the proof of his inspiration; and when he does, we more correctly state that the work itself is inspired.

Our preference for the latter interpretation is not an unfounded prejudice. In calling the work "inspired," we avoid the intentional fallacy in making a judgment upon it and we adopt the creative model of communication as the more general explanation, of which the Platonic is only a limiting case—the one in which there is no distinction between subjective and objective intention; it also allows us to associate "artistic problem solving" with active, or productive, manipulation of sensuous materials—the only process over which a critic or a teacher in the role of critic may have some influence in suggesting to students that their own aesthetic judgments be reflective. Finally, if there is a seeming disadvantage in likening a student's halting performance to that of an established artist, this result is attributable to our prejudices, not to an understanding of efficacious human productive action. The ultimate check on our judgments, of course, is not the result of our knowledge concerning its authorship but an experience of the quality produced.

But for this explanation, we must move on to a description of works of art and, therewith, to an exposition of the relevancy principle of aesthetic education.

V

Relevancy as a pedagogical principle of aesthetic education closely parallels a similar principle of aesthetic discourse in general. We have in the foregoing discussion of autonomy already eliminated a principal source of irrelevancy in aesthetic discourse by disallowing any reference by student or teacher to the purely subjective intentions of the student's project. Since any unsuccessful attempt at embodying an intention on the part of a student artist must remain a mystery—or be expressed in some medium other than the one in which it had been aborted—all relevant discourse will be found to be about an embodied intention as that towards which one is striving, or as the effective aesthetic quality one has in fact produced. In either case, both the student and the teacher must be in possession of a set of aesthetic categories capable of application to the structures of the work in question: in the one case, to explain the failure; in the other, the success, of the student project. Judgment on the value of the embodiment of an intention is possible only in terms of an experience of the state of completion achieved in the physical artifact.

We move, then, from a discussion of intentions to a range of possible responses called out by an encounter with the artifact. It is the purpose of our aesthetic categories to indicate the degree of relevancy in this range of aesthetic responses. Whence, the relevancy principle in aesthetic education.

The point may be put simply and in nonphenomenological terms: correlative to the intentional fallacy on the part of some creators of artworks, we find an equally tempting "affective fallacy," usually committed by some of the most sanguine of the work's appreciators (see Parker, 1945; Pepper, 1953; Wimsatt & Beardsley, 1949). If the work does not, strictly speaking, "mean" the intention of its author, perhaps we, as appreciators, are free to interpret its "meaning" in terms of whatever we find there, in an experience of it. Since one is perfectly free to associate any two elements of human experience, and there is a tendency to do so, depending upon the suggestibility of the subject of experience, it could be said that a work of art expresses anything at all. Theoretically, then, each individual work of art would be a microcosm possessing macrocosmic significance, like the individual "monads" of Leibniz's cosmological system, which were claimed to mirror the entire universe from their own points of view. The difficulty with this hypothesis is that there is no way of determining what an individual work is, short of an intuition of the total structure of the universe. And since at least a part of what may be known in the universe is being created from day to day by individuals and the institutions of society, our hope of ever gaining a point of view on the totality of the universe's structure must be frustrated at any given moment of inquiry.

In other words, where an appeal to the intentions of an artist is a fallacy because it posits a null hypothesis for aesthetic significance—that is, nothing is expressed in the only situation in which it is necessary to look for an intention—the affective fallacy likewise inevitably leads to failure because it posits an infinity hypothesis for the same thing. The truth of the matter, we can be sure, lies somewhere in between. Rather than considering the work, then, as an expression of the artist's subjective intention, or as the locus of an infinite range of aesthetic responses, we must develop a set of aesthetic categories, approximately minimal yet quasi-complete for the determination of significance in aesthetic discourse. But here once again I shall proceed phenomenologically.

Not all philosophers of art can be persuaded to make this move. Upon reconsideration of the issue at stake, however, their hesitation constitutes only a detour back into the heart of the matter. Consider first of all the position of the "analytical" philosophers of language, who claim to make no substantive pronouncements on the nature of aesthetic experiences or on the aesthetic objects that are their correlates (Ziff, 1954). Their job is merely to analyze the way in which the ordinary person uses language to describe or evaluate works of art. Such a task is no doubt possible, but it does not of itself establish a criterion for distinguishing between informed and noninformed aesthetic discourse; and although, as a metalinguistic discipline, it can distinguish between descriptive and normative discourse—as it does by continually reminding us that the word art has these two basic uses and that to confuse them is to engage in "fuzzy" thinking—it cannot, once again, provide the criterion for judging the correctness of the usage in question.

We may all know that we are merely describing the structures of an artwork and still maintain some doubt that our description is fitting; we may also be aware of the fact that our language is evaluative, only to be faced with the doubt occasioned by somebody else's contrary judgment. The only solution to these dilemmas, of course, is to have some criterion for the empirical adequacy of our descriptive categories and some knowledge about what one could reasonably say in justifying aesthetic judgments. Whether or not our general categories do justice to the particular case can be tested only on the basis of an experience of a particular work; so whether we are describing the structures of an individual work or attempting to elicit some reason for our estimation of its value, we must possess a set of empirically adequate descriptive categories.

The limitations of the ordinary person's aesthetic categories are for the most part patent: "content and form" (or, variously, "matter and manner," or "stuff and style") are found not to be universally valid antitheses (Weitz, 1950); even "elements" and "principles of organization" bring with them an air of false authority. For, if an element of an aesthetic object is anything that be discriminated in context, then the principle of organization that unites such elements is likewise an element, and there is no meaning in the disjunction of the terms. In order to avoid this embarrassment, along with that of not being able to point out the "matter," "content," or "stuff" of a nonobjective work, I propose the term *counter*. It is value-neutral, as *form* and *style* are not; and since it is used merely to refer to something discriminable in the aesthetic context, it may be used to refer to both representational and nonrepresentational contexts.

If we can be persuaded to adopt such value-free terminology for our basic aesthetic categories, the problem of determining relevance in the discourse used to describe works of art comes down to being able to find ways of categorizing the manner in which "counters" function in the determination of significance in the particular context. But before the individual case may be considered, we must attempt to ascertain the various ways in which aesthetic counters have been observed to function in well-attested sample cases. These need not be "touchstones of excellence," as per Matthew Arnold, or even "paradigm cases" of linguistic usage; all we need to know is whether the word *art* is correctly used to describe such things as musical compositions, traditional and modern paintings, dances, and the like, and our investigation may begin.

It will begin when we learn to "bracket out" the nonessential characteristics of the physical artifact. But this move may be justified by considering once again some of the leading tenets of analytical aesthetics. It has been said, for example, that any distinction between a "physical artifact" and an essential "aesthetic object" is a metaphysical confusion. In the best-known treatment of the problem, Paul Ziff (1954) has maintained that there are not two "objects" but only different ways of describing the same object. His point is well taken: any description of the so-called aesthetic object must certainly be linked with what we perceive of the thing made by the artist. Yet he gives us no clues for distinguishing the two sorts of descriptions. Presumably, we know when we are talking about a physical thing; it has weight, location, and all the other properties associated with natural objects. But to call a painting, for example, a spatial arrangement of colors is systematically misleading; for we experience the spatial arrangement in terms of the intrinsic values of the colors or forms used to arrange the spaces of the painting. We are talking in the physical language when we describe a painting as possessing reds and greens; we are using the aesthetic or phenomenological language when we describe the tensions created by juxtaposing a red and a green on a picture plane. A difference of language, indeed, but one that makes all the difference in the world: it is that which allows the teacher, who has experienced the space tensions within the painting, to inform students, who have arranged the blobs of red and green pigment on a canvas, that their paintings are either functioning or not in the creation of a significant visual context (Ingarden, 1967).

Our awareness that some descriptions are only physical and others purely "aesthetic" may already be understood by everyone who has had any kind of experience of paintings, but unless we can point out what makes the difference, we can hardly be effective teachers of art. Phenomenologists, following Edmund Husserl, claim to make the difference between physical and aesthetic descriptions clear by their practice of the "phenomenological *epochē*" (see Chapter 7). They place brackets around the single physical object as it appears to our attentive vision by a typical change in attitude. Beginning with the natural attitude, in which an object appears as it exists in nature, they reduce it to its manner of appearing. We can remain within the natural attitude and explain the existence of the physical artifact as an effect, cause, reason, or consequence. The explanation may be given in terms of commonsense assumptions about the nature of physical reality or in the more sophisticated language of the appropriate empirical science. In either case, however, our descriptions will tend to obscure the issue under discussion: the specific manner in which the object affects us in perception; and that is precisely where we must learn to place our "brackets" around our own perceptual field. When we do, not only will we have performed the phenomenological *epoché*, we shall also have determined the scope of relevancy within our "aesthetic" descriptions.

Discussions of "the aesthetic attitude" have been as profitless as those of the "aesthetic object." George Dickie (1966) was once engaged in a long discussion with Virgil Aldrich about the propriety of the former term. He gave the impression that any reference to an attitude on the part of a perceiver represents some sort of mystical state into which one might throw oneself prior to one's actual perception of the values in a work of art. Obviously, there is no such state.

Whether we are in the natural or in the phenomenological attitude, our consciousness is intending some kind of object; otherwise we should not have experience of either kind, the physical or the aesthetic. All we do in effectuating the *epoché* is to place brackets around the appearance of the object, so that the physical characteristics it displays, from the standpoint of the natural attitude, are held to be irrelevant. Bracketing the phenomenological characteristics of an object means only that we attend to an object as it appears to us.

Once we have performed the reduction, we may observe the following sorts of counters. All works of art display some sort of organized sensuous surface, capable of expressing some sort of vague feeling or mood. In addition, some works have surfaces so organized as to suggest further interpretation: an object may be represented, or an idea, by the relationship between represented objects; and ideas may call out further images, purely psychological in nature, which are gauged to be relevant or irrelevant on the basis of their fittingness to the context being developed. We may refer to the representational elements—objects, ideas, and images—as "experiential depth" to distinguish them from the purely surface counters of the medium. And, lastly, since surface and depth, when they coexist in a single context experienced as a pervasive quality, are obviously related, we need a further category to refer to this relationship: whence, the necessity for a concept of "total expressiveness."

Surface, depth, and total expressiveness were explained in Chapter 6 of this volume. They were used to define the postulates of aesthetic significance as contextually determined. The postulates themselves, four in number, were (1) the context-boundness of aesthetic significance; (2) the constitution of an aesthetic context by its counters; (3) the Gestalt principle, by which significance is denied to any counter taken out of context; and (4) the determination of the significance of the context by the qualities of an experience funding into some determinate quality pervading the whole. The four postulates, taken together, constitute an eidetic description of works of art as these determine our aesthetic experiences of whatever physical object the artist may have constructed.

The point to retain is that the language of aesthetic counters and their relations is categorial, that is, descriptive of the general characteristics of possible aesthetic objects. How particular counters function in coming to closure in a single, successive experience is an empirical matter, concerning which any kind of ordinary language description that actually fits the case is licit. Thus knowledge of the categories serves merely to judge the relevance of statements made about art objects in our ordinary, day-to-day linguistic references. Once having constructed the categories, we should be willing to "throw them away," if only we were convinced that all experients' descriptions of their aesthetic experiences were both relevant and empirically adequate.

The purposes of an adequately developed set of aesthetic categories for aesthetic education, therefore, is to guarantee the possibility of communication between the teacher and the student when both are referring linguistically to the work of art being developed as the student's project.

Pedagogical aesthetic behavior, then, is relevant when the student and teacher are engaged in communication—either directly through the creation and the appreciation of the student's work or indirectly, that is, linguistically, when either party to the communication is referring meaningfully to some phenomenologically observable characteristic of works of art. When the student's role is that of appreciator or critic, the teacher's is that of metacritic. Whichever the roles of the moment, the dialogue concerns the communication of aesthetic knowledge and so is based upon a set of shared aesthetic categories. According to the autonomy principle explained earlier, all other behavior in the classroom must be ordered to this end.

VI

One more principle remains in our inquiry into the phenomenology of aesthetic education—completeness.

From one point of view, pedagogical completeness is not as closely tied up with aesthetic completeness as pedagogical relevancy is with aesthetic relevancy. If our experience of a work of art comes to closure in the funding of aesthetic counters, the experience may be said to be complete with our consciousness of their closure. This is what Dewey meant when, in *Art as Experience* (1934), he claimed that an adequate perception of the work of art is already an implicit judgment of its worth. According to the last aesthetic postulate of contextual meaning, the significance of a work of art is precisely the felt expressiveness of the funding counters; and any verbal expression concerning the value of that expressiveness merely gives the added bit of information: that in the light of the given experience the counters had funded, or failed to do so, or even tended to do so or not. Thus when we say, "this work is good, bad, or leaves us indifferent," we mean to convey the corresponding information concerning the functioning of aesthetic counters within the experience of the work; if there is any doubt about the matter, we can always refer back to the context of that experience, in the light of an observation performed according to the categories of relevance, in order to determine whose judgment on the work is better founded in any case of disagreement. Where there is no disagreement, the act will be complete with the concomitant experiences, on the part of the teacher and student, of the goodness or badness of the work. The communication is completed in the similarity of the judgments.

In any case of disagreement in the judgment of an artwork's value, however, the inquiry must continue beyond the stage of relevancy in the two perceptions—or of applied descriptive aesthetics—and proceed to an analysis of the ways in which aesthetic judgments are justified; the move is into normative aesthetics. The critical case arises, therefore, when students claim their artwork to be completed and the teacher must explain that, if so, the work is good, bad, or relatively either. In those cases in which the students themselves are uncertain of the value of the expression, the inquiry is not complete until a normative analysis of the situation has been given; and in the prevailing circumstances, pedagogical completeness and aesthetic completeness are once again more strictly analogous. In making this reservation, we are maintaining that the goal of aesthetic education is not merely the production of successful "artists" but rather of creative individuals fully self-conscious of the value to be found in the experience of their creations.

One further caution, however, is still in order. It may be psychologically damaging to put too much weight upon aesthetic completeness too early in the careers of students. Harsh, nonconstructive criticism may serve to inhibit further trials at creativity, especially upon extremely young students. Yet it seems apparent that a "work of art" has to be something more than just "nice"; if we do not, at some point in their careers, lead students to an understanding of the actual niceties at work in their works of art, then we obviously will have failed to develop the purpose of the aesthetic institution to its fullest—which, it will be recalled, is to liberate the aesthetic impulses of individuals under the constraints of the aesthetic perception of values, whoever the creator. Moreover, with the proper sort of constructive criticism, there seems to be little danger of destroying students' motivations to express themselves. All this does is to put the burden of demonstration on the professional consciousness of the teacher.

According to analytical philosophy, once again, aesthetic judgments are justified by eliciting "good reasons" for a given appraisal (Ziff, 1958). Some care must be made, however, to distinguish aesthetic judgments *per se* from psychological reports, such as aesthetic preferences, which have nothing to do with the value of a work. Always, as before, we shall claim that the statement "I like *x*" is a psychological report and may or may not give some evidence of an acceptable value judgment. If someone having a sufficient background in the creation and appreciation of works of art of the kind in question makes the statement, we should be more inclined to look for the relevant reason that could be maintained as grounds for making it. The practicing artist or critic usually expresses a kind of liking wherein the "qualification" is determined by the bias for correctness in judgment and wherein this "correctness" is underwritten by the experience of the judge in question. Where these conditions do not obtain, as they do not when judges prefer works that most closely resemble their own, we should be led to doubt the accuracy of the judgment. Aesthetic judgments must be made upon the basis of relevancy guiding an actual perception of the functioning contextual counters.

A bare liking statement almost always violates the relativity, or Gestalt postulate, governing the interpretation of aesthetic significance. Preferring certain kinds of objects or experiences in the natural attitude, the biased judge tends to give an absolute value to any context in which such counters may be found. A religious work is good because it possesses representational counters depicting a religious subject; a socially realistic work is good because it represents an approved ideological position. And the same sort of falsification may be perpetuated by an illogical (or nonaesthetic) preference for a given technique. Other false judgments are given on the basis of peer-group approval or of the reverence for the mystique of an artist's personality. But there is no way of guessing what can be given in lieu of an aesthetic judgment on a work of art. That the states of affairs alluded to in the latter sorts of judgments are so widespread attests only to the heteronomous grounds used heretofore in aesthetic education.

In order to avoid these extra-aesthetic judgments on works of art, along with any unfounded appeals to authority, the teacher may redirect any statements of a personal liking by posing a different sort of question: not "do you like *x*?", but "what is it, exactly, that you like about it?" Inevitably, if the rules of aesthetic relevance are followed, the answer will be couched in perceptual terms: either the counters fund or fail to fund at some level of significance, because tensions are set up that are resolved or fail to be resolved when one attends to the working of the work. As long as one leaves oneself open to this phenomenon—without making any elaborate or unfounded claims—there is a good chance of agreement on the part of equally qualified observers.

It is for this reason, I hypothesize, that persons trained in art, criticism, or aesthetic theory tend to agree on the value of a given work of art; and why, paradoxically, "objective" inquirers into the aesthetic preferences of their subjects wisely exclude those having some knowledge of aesthetics: the judgments of such individuals are biased toward the correctness of aesthetic judgment and would tend to falsify the results obtained in a study of nonsophisticated "judges." For similar reasons, some defense counselors refuse to accept jurors who profess any knowledge of logic, since that would be to prejudice a jury against any purely emotional pleas they would like to make. Certainly if our teachers of an aesthetic subject matter are not so biased, they are not fulfilling their function of bringing about the complete aesthetic development of their students.

In general, the procedures for making an aesthetic judgment are easy to define: we have an experience of a given work; we analyze its distinctive counters, resynthesize the counters into a whole context, and thus find ourselves in a position to judge the degree to which our consciousness is controlled by the artist's productive work (Dewey, 1934). A good rule of thumb for this procedure is that any work which "resists analysis," that is, which yields a postanalytical experience of the same or richer quality than the preanalytic, is good; and if the postanalytical experience is of a poorer quality or the same, if the preanalytic experience was negative, then we have presumptive evidence that the work is unsuccessful.

A judgment is also possible on the basis of difference by degree. Some works tend to closure, but never quite make it; while others diffuse any attention paid to the context to a greater or lesser degree. If, however, our prior postulate of relevance is correct, that all expressions are limited to their contexts of funding counters, it is impossible to judge the value of one work on the basis of a comparison with that of another. We can, of course, compare two works, once judged, and pronounce one better than the other; but if aesthetic contexts are truly autonomous, no sense can be made of the comparison. To call a work "good" is to pronounce a judgment that claims the student or artist has managed to bring the counters he or she has elected to use to some sort of closure, some sort of successful completion. That is the reason for the necessity of a completeness principle in art education. The only test for the validity of an aesthetic judgment is an experience of a closing aesthetic context.

The expected success of the pedagogical principle of educational completeness therefore depends upon teachers' abilities to make valid judgments of the creations or appreciations of their students, as well as upon their abilities to make them stick by an analysis of the context in question. In this sense, educational completeness depends upon aesthetic completeness.

If the foregoing analysis is correct, it would be impossible to be an effective teacher of art, either of its creation or its appreciation, without some training in philosophical aesthetics—an argument which at the present time lacks only a succinct summary, which is given below.

VII

The foregoing argument is premised upon the assumption that a close correlation exists between aesthetic knowledge and the pedagogical procedures one ought to adopt in aesthetic education. There surely can be no argument with the statement that one ought to adopt that method which produces the best essential results. In search of some kind of result, I have proposed an educational program based upon four principles: in sum, aesthetic education is to be projectional, autonomous, relevant, and complete. The first of these principles is drawn from existential phenomenology as an account of human self-determination; the other three, from the stages of aesthetic communication.

If a human being is properly characterized as a transcendence, defined in part by its openness to new experiences and its ability to transmit the significance of such experiences to other beings of similar structure, it is properly understood as a projection toward value fulfillment, and the overall context for this personal fulfillment is social, worked out within the institutions of a given society. The development of transcendences within the context of social institutions was stipulated earlier as the end or objective of the general educational process.

Moving on to the means by which this development is to take place, in the particular instance of aesthetic education, I found auton-

omy to be achieved by the selection of the process of artistic communication, in which creation and appreciation of created values occur,
as that which makes "education" specifically "aesthetic." For purposes
of shortening the description, the act of creating was selected as typical of the concerns illustrating autonomy. If courses where the means
selected are not strictly creative, but only appreciative, of course, the
creation has already been performed by another artist, and instruction
must begin with response to the created object. Where the student's
behavior is critical, the teacher's is metacritical; and we still remain
within the functioning of the aesthetic institution. But whether the
student's behavior is creative or appreciative, the process is governed
by the appearance of a work of art, the central concept of aesthetic
communication, as that by which the communication takes place. A
model other than the traditional Platonic one was suggested for depicting the centrality of the work of art in aesthetic communication; it
is the work itself that mediates the communication.

The relevance of aesthetic categories to aesthetic education is
therefore apparent, although the tendency of educationists has always
been to favor the kind of eclecticism (see Smith, 1966) it has been my
purpose to avoid. However they are to be gained, a consistent set of
aesthetic categories is needed to establish the aesthetic relevance of
statements descriptive of works of art. Developing such a set of categories has always been one of the traditional domains of philosophical
aesthetics. And if the danger of looking to too many sources for the
opinions of the "experts" brings to mind the old story of the difference between a camel and a horse, that would not be an evil consequence.

Another problem of traditional aesthetics is that of justifying aesthetic judgments; and it must be solved if the teacher is to function
suitably as critic of a student's work or criticism. Aesthetic experiences
are brought to closure by an act of perception, which lays the ground-
work for approval or disapproval; and all perceptual acts are amenable
to phenomenological analysis, which culminates in a linguistic description. When disagreement in the verbal expression of one's ap-
provals or disapprovals arises in the contact between student and
teacher, educational completeness demands that the disagreement be
reduced by an actual justification, through the analysis of the aesthetic
object in question.

Thus where the projectional principle is established through the
existential analysis of human subjects, the autonomy, relevance, and
completeness principles are established through the phenomenological
analysis of aesthetic objects. By performing such analyses, I have hoped

to succeed in my own project, which was to produce an existential-phenomenological account of aesthetic education, considered as a model, and hence prescriptive, account of aesthetic education.

Two last reservations must be voiced. The first is that the method prescribed has only clarified the objectives and means of aesthetic education; as far as practice is concerned, I have used the method only from a critic's, not an artist's, point of view. Should others be persuaded by whatever clarity has been produced here to attempt the method from the creative aspect, some objective studies of its results may be made and tested against the results, similarly determined, of other methods. Then, on purely pragmatic grounds, one should be in a position to make a rational choice between alternatives. Experimental and control groups are relatively easy to devise for testing the workability of methods; but surely this is the business of professional educationists.

Secondly, while it is also relatively easy to describe autonomy, relevance, and completeness as principles, it is not quite so easy to apply them to particular cases of analysis. Only experience with the method is capable of producing this kind of "knowing how"; and until professional educationists become more proficient as phenomenological analysts, it would seem more profitable to lay this part of the teachers' training on the shoulders of a professional, phenomenological aesthetician; and the only place this is happening, at the present stage of our culture, is in departments of philosophy open enough to external currents to be influenced by the European sources of this philosophical movement.

9

BETWEEN THE INNOCENT EYE
AND THE OMNISCIENT MIND

PHENOMENOLOGY AS A METHOD
FOR ART-CRITICAL
AND AESTHETIC ANALYSIS

This essay, under a slightly different title, was commissioned as a lecture to be delivered before a summer institute at New York University in 1980. The subject of the institute was phenomenological aesthetics. I chose as my task the explanation of the "deepening" of an aesthetic experience from the surface characteristics of a work of art to the deeper structures called forth in an engaged consciousness by the objects, ideas, and imagery of representational works.

In the same breath, I took on, for the first time, a phenomenological explanation of the linguistic functioning of critical discourse in its full scope: description, interpretation, and evaluation. If I am right in this matter, each of these procedures is another form of phenomenological description. Only the object of consciousness differs in the so-called three "distinct" activities. The sameness of the consciousness—a single spread of conscious temporality spanning one's remembered past and an anticipated future of an experienced aesthetic value—changes character as the object of its intentions change; it depends and is suffused with what used to be called by aestheticians "an aesthetic satisfaction."

Since my account was highly technical, my hosts invited me to append a selective bibliography and a glossary of the unusual terms. Both may be found appended to this entire collection of essays.

This essay (1980) was published in-house in a collection of lectures that served as record of the institute.

I

When contemporary American philosophers speak of phenomenology, they may be referring to any of a number of highly technical methodological procedures for analyzing the meanings implicit in human behavior. Dominant among these are the "descriptive" phenomenology of Edmund Husserl and the "hermeneutical" phenomenology of perhaps his most famous student, Martin Heidegger. I shall be maintaining, after a brief description of these two methodologies, that both have their rightful place in a complete account of aesthetic analysis and that, with a slight modification I shall myself introduce into the procedures, a single method I yet call "phenomenological" will enable us to account for the qualitative evaluations that a good critic and other informed viewers of works of art actually make as a matter of daily habit. The clue for my interpretation is to reconsider hermeneutics, itself a theory of making interpretations, as a special case of phenomenological description—as a description of the deeper associations brought to bear upon certain organizations in a surface design.

These two structures—the surface design and the depth associations—constitute two orders of controlling human interest in aesthetic expressions. The first is markedly perceptual but may be the object of an artist's imagination prior to being realized in colored pigments; and the second is primarily imaginative as the perceptual counters of the experience fund into a representation of an object, which may or may not be a part of nature but which is always constituted solely in accordance with an artist's conceptual understanding of such a thing, even if the artist's rendering is the only clue for the understanding. Something similar to a geometer's proof by "construction" is involved here.

The problem posed to phenomenology is the proper way to describe an experience that is partly perceptual and partly imaginative and yet, for all that, a single experience (Dewey, 1934).

I begin my account with an exposition of Husserl's methodological claims.

II

The first principle of the Husserlian methodology is to return to the things themselves, that is, to abandon all preconceived notions of what must or only might be the case in favor of an unbiased observation of what actually is the case as a phenomenon occurs to our attentive consciousness. Thus if the phenomenon in question is the appearance of a work of art, our decision must be to let ourselves open to the manner of that appearance, which is what it is no matter what the object may be "in itself." Indeed, in yielding to appearances the phenomenologist arbitrarily suspends any interest in the reality of objects or of the world in which they are habitually encountered. Sometimes this suspension of our interests in reality is referred to as a change in attitude: from the natural attitude, in which things are noted for their possible use or explained in terms of the causes that have produced them or the effects they themselves may cause, to the phenomenological attitude, in which things are observed only as they appear. This change is said to be attitudinal since only the consciousness of the perceiving subject is involved in the change: the object of nature is "reduced" to a meaning "object" related to a meaning "nature"; a tree as one such object is thereby reduced to a "tree as perceived."

The perceiver who has adopted this particular conscious set is said to have practiced the "phenomenological reduction"; the suspension of belief in the existence of the object meant constitutes an *epochē* within which attention is no longer placed upon the physical characteristics of a thing but rather upon the manner of its appearance as a set of meanings by which our consciousness is related to that thing. The next step of the method is to describe what appears within the reduction. A similar technique used in elementary pedagogical situations goes by the name of "show and tell."

The descriptions used by phenomenologists in their telling may be either general, in terms of repeatable characteristics, or particular, in terms of specific properties of the phenomenon in question. Since the repeatable characteristics are called *eidē*, or essences, the general descriptions are called "eidetic." Most of Husserl's own descriptions were of this nature. Descriptions of particular phenomena, on the other hand, although less philosophical than eidetic descriptions of the conscious structures of experience in that they are lacking in generality, are still necessary components of the phenomenological method. They provide the basis for a future judgment on the repeatability of essential characteristics. Within the area of aesthetic descriptions, those of aestheticians proper are eidetic and those of literary critics are phenomenological.

Essences may be intuited through the technique of consciousness variation. Those characteristics of a phenomenon that remain unchanged throughout a change in consciousness, say, from perception to imagination, are of essences. Consider, for example, the *eidos* "red." It is a species of another perceptual *eidos*, "color." Whether I am perceiving the red of an object in nature or on a painted canvas or only imagining the red of the same sorts of objects, my attention has not been changed from the color of the object to its shape, nor has the hue, brightness, or saturation of the color undergone any change for the change in my intentional acts. These invariant essences are the repeatable characteristics of experiences deriving from the immanent structures of consciousness itself, a part of the so-called noematic nucleus by which our consciousness intends its objects. A noema is a meaning structure, the means any consciousness possesses for intending any sort of object whatsoever; and for each noema there is a corresponding noetic act. Perception, conception, and imagination are different noetic acts, different ways for consciousness to relate itself to the objects of its world.

When we reflect upon the eidetic structures of a particular act of consciousness, our consciousness is no longer related to a transcendent object but rather to the immanent structures of the original conscious act, either to a noesis or to its correlated noema. It is of some advantage here to limit our attention to noematic structures. They may be described by using names for qualities or things that, as a result of prior intendings, have become "sedimented meanings"; by using names that have been stipulated for the purpose of identifying qualities or things; or by using the metaphorical extension of names for prior sedimented meanings. This is a fact of extreme importance for art criticism, which may be directed toward a work of art of almost infinite subtlety wherein the nuances of expression may be so finely drawn that an equally powerful technique must be devised to provide descriptions of their effects. And here, if stipulation fails, then metaphor operates whenever we apply a single name to variously similar qualitative structures.

However metaphorical, for a description to be adequate its component meanings, either nucleic or peripheral, must be understood; and the criterion for the understandability of an *eidos* is whether a given description guides an observer's attention to the properties of the phenomenon described. Both phenomena and their essential structures may be intuited, and the appropriate test for the claim that they have been intuited is whether a description may be given that is understandable in one of the senses indicated above.

In general, as was indicated above, philosophers are concerned with eidetic descriptions and critics, with phenomenological descriptions. But one cannot move to the intuition of essences given in eidetic description without having first practiced the phenomenological reduction on the qualities of experience. Consciousness is said by Husserl to "constitute" the meanings by which we interpret our experiences insofar as it finds objects to fulfill its intentions. Indeed, the defining characteristic of a consciousness is its intentionality—as expressed in the axiom that every consciousness is a consciousness of some thing.

That principle was borrowed by Husserl from his own teacher, Franz Brentano, who was attempting, in his *Psychology from an Empirical Standpoint* (1874/1973), to differentiate the physical and physiological structures of human behavior from the "purely psychological." An accomplished medievalist, he settled upon the notion of "intention" developed by the medieval logicians to express the relations between a term and its reference as a convenient model to conceive of the relation between a consciousness and its objects. Within the medieval logical traditions, terms of the first intention were those relating to an object of nature, while terms of the second intention, such as *genus, species*, and the like, referred to those "beings of reason" by which human consciousness ordered its own knowledge. The historical irony of Brentano's decision is that his own approach to logic was itself criticized by Husserl as being "psychologistic," that is, described in terms of the psychological processes by which inferences are made rather than in terms of the logical relations themselves. But, then, given the source of Brentano's inspiration, this charge is very easy to understand.

Husserl's career began with the attempt to rid geometry (and logic) of its psychologism. If the defining property of a consciousness is its intentionality, then a method had to be devised by which the structures of this intentionality could be described as they showed themselves in the phenomena of our conscious experiences. And how was this to be done? By the practice of the phenomenological *epoché*, by careful reflection, and by eidetic description.

The principal error promulgated in the history of philosophy, Husserl thought, was the doctrine of a soul-substance. Had Descartes not been burdened with this bit of ancient lore, his *Meditations* would have led him to the discovery of the truth—that all our acts of consciousness intend objects in essential ways. Descartes' dream hypothesis alone elicits the structures of perception, imagination, and conception (three different noetic acts); and his variations of these acts, intending different objects in different ways, led him to the intuition of a simple nature or essence. According to Husserl, consciousness is not a substance but an act, an act of relating an ego to an object in its world. And this "transcendental ego" is itself intuited as an object that is left over—as a residue within the transcendental reduction—when the world has been placed "within brackets" or put out of the question. The ego is only a conscious act of intending a world through a set of meanings appropriately definitive of that world; but, as reduced, it is cut off from its actual connection with the real world. Throughout its separation from the objects of its transcendent world, it too remains the same: a more or less tensely felt correlation between an act and its noematic, immanent, meaning structures.

There are, moreover, as many transcendental egos as there are conscious subjects capable of making the phenomenological reduction, and anyone capable of reflecting on a prior conscious act is capable of understanding the various roles played by one's transcendental ego in the organization of experience. Husserl wrote his own *Cartesian Meditations* (1926/1969) to explain what these roles were but did little to convince other philosophers that his phenomenological demonstration of the existence of other persons was cogent; for, from the sphere of one's own transcendental ego, all that one has, in fully intuitive evidence, is the idea of another, that is, the other as an idea or meaning, which may or may not be fulfilled in our conscious experience of interpersonal relations. The reason for this lingering doubt concerning the actual existence of another person is the effect of the first, or phenomenological, *epochē*, which has put the world into brackets, and along therewith the bodies of all human beings, those of the others as well as those of the meditating philosophers.

This brief survey of the range of the Husserlian methodology gives little explicit advice to would-be critics of art. Husserl made little use of the phenomena of art in developing his methodology, since he was primarily interested in establishing an indubitable basis for human knowledge on the strength of intuitive evidence of the various acts of consciousness by which knowledge is gained. The most basic of these processes is perception, and imagination comes on the scene mostly as a means by which consciousness is varied to allow the intuition of essences. But to illustrate the difference between perceptual and imaginative intentionalities he did, in *Ideas* (1913/1962), refer to an experience of Albrecht Dürer's *Ritter, Tod, und Teufel*, an engraving depicting a knight, his horse and dog, a personification of death, and a monster representing the devil. All these terms, *knight, horse, dog, death,* and *devil,* are sedimented meaning structures of the intending consciousness or may be defined by pointing to the figures they refer to. The perceptual consciousness intends the surface of the etching as a set of lines and forms, but these lines and forms are seen as representations of the objects named above and, as such, refer the consciousness to the imagined objects: a knight in flesh and blood, the figure of death, and the animalistic incarnation of the devil.

In these descriptions, the surface presentation is said to have the same psychic matter as the representation—the same lines and forms as seen but now *seen as* representing transcendent objects. Only the manner in which consciousness is directed to its object differs in the two attitudes: perceptually, consciousness intends the lines of the drawing; imaginatively, it intends the transcendent objects, which are not present as flesh and blood but are merely referred to as so existing. As Sartre will later say, such objects are "present" in their absence.

The differences in these two conscious attitudes constitute the basis for the phenomenological aesthetics of the two Frenchmen, Maurice Merleau-Ponty and Jean-Paul Sartre, whose theories make up the subject matter of my next section. Now that two of them have been united in death—or in objective history, if you prefer—their theories may be considered as fixed.

III

Merleau-Ponty, we recall from prior studies of his "aesthetics" (Kaelin, 1962), developed his entire philosophical career on the theme of the primacy of perception for the determination of human significances—a thesis admirably suited for explaining the expressiveness of the "aesthetic surfaces" (see Prall, 1929/1967a)—presented to us by the the objects of our world. Although this theme was developed out of a thoroughgoing study of Husserl's phenomenology and a lifelong habit of reflecting on his own perceptions, he could find no evidence that a transcendental ego constituted the meanings of our perceptual experience. When he himself tried to perform the transcendental reduction, all he succeeded in intuiting was the relation between his body and the objects of the external world. Aspects of these objects tended to fund into significant Gestalten, depending upon the way in which the living body expressed itself relative to these objects, and a complete theory of the body would contain descriptions of all the ways in which different behavioral structures are embodied in the intentional-arc uniting our bodies to their habitual worlds. Some of these structural behavioral forms, for example, are syncretic, determined by the physical and physiological makeup of the organism; others are amovable, proper for one situation but transferable to others; and still others are symbolic, in which the behavioral response is for the purpose of creating a significance not tied to any particular environment, but which projects the possibility of an understanding by virtue of an arrangement of the elements built into the autoaffective response.

The individual parts of a stimulus never determine the response to a symbol, since that response is to the whole, which is always greater than the mere sum of its parts. Thus it is the pregnancy of the Gestalt that constitutes the significance of a symbol; and that pregnancy is found in the configuration the same way that a theme is found in a melody, as a single recognizable Gestalt: a moment made up of smaller moments, none of which has any meaning apart from a relationship to an other. In this way, aesthetic behavior, dedicated to the creation and appreciation of such forms, comes to crown the highest moments of our "conscious" lives; and what Husserl thought he had intuited as a transcendental ego was nothing more than his body caught in a moment of chiasmatic self-affection, as stimuli coming in from outside the body were modified, arranged into a symbol, and redirected outward as an expression, in the world, of a human being's drive to self-transcendence.

The unity of body and consciousness is established by the continuity in these orders of human response: expression, the body, and human significance are all variations on a single theme—that indestructible relationship between a living body and its world.

Within this demonstration Merleau-Ponty (1948/1969a) refers to Cézanne as the painter who, more than most, had taught us how to look and see. But that was only because he had such a difficult time teaching himself how to see, that is, how to let the phenomenon show itself in all its visibility. He learnt that lesson the day he realized that in order to paint the Gestalt features discovered in his field of vision he had to find the simpler features of which they were the symbolic significance; if he tried to paint right off the "woolly" aspect of a piece of material, he botched it every time; he could pull off the trick only if he was capable of rendering the aspects that fund into that sensation of woolliness—the hues, the values, the tones, in the background as well as in the foreground—and only when he was patient enough to discover the laws of their organization.

Such was the aesthetic theory many of us found so full of promise. But beginning with "The Eye and the Mind" (1969b), Merleau-Ponty's reflections on the art of painting took a turn for the worse. His recent reading of Heidegger's ontology had convinced him that the "meaning" of the objects of experience, and even of their representations, is determined by the manner in which things are disclosed to an inquiring subject as being what they are. In this scheme of things, entities get interpreted—whence the name of "hermeneutics" for this form of phenomenological analysis—as something lying present-at-hand; their being, as their manner of presencing.

Stated in this way, there seems to be only a slight difference from the account given above. Where before vision was described as the closure of surface characteristics of an object into a significant Gestalt, now it has become a means for unveiling the deeper and usually hidden structures of reality, both human and natural, that make possible the appearance of such characteristics. In short, there has been a shift from an interest in describing the ontics of a visual experience—how such experiences take place under standard conditions—to one in describing the ontological structures that constitute the possibility of such experiences: from a simple account of our seeing to a very complicated account of our own being as disclosing the being of those entities that are disclosed.

The title of this later speculation on the ultimate—ontological—significance of paintings still seems relevant enough. "The Eye and the Mind" is a simple metonymic reference to the functional differences between perception and conception—the same that had produced the difference in emphasis in empirical and rationalistic theories of knowledge from the seventeenth to the beginning of the nineteenth century. Both these conscious sets are brought to bear in our creative—read "symbolic" here—and our appreciative— read "perceptual" or "interpretive" here—responses; but his descriptions of the depth structures of painting by now have become rife with ontological references: not only to objects in their essential appearance, as before, but to their being as appearances, and even to the Being of such beings.

I am not questioning here the possibility of such an inquiry. To my mind, Heidegger himself was quite successful in this manner of inquiry. I mean only to point out the differences between an ontological and an aesthetic inquiry and to suggest, perhaps, that either of these philosophical disciplines may be subordinated to the other and that in finally subordinating aesthetics to ontology, Merleau-Ponty had made the wrong choice, at least for an aesthetician. Later on, in showing how Roman Ingarden developed Husserlian description into a full-fledged aesthetic methodology, I shall show how ontology is correctly subordinated to aesthetics. But for now that must remain a promise.

Suffice it to repeat here that Merleau-Ponty himself had succeeded in devising one of the most promising theories of surface aesthetic expressiveness only to later break that promise by introducing irrelevant elements—those transcending the issue of what makes a situation aesthetic (Urmson, 1962)—into his descriptions of paintings considered as works of art. There is nothing inherently wrong in using our experience of paintings to illustrate ontological structures, but there is nothing particularly aesthetic about it either.

Where Merleau-Ponty had begun his aesthetic analysis with an explanation of the determination of significance within a perceptual field and then moved on to an interpretation of such experiences in terms of the meaning of Being itself, Sartre, for his part, began with the depth structures of the imagining consciousness. Although interested much earlier than his longtime personal friend in Heideggerian ontology and "existentialism," Sartre never betrayed his inspiration in Husserlian phenomenology for his account of aesthetic objects. His choice for the dominant mode of an aesthetic consciousness was the imagination, whose eidetic structures were described in his *The Psychology of the Imagination* (1940/1948).

The conclusion of that book is devoted to a matched set of observations: the imagination as an act of consciousness and works of art as objects of the imagining consciousness. Like all other acts of consciousness described by Husserl, images were said to be of objects. Unlike the objects of a perceptual consciousness, however, imaginary objects were described as "unreal," that is, intended in their absence, or as existing outside the real world of time and space, on the basis of the perception of a physical "analogue." The analysis follows pretty closely Husserl's own analysis of Dürer's etching mentioned above.

The surface characteristics of paintings are real enough—as real as pigments on a canvas; and when organized in such a way as to represent another real object, these perceived surface characteristics motivate the human imagination to intend the objects represented. The difference between our perception of a sensuous surface and our imagination of a representational depth is a difference of conscious attitude—a change of conscious act, if you will, between the realizing thesis of the perceptual consciousness and the "irrealizing" thesis of the imaginative.

There were two difficulties with this distinction in aesthetic attitude.

First of all, although it enabled aestheticians to refer both to surfaces and to the depth of figurative works of art, in stressing the irrealizing features of the imaginative consciousness Sartre tended to ignore or to discount the aesthetic values of the perceptual surfaces in determining what makes an artwork good. Where surfaces have been reduced to the role of an analogue of the imaginary object, their only role is to motivate the appearance of such objects: actual seeing and its values have been traded off against "seeing in the mind's eye alone," whose aesthetic values are never given a rational explanation.

The second difficulty lies in the generalization of the imaginative thesis to cover cases of nonfigurative art. Sartre does not avoid this one, pointing to architectural monuments and musical symphonies to make this point. We do perceive the stones of buildings and the sounds of music, but these perceptions, too, are only of the analogues of the purely intentional aesthetic objects. Aesthetic objects *qua* intentional exist only as intended by some consciousness. For this reason, the stones or the sounds we perceive are mere signs, albeit iconic, of the objects first imagined by the architect or the composer. Beethoven's Seventh Symphony, for example, does not exist in the space and time of our one real world; it may be said, as by Suzanne Langer (1953), to create its own space and its own time, but our access to it is only through its enactment or performance. But each enactment, each performance, is only an analogue of the imaginatively conceived object.

Such analogues may be more or less resemblant, more or less faithful renditions of the imaginary object, but they are not to be equated with it. Each exists in a different context. Although in these cases the aesthetic values of the perceptual objects are not ignored, in that they transfer along with the visual or auditory basal elements in the shift from perceptual to imaginative mode, it now becomes a mystery how anyone may be assured that the object of one's imagination is the same object intended by another person, including the original composer. That, of course, is the consequence of answering "nowhere" to the question, "where is the work of art?" Two intentions of the same imaginary object could be the same only if there were no differences in the physical analogue, which is the only access we have to any further "reduced" object.

But let us suppose this predicament is resolvable; let us suppose that our perception of the physical analogue is the exact equivalent of an ideally constituted imaginary object. Why in the world would anyone appeal to the aesthetic qualities of the imaginary object when these are already given in our perception of the real object? Although it is easy enough to change attitudes—from the realizing thesis of perception to the irrealizing thesis of imagination—why should one be motivated to do so in this particular case? I conclude, therefore, that for all cases of nonfigurative art there can be no assurance that the object of my imaginative consciousness is the same as anyone else's and that on the highly improbable case of exact likeness between the objects of perception and objects of imagination there would be no necessity to appeal to acts of the imagination to explain the existence of aesthetic qualities. This is the phenomenological equivalent of the traditional explanations of the "intentional fallacy" (Wimsatt & Beardsley, 1946).

In general, I perceive real objects, and when I attend to the surface characteristics of these objects I also perceive their aesthetic qualities funding into an expressive or felt qualitative unity. This is Merleau-Ponty's thesis of the primacy of perception applied to aesthetic objects. But our aesthetic perceptions become more complicated with the introduction of figurative elements; our consciousness "deepens" as we contemplate represented objects and ideas along with the surface designs: the same form perceived as a long lyrical line lends its sensuous character to the undulating figure of Botticelli's Venus-on-the-half-shell. Here perception and imagination are fused; the imaginary object is given precisely these perceptual characteristics. Can this process be given a single phenomenological description? And if so, how?

Merleau-Ponty's perceptual thesis falls short of explaining the experiences of figurative art, and Sartre's imaginative thesis, although applicable to the representational elements of figurative art, must be strained beyond belief to be applied to nonfigurative art. The search for a synthesis of these two modes of conscious behavior must go on.

In the following section, I shall examine Roman Ingarden's adaptation of the Husserlian methodology.

IV

Where Sartre and Merleau-Ponty developed an aesthetic component to their general philosophies emphasizing the noetic structures of human conscious behavior, Roman Ingarden, perhaps the best known phenomenological aesthetician, built his reputation by his eidetic descriptions of artworks as noematic constructs. Whether he talked about the literary work of art (1931/1973a) and our manner of cognizing it (1937/1973b) or about the objects of music, painting, architecture, and film (1933, 1946, 1947/1962a), his basic move is to distinguish the physical thing (a text, sound waves, painted surface, and the like) from the phenomenologically reduced "intentional" object. I shall pass over his purely epistemological dispute with Husserl concerning the latter's alleged "idealism," since that issue has no relevance for an aesthetic inquiry. In talking about works of art we have no need of referring to "ideal" objects of the mathematical sciences, which are determined by their definitions and have only those properties that may be deduced from an essence; nor to the physical objects of nature—it was concerning these that the dispute about idealism arose—which suffer the same fate in phenomenological analysis whether it is Husserl or Ingarden or anyone else who practices the reduction: their existence is "bracketed out" of relevance when one attends only to their manner of appearance. Artistic values may be said to attach to the physical object *qua* made, but they are relative to the ulterior purpose of building the "strata" of their associated intentional objects and their component aesthetic qualities. Perhaps the easiest way to make this distinction clear is to enumerate the four strata of the literary work of art and then to contrast that description with the one given to paintings.

Once the physical aspects of a written text have been laid aside, the first stratum of significance in the literary product is the order of phonological sense, that is, the phonemes, made up of the vowel and consonant patterns that bear a semantic meaning when perceived in some syntactic whole such as a phrase, a clause, a sentence. One can, of course, hear the words without thinking of their meanings; and a good exercise for attending to the phonological stratum of a literary artwork is to have someone who knows how to, read a poem or novel in a language one does not understand. Literature is indeed a performing art. What one "hears" when one does not know the language suous surface of the poem or novel being performed.

As an organization of heard sounds, a literary work can be metered, measured, numbered; but these terms are names for the abstract relational patterns discernible between qualitative phonological "units," the phonemes that are the basic, repeatable structures out of which all other, more complex, linguistic units are constructed. Since these sounds may already possess aesthetically determined value qualities— such as their sharpness, mellowness, relative highness or lowness—and since these qualities may themselves control other value qualities in combination, either as flowing into a harmonious sequence or only as marking a staccato beat to an increasing tempo, the phonological stratum may be considered a miniature work of art in itself.

Essential to be remembered is that the stratum of sound has two functions: to create a set of aesthetically valent properties and to "found" the appearance of a second stratum, that of the semantical unities brought to consciousness when one hears a language that one knows spoken. Possessing no sensuous characteristics in themselves, the elements of this stratum have as their principal function the founding of the third stratum of "represented objectivities," that is, persons, things, and events as denotations that fulfill the intentions of the various connotations conveyed by the words themselves. It is the sum of such persons, places, and events that constitutes the "world" represented in the literary work and, as such, possesses properties befitting only the world as represented. For this reason, Ingarden refers to these properties as "metaphysical" qualities. Examples are the sublime, tragic, grotesque, and horrific aspects of some depicted worlds.

Moreover, since no world may be totally depicted, some aspects of these represented worlds are left undetermined; and in an effort to make these depictions as concrete as possible, authors usually prepare the reader by indicating some further "schematized aspects" of the represented objectivities. These aspects may be images deriving from any sense modality, and they are relevant to the growing aesthetic object as long as the semantic unities bring them to consciousness. But even where the author is careless in preparing the schematized aspects of the objects in this represented world, the reader will tend to make such associations among the aspects. However this stratum is constituted, either explicitly by the author or by an act of complicity on the part of a reader, once the aspects are introduced they may be held in readiness for repetition in any other part of the representational whole.

An aesthetic object results from a concretization of these various strata of intentional significance, but not as separate from one another, nor merely as a collection of disparate acts of meaning. In each specific reading the four strata are grasped as disparate voices in a single "polyphonic harmony," in which each voice maintains its own distinct quality as it contributes towards the mutual determination of the whole.

Paintings are similarly described, with the proper modification for the change in medium (Ingarden, 1962a). The analysis begins with a phenomenological reduction that brackets out of relevance the physical object hanging on a wall: what makes its appearance is a purely visual object, the first stratum of which is an organization of reconstructed (visual) aspects, such as line, contour, surface, color. And just as there is nothing in a literary work that is not founded in the two basic strata of sound and sense, there is nothing in a visual work that is not founded in this stratum of "reconstructed aspects." Ingarden uses this expression to indicate the degree of freedom an artist possesses in selecting the aspects useful in determining a desired effect. The "effect," again, is a set of aesthetically valent qualities embodied in the organization of these aspects. If there is nothing more than these aspects and their qualities, we are concerned with nonobjective painting and our grasping the Gestalt tendency of the aesthetically valent qualities is the total experience of the painting.

The second stratum is that of represented objects: things, persons, events once again, with the same potentiality of "metaphysical qualities" attaching to the "world" depicted as a whole. Still-lifes, portraits, land and seascapes are all examples of the "pure painted image" (das reine Bild). The space modulations resulting from an organization of the plastic values afford a painter the same opportunities for creating a polyphonic harmony between the reconstructed aspects and the represented objects as was found in the literary work of art. James McNeill Whistler often titled his painting as "harmonies" or "symphonies" to suggest just this kind of viewing for his works.

A third possible stratum in painting is found in pictures having a literary theme. Here the objects represented by the stratum of aspects themselves may represent other objects or, by virtue of a relation between themselves, an idea. When they are other objects, they are symbols—as a painted Venus is a symbol of love, where the metaphorical connection between the two is represented by the sensuous characteristics (the reconstructed aspects) of the goddess's material form (the represented object).

The danger of introducing literary themes in painting—endemic in both medieval and Renaissance times—is the tendency of some viewers to value the literary content of a painting for its own sake, rather than as one painterly device to permit the construction of a single aesthetic object in which each stratum of the medium may contribute to the polyphonic structure of the whole. Without its specific religious theme, Leonardo's *Last Supper*, which is currently in danger of pealing off its wall, would only be a picture of thirteen men breaking bread; one might even wonder while looking at it where the women were!

This Ingardenian account of the intentional structures implicit in an essential work of art is not without its difficulties; I shall mention three of them. First of all, his metaphorical use of "polyphonic harmony" to suggest the principle of closure for all works of art is suspect, since it is derived from one specific medium, music, in which the closure is limited to the field of sonic phenomena. Secondly, his account begins directly with eidetic description without the preparatory passage through a phenomenological description of any one work of art. And, thirdly, his description of how "metaphysical qualities" attach to only one of the noematic strata of the aesthetic object—that of the represented objectivities—rather than to the whole object, seems unclear, to say the least.

What we gain from Ingarden, on the other hand, and in particular from his description of the stratified aesthetic object, is an insight into the differences between Sartre and Merleau-Ponty: each, for different reasons, had taken too narrow a view of the phenomenological method as it is applied to aesthetic objects. Obviously, Merleau-Ponty's thesis of the primacy of perception accords with our experience of the various strata of sense, that is, of the manner in which the human subject grasps the holistic properties of organized patterns of sensed properties. What he lacked, it now seems obvious, was not only the conception of how various elements of imagined entities (represented objects and schematized aspects) are relevant to the visual work of art, but how the perceptive consciousness "deepens" into further acts, which yield further levels of significance (further strata of intentional structuring).

Although Ingarden referred to *The Literary Work of Art* (1931/1973a) as an exercise within the intersecting fields of aesthetics and ontology, his later work is entitled *Investigations into the Ontology of Art (Untersuchungen zur Ontologie der Kunst)* (1933, 1946, 1947/1962a). There is no evidence that his interest in a philosophical determination of the kinds of beings an individual human being may relate to—ideal, real, or purely intentional—has falsified his account of the structure and functioning of aesthetic objects in human experience. It just so happens that artworks are paradigm examples of intentional objects, and in describing the structures of such objects one man, Roman Ingarden, has produced a theory of aesthetic objects with sufficient power and cogency to found an informed critical practice. But of that, more later.

V

Unlike Ingarden, Heidegger's contribution to aesthetic theory has been minimal. *Being and Time* (1927/1962), his magnum opus, purports to be a study in fundamental ontology whose ultimate achievements were to be, in descending order of importance, an answer to "the question of the meaning of Being in general," a "destruction" of the history of ontology, and the demonstration of a method of "existential analysis." Only the last of these three aims, the derivation and exemplification of a technique for analyzing the structures of human existence as "being-in-the-world," was given full explicit development in that text. Yet the book remains the one best source for an understanding of how phenomenology took the turn toward hermeneutics. Although Husserl was himself the first editor of the text, he was surprised to read in its introduction that phenomenology had always been an ontology. That identification was established by Heidegger's explanation of the etymology of the term: a phenomenon was that which showed itself, what was brought to light in the appearance of a thing; the *logos*, discourse that allows things to be brought into the light. Together they suggest a method for using language in such a way as to permit phenomena to show themselves as they are in themselves, from themselves (Heidegger, 1927/1962). Since that use of language is descriptive, it is interpreted as the equivalent of Husserl's admonition to return to the things themselves.

Hermeneutics is the science of interpretation and has had a long history as a formal method for reading symbolic, hieratic literatures, in which a first-level, or apparent, signification is purported to convey a second-level, or symbolic, content. Separating the moral and spiritual content from the purely historical events recounted in the Bible is a frequent use of the method.

The issue becomes compounded in Heidegger in that interpretation is a technique of understanding, and understanding, along with
affectivity and discourse, constitute the human subject's "disclosed-
ness," that is, its manner of opening itself to the significance inherent
in its relationship to a world. Feeling, understanding, and discoursing
are the three ways such significance may be expressed in human behavior. Since understanding is basically a projection of significance (one
which is to be determined as fitting the given context), that context
must itself be laid out in such a way as to permit the application of what
is already known, in its structural components, to the context that is
held open for interpretation. Heidegger refers to the structural components of what is already known in general as the "forestructure" of
interpretation.

The interpretive forestructure is composed of a forehaving—that
which is already had before, a whole past life of experience and a specific, albeit vague contact with the whole context to be interpreted—a
foresight, and a foreconception. If it is a text we are dealing with, for
example, our interpretive hypothesis is based upon a prior reading in
which the first-level significations are clear enough on the basis of our
understanding the language, but whose second-level import remains
to be determined. The forehaving (Vorhabe) is the general intent of the
disclosive projection. The foresight is a specific intent, picking out one
element or group of elements from the more general context, which in
later stages of the interpretation will become the bearer of specific
qualities and, still later, a subject of attribution. The foreconception is
our prior understanding of the aspect or aspects picked out in the specific intent of our observation, the foresight. Eventually these will become the predicates used to denote the aspects attributed to the subject.

It will be of some purpose to exemplify how an application of the
forestructure of interpretation constituted the very method by which
Being and Time was itself composed. Each subject interested in pursuing the ontology of human existence already has at its disposal a language with which to communicate and a vague understanding, by its
feelings, if nothing else, of its own situation. Heidegger refers to this
as a "pre-ontological" comprehension of our own being. This comprehension is what needs interpretation to be brought to the light of an
explicit understanding, and the writing of the text is the discourse used
to communicate this understanding. The writing and the reading of the
text are correlative acts of ontological comprehension. The foresight
picks out a single entity, the human subject itself, whose significance
is to be determined and explained in terms of the conceptions it already possesses such as "the world," "who," and "being in." We

move, then, from our basic pre-ontological comprehension of our own being in the world to the preliminary analysis of the structures of human existence; and from these, as a new "forehaving," to a description of human being as care and to its meaning as temporality, through ever-widening circles of hermeneutic analysis. In each case, we end with exactly what we had begun with, but the character of the knowledge is always changed from the vague and only implicit status of a preliminary to the completely determinate and explicit status of knowledge gained through the interpretation.

As far as I know, no one has applied Heidegger's doctrine of hermeneutics to anything but the literary work of art (Magliola, 1977); and most of his own interpretations have been limited to poetry. His essay in general aesthetics, "The Origin of the Work of Art" (1935-36/1964), may be interpreted as a generalization of his contention that poems create a context in which Being, as presencing, is brought to a stand. He makes his point by discussing a painting by Van Gogh, a poem (C.F. Meyer's der Römische Brunnen), and an unspecified Greek temple (Heidegger, 1935-36/1964; Kaelin, 1967). Van Gogh's painting, the subject of Heidegger's discussion of how and what paintings communicate, is Les Souliers, a picture of a pair of peasant's field shoes. Heidegger pretends to see the serviceability of the shoes, the oppressiveness of the labor that has worn them into their apparent condition, the somberness of the peasant life—all qualities that he has read from the visual characteristics (reconstructed aspects) of the painting.

In the represented world of the painting there is only a pair of shoes in a middle ground, resting on the soil and surrounded by an indefinite horizon of the surrounding atmosphere. Much of the "somberness" and "oppressiveness" of this world, however, is communicated through the surface: the blended dark tones of the dominant brownish hues. This surface and this depth constitute the "work-being" of this work of art, that is, the working of the work as an intentional object of our perceptive consciousness. Other than from the point of view of its being-as-a-work, the painting could be considered as a thing, as a compound of matter and form, as a Gestalt of visual properties, and the like; but the history of aesthetics, it is said, reveals the emptiness of these approaches to the subject.

Our perception of the painting's qualitative essence reveals to us, not the pair of shoes as equipment used in a peasant's everyday existence, not just two things having precisely the properties they are shown to possess—that is only one half of the picture; the other half is constituted by the aesthetically valent qualities of the colors and forms themselves. And it is the qualitative distinctiveness of this surface that replaces the foreconception in a purely linguistic characterization: we say "sombre" or "oppressive," but that is only a metaphorical way of interpreting the quality we have already perceived in attending to the working of this work. In the working of a visual work of art, it is our own being—our own affectivity, our own understanding, our own critical discourse—that manifests itself as a phenomenon. And the discourse of aesthetic theory is only an explanation of how such phenomena may reveal themselves in the first instance.

Meyer's poem is treated in similar fashion. It consists, within the stratum of represented objectivities, of a series of images: water first spouting up, and then falling down through successive tiers of marble dishes until it reaches the bottom of the fountain, only to be thrust up through the upper jet once again. Throughout, the water is described as flowing and resting. Here there is no workaday world of tools that constitute the object of representation, only a rather useless display of formal spatial relationships between various levels of the fountain and its base and the play of water passing through negative spaces of the arrangement. But as the last strains of the descriptive phrases attached to the falling waters catches our attention—they flow and they rest—a concomitant phenomenon finds itself reinforced: the flowing and the resting of the represented waters strengthen the impression created by the flowing and resting of the sonic surface of the poem's resounding syllables. It, too, is a qualitatively distinct tension felt in the working of the work as the intentional object of our consciousness.

The last work discussed is an unnamed Greek temple. On the surface, the temple is a heap of stones placed upon the earth and rising into the enclosed place that will, by later invocation of the human community, become the abode of the gods. Rising from the earth, the stones create a world—both symbols, now, of the surface and depth of aesthetic expressiveness—that exists in a tensely felt unity of opposition. The surface is "serene," to apply our foreconception of its qualitative distinctiveness, and is as fitting an expression as might be devised for the perfection of form usually associated with the divine essense.

Contrast this serene contemplation of a perfectly formed being with the aspiring drive upwards in the basilicas and cathedrals of medieval Europe: the Greek was content in religious celebration to invoke the descent of the gods and to contemplate the perfection of their forms; the Christian put all energy into the upward sweep into the celestial abode above. We thus have two different "worlds" associated with the Greek temple and the Christian cathedral.

But to return to the temple, it, too, exhibits the essence of the work of art: a tension felt between expressing "earth" and expressed "world" (read "surface" and "depth") that reveals the disclosive structures of our own being: a feeling, and understanding, and discoursing being living in a world in which new significances are being instituted by the creativity of our artists. They, too, live in a world and act in such a way as to disclose "the truth of Being" as it reveals itself in the workings of their works.

The danger with this kind of ontological analysis of artworks is illustrated in the later Merleau-Ponty's work. We can become so interested in the ontological meanings expressed in paintings that we tend to overlook the apparent properties of their ontic distinctiveness; and when we do, our interest in the aesthetic properties of artworks has been replaced, changed into something it is not and cannot be. If we wish to solve the problems of the eye and the mind in the experience of a painting, we should limit our explanations to how a sensuous surface relates to a representational depth. Should any question at all arise about what the objects of the representational stratum of a work of art mean, then it is proper to proceed in a strict hermeneutical fashion. Heidegger has given us an example of how this procedure can be used when he used it to write his fundamental ontology, but it should not be forgotten that within his fundamental ontology hermeneutics is an explanation of one way in which a human subject may be in its world—that is, understandingly.

It remains for me to show how in interpreting the depth significations of works of art the critic relates himself understandingly to the work of the artist. This process is descriptive, I maintain, and makes it possible for "the evaluative process" of the critic to be as descriptive as his account of the surface characteristics of the works he criticizes. But to show this process I must move on to my own appropriation of the phenomenological method.

VI

The history of art criticism has been long and varied. Since most of it has been uninformed by a viable theory of aesthetic objects, and of how such objects affect the consciousness that subtends their very existence as intentional objects, much of it has been incorrigibly bad. For the most part, the aesthetic judgments of art critics have followed the fashions initiated by the artists themselves—a practice that would not necessarily be pernicious, unless the artists were engaged in a monumental scam and the critics had no eyes with which to see. Even the least sophisticated person knows what he or she likes; what such persons do not know is that their likes have nothing to do with what makes an artwork good. Within the artworld, judges are chosen because they are supposed to know what makes an artwork good. But even they—the artists themselves, thoughtful critics, museum curators, art historians—may be prejudiced in their likings, so that the little qualification their expertise brings to the ordinary liking standard is hardly enough to persuade us to accept their authority as a guide to aesthetic judgment. What makes them experts, after all, is their acquaintance, owing to their special training, with the aesthetic qualities artworks are presumed to have. But the qualifications that accrue to such training are predicated upon a simple supposition: only the person who has had the experience of the qualities inherent in an aesthetic object is capable of giving an unbiased account of their value; and then only when the descriptions of the structures of those intentional objects accord with another's experience of those same structures. As a result of this system of qualification, two persons who disagree about the qualities of an aesthetic object are necessarily directed back to a mutual experience of those qualities.

Judgment of aesthetic qualities has nothing to do with establishing the worth of an object. That has already been done by an act of perception in which those qualities inhere. The two greatest aestheticians to have been aware of the distinction between the perception of aesthetic qualities and the estimation of the worth of aesthetic objects have been Immanuel Kant (1790/1951) and John Dewey (1934), the one a transcendental idealist and the other a pragmatic naturalist.

Kant's doctrine of aesthetic judgment distinguishes clearly between a logical or determinant judgment, in which the person making the judgment already possesses a concept (say, of a norm) and then, by virtue of the logical connection between genus and species or between species and individual, subsumes the latter under the rule of the former. Such judgments explain how we identify particular intuitions under general determinations; the concept constitutes a rule for the interpretation of the particular. Aesthetic judgments, on the other hand, are not determinant, but reflective.

In aesthetic judgments, there is no concept adequate for the status of a general rule, and hence no possibility of describing a norm by which particular aesthetic objects are judged. Instead, aesthetic judgments are reflective in that an intuition is given for which some kind of concept is sought; it itself must remain "indeterminate." That such a concept will have been found would be attested to by the felt harmony between the faculties of sensibility (the source of the intuition)

and the understanding (the source of all conceptual awareness), between the stimulated eye and the operating mind.

Between 1790, when Kant's doctrine was promulgated, and 1934,
when Dewey published his *Art as Experience,* aestheticians continued
to argue whether our aesthetic judgments were controlled by our
knowledge of the norms of aesthetic goodness or whether there were
no such norms and individual connoisseurs were delivered over to their
own impressions. Criticism was either "judicial" or "impressionistic,"
depending upon one's attitude concerning the possibility of obtaining
knowledge of aesthetic norms. Dewey's insightful writing on the relations between perception and criticism is a masterful piece of philosophical analysis.

Classical, or "judicial," criticism is predicated upon the existence
of so-called objective norms or criteria, which can be known inde-
pendently of the context to be judged. The standards themselves are
physical and determine the quantitative measurement of purely physical properties, such as length, weight, temporal duration, and the like.
These are precisely those properties that are excluded on the principle
of the phenomenological reduction of the physical object into a set of
phenomenal appearances. An organism, it appears, has already "criticized" its environment, that is, sized it up for a possible biological
significance when it has perceived an object therein. What is given to
the "live creature" for judgment is the experience of a pervasive quality (Dewey, 1934, 1931/1968) that defines the situation for what it is—
just as one's being-in-the-world is known primordially through the
significance of that world as an affective state of our consciousness
(Heidegger, 1927/1962). To make a judgment one must learn how to
reflect upon the conditions that have controlled the subject's experience—either as a live creature or as a conscious individual.

Thus if the judicial critics were wrong in their suppositions, so,
too, were the impressionists, since their denial of the possibility of a
judgment on aesthetic qualities was a result of the assumption that an
object is known through its fleeting impressions on a particular consciousness. But our impressions endure; and, once we attend to them
with the physical characteristics of the objects causing them to be
"bracketed out" of relevance, they themselves reveal the qualitative
distinctiveness of the objects perceived.

Another route to the conception of the internal conceptual determination of aesthetic qualities is to consider the ordinary question often
posed to critics about an artwork's significance. What is expressed in
a work of art? The intention of its creator? If so, we can answer that
question only by pointing out what properties the artwork actually

possesses; for, if for any reason, the artist has not succeeded in achieving his purely subjective intention, there is no way of knowing what he actually intended. Can we say for this reason that the artwork "means" the response of some audience? If so, only those responses would be accepted whose descriptions accord with the responses of others, that is, as each set of responses is observably controlled by the structures of the object of criticism.

We are by now long familiar with both the "intentional fallacy" and the "affective fallacy" (Wimsatt & Beardsley, 1946, 1949). We can avoid them by introducing restrictions on the applications of the two hypotheses—of the null hypothesis of the intentionalists and the infinity hypothesis of the affectivists—and by stating as our principle of procedure that we shall accept only those explanations that accord with *an experience of* the qualities of an artwork as they appear to our attentive consciousness (Kaelin, 1964a, 1970b). We find ourselves here stipulating the necessity of the phenomenological reduction as the grounding principle for the judgment of aesthetic qualities, just as in Chapter 7 of this collection I pointed out the connection between practicing the reduction and establishing a principle of relevance in our aesthetic discourse.

By now it is no longer a secret how I suggest we interpret what is bracketed *into* our phenomenologically reduced consciousness. The reduction establishes the "aesthetic context" within which the given aesthetic expressiveness has taken place. Such was the first postulate of the four constituting my own eidetic description of an object of criticism (see Chapters 7 and 8 of this volume; Kaelin, 1964a). At the same time, the postulates constitute an eidetic description of works of art to be criticized; however, they also delimit the situation in which aesthetic properties are experienced for what they are: that is, for what they appear to be. The term to be defined here is *aesthetic judgment*; the technique will be Heideggerian.

The forehaving that constitutes the basis of my interpretation is determined by some 53 years of aesthetic experiences and all the phenomenological aesthetics mentioned in the prior sections of this article. The foresight is the object of criticism, that is, the structures of our conscious experience as they are implicit in the "constitution" of an intentional object we call "a work of art." The foreconception is the attribute "quality," when that notion is understood as the essentially determined distinctiveness of a thing as it appears to our attentive consciousness.

To understand the first postulate, that *all aesthetic expressivenss is context-bound*, all we need do is to place the necessary restrictions on the intentional and affective fallacies mentioned above: upon intentionalism, that we attend only to those intentions actually expressed in a given work, and upon affectivism, that only those affective responses be admitted that are controlled by the intersubjective structures of the work. Accordingly, we limit our critical attention to what has transpired in the interaction between ourselves and the object perceived.

As for the second postulate, that *aesthetic contexts are composed of counters, either surface alone, or both surface and depth, and their relations,* we need only recall Ingarden's account of the strata of an intentional object: sensations and feelings (the basic founding stratum of the various art media plus their "aesthetically valent qualities"), meanings (connotations and denotations); represented objectivities; psychological images (schematized aspects); and the "depth feelings" of the meanings, objects, and images—the emotional state of the consciousness contemplating the patterns of relatedness obtaining between the strata, but not necessarily the "polyphonic harmony" referred to by Ingarden. Once we refer to these strata as "counters," we may identify the "founding" strata as the surface counters and the others as depth counters. And where there are no depth counters, the work being criticized is nonobjective.

The third postulate, that *no counter has an absolute significance,* eliminates the fallacies Dewey (1934) called "reductionism" and the "confusion of categories." By stating that every counter has only that significance which accrues to it by virtue of a relation to some other counter, we preserve the unity of the aesthetic context and the Gestalt principle by which it has been experienced. For example, on the surface, the existence of a green has no absolute significance, but only the relative pull of that green against the hue of some surrounding color; and no object represented within the depth of the expression has the value it would possess in an extra-aesthetic context. Art objects are not good or bad because they possess a religious theme, for example; the religious (or sexual or political or scientific) object or idea has only that significance which attends upon its surface expression or upon its concretization in fulfilling imagery (the "schematized aspects" of Ingarden).

If the viewer is incapable of perceiving the meanings implicit within the stratum of represented objectivities, then, following the Heideggerian procedure, one must entertain—either imaginatively or purely conceptually—a hermeneutical hypothesis for interpreting that significance; but even this must then be related to the other strata of the intentional object. Since, in making our judgment, we are describing the structures of the intentional objects of our consciousness, surface descriptions and depth interpretations are of a similar nature. Their objects, of course, differ; but they are all intentional. A hermeneutical hypothesis is a description of the way represented objectivities are related to suggest the presence of a relevant idea.

The final postulate, that *the significance of an aesthetic context is the felt expressiveness of all the counters as they fund, or come to closure in our experience of them,* summarizes in Dewey's terms how the experience of an artwork is *an* experience: the closure principle marks the controlling factor of an artwork's qualitative distinctiveness; it determines what our art experiences are experiences of. As noted above, we should retain the practical equivalence of Dewey's (1931) "pervasive quality" of a situation and Heidegger's significance of a worlding world.

If aesthetic judgment is the reflective determination of what has constituted the quality of an experience, as both Kant and Dewey have maintained in nonphenomenological contexts, then our aesthetic judgments are likewise descriptive of the manner in which the various counters of the context achieve closure, that is, in which they fulfill a sense. Since we have already experienced the "pervasive quality" of the closing context, our mind has already judged when our eye has seen. The reflective judgment is only an attempt to explain to ourselves or to others what this sense "seen" has been.

Aesthetic judgment: an affair of the innocent eye or of the omniscient understanding? Neither; it is an affair of a complete consciousness capable of reflecting upon the constitution of its meanings. And without an awareness of what our consciousness of quality portends, we should no doubt be reduced to an ignominious silence—or what is worse, by far, to an analysis of the terms used by others to express their reasons for attributing value to works of art.

10

THREE THEMES FOR DETERMINING
A MEASURE OF AESTHETIC LITERACY

What is the short-term value of education in the arts? We assume for the moment that the aesthetic literacy of a student population is the primary goal of the process. But what is aesthetic literacy? Answering the question is another task for the conceptual analyses of aestheticians.

The following essay was read for the first time before a meeting of art educators assembled in the Florida State University Conference Center on April 3, 1987. The event was sponsored by the department of art education of that university, under the direction of Professor Charles M. Dorn.

I

The three themes I have in mind are taken, in the first place, from the history of art in the nineteenth century; next, from contemporary educational psychology; and, lastly, from recent theories of aesthetic judgment in art education. If I succeed in my plan, the last theme will be understood to have been contained *in nuce* within the "conceptual framework" I shall have used to interpret the significance of the first two themes.

From the history of art, I choose a single phenomenon exhibited in J. A. McNeill Whistler's habit of giving two titles to some of his most well known works; from contemporary educational psychology, I shall note the discussion of "reflective judgment" reported in *Time* (1987); and from recent accounts of aesthetic judgment in art education, I shall examine the common distinction drawn between description, interpretation, and evaluation as distinctive components of the critical judgments of artworks when they are considered the objects of aesthetic appreciation. Here, I shall examine the theories of my colleagues and friends, Elliot W. Eisner and Edmund Burke Feldman.

As for the term *aesthetic literacy*, I acknowledge its metaphorical nature, hoping that it will be understood that I intend the same kind of proficiency in giving reasons for our aesthetic judgments as in the

163

more distant past rhetoricians expected of their students who were being instructed in the effective handling of their "letters." Using the metaphor in this way enables me to express my sympathy for anyone whose job description entails instruction of the so-called principles governing the arrangement of elements into the patterns of sense. In spite of their best efforts, and many times because of them, such teachers find it difficult to overcome the functional illiteracy of their students—not to mention the ever-present temptation they experience of foreclosing on a student's creativity by applying rules to something that is not essentially rule-governed. Art educators merely find themselves in a similar predicament: knowing the difference between knowing something to be true, good, and beautiful and being able to produce something having those same characteristics. What still is not too clear, to some of us, is precisely what is properly described as being true, good, or beautiful.

Philosophers, who sometimes love to shorten their explanations, insist upon describing the difference between the cognitive competencies of *knowing that* and *knowing how*; and surely such a difference exists in most areas of human judgment. What some philosophers have forgotten, however, is that, although cognitive and practical judgments may differ, knowing what and how to do something may be an essential component of coming to know anything whatsoever; and knowing where to look for one's evidence to support a plan of action would seem an indispensable condition for making such a plan succeed. Human judgments are complicated projects, and to simplify our descriptions of them beyond necessity is a sure way of introducing error into our methodological decisions. At present, I shall insist only upon the fact that not everything we know—including about the history of art—is relevant to the problem of justifying our aesthetic judgments concerning works of art.

Of those things we know to be true, only some can be used to support criticism; and knowing how to decide between the relevant and irrelevant facts at our disposal to ground aesthetic judgments is itself based upon a cognitive procedure operating at a higher level of significance—as when language is used to describe a lower-level use of language as simply descriptive, interpretive, or evaluative. But to say this does no more than give warning that applying critical concepts to particular works of art is made theoretically possible by a set of aesthetic categories that allows us to explain the difference between aesthetic and nonaesthetic behaviors. Any conceptual framework for making critical judgments on aesthetic objects must stem from the same sorts of experiences that are themselves the objects of aesthetic appreciation—a truism that has led at least one artist to declare that aesthetics is like ornithology, in being for the birds.

Critical ineptitude may have many causes—from simple blindness or inattentiveness to detail to the ambiguity of one's critical concepts; from the inappropriateness of one's aesthetic categories to a peculiar birdlike fear of ornithology and ornithologists who may view our behavior in a slightly different way from the one we habitually use for ourselves. Yet all this possibility of error should not deter us, for the discovery of any error we ourselves may have made should be the first step on the way to further inquiry and ultimately toward the truth of the matter.

There is no rational ground for denying that human beings have and enjoy aesthetic experiences or that making and appreciating works of art are common among such experiences. All we have to do is to be careful in explaining why a given work is worthy of someone else's appreciation, while some others may not be. Here is where we need effective critical concepts—ones that give good and appreciable reasons for our own critical estimations and actually lead others to experience the same qualities we ourselves have appreciated. Aesthetic categories, on the other hand, are more general in reference and apply to objects, experiences, or situations as these constitute the loci (within human behavior) of possible aesthetic values. The word *value* here means nothing more arcane than any feature of an experience that satisfies an interest or drive of the perceiving organism. The difficult term is *aesthetic*.

I have chosen two of Whistler's works because they will help me make clear what might be said about works of visual art in our attempts to make aesthetic judgments about them. In effect, what I must do is to show what features within our experiences of these works might be claimed to fulfill our drives to perceive their qualities as determining the experiences we have of them. If our experience of a visual object is what fulfills our drive to perceptual clarity and, for the moment, our interest in being alive, then, quite obviously, having such experiences is the value pursued in our aesthetic behavior.

Criticism is an attempt to explain how a given object has produced our aesthetic experiences, and good criticism leads others to share our judgments by leading them to the same sort of experience. The role of aesthetics in this process is merely to provide the categories necessary for viewing the objects of critical judgment in the same way—with some degree of perspicuity, it is to be hoped, and somewhere between the lower bound of relevancy and the upper bound of completeness.

II

James McNeill Whistler produced a prodigious amount of visual art: about 528 catalogued paintings (including oils, water colors, pastels, and drawings), 161 lithographs, 426 etchings, and at least one completely decorated room (Cary, 1971). Among these are landscapes, seascapes, portraits, cityscapes, and so many "nocturnes" that he was at one time referred to as "that night painter." Scanning the names appended to these various artistic constructions, we perceive a number of so-called musical pieces: in addition to the already mentioned "nocturnes" (in music, moodily pensive pieces written to be performed at night), almost as many "caprices," "variations," "symphonies," "arrangements," "harmonies," and the like. Had the expression not been first used by Walter Pater (1873/n.d., p. 111), his contemporary and fellow aesthete, he might have formulated the dictum so dear to all formalist critics, that "all art . . .aspires to the condition of music," that is, to attain whatever expressive qualities it does by virtue of the relationship between elements of its composition.

In music, compositional elements are all tonal, and tonal differentiations are perceived in relationship to one another in changing sequences of patterned sound. Harmony is the pattern of consonant repetition; balance, of contrast; and rhythm, of repeated contrasts within the overall acoustical image, which may be as simple as a single tone or as complicated as a toccata and fugue, symphony, or operatic score. All these are forms, as indeed all objects of perception are forms, or patterns of relatedness.

Moreover, both the primitive elements and the patterns of their relations are forms in the same sense of the term: a simple tone is a relational pattern perceived as a tension between a sound and a silence; a musical phrase is a pattern of change in a tonal system from tone to tone, with its horizontal distance measured in the differences between successive tones and its vertical spread, by the differences, if any, in their pitches and in the complexity of their accompanying overtones, all experienced in the measured pulses of time. Nothing in such organized perceptual wholes is anything but a form—a relatedness between one discriminable thing and another, whether it be a pitch, a loudness, a timbre, a duration. Even the evolving harmonic mass of "tonal" materials delineating motives and themes achieving a partial wholeness, which, developing in concert with other such wholes, determine some greater whole that possesses its own specific quality of affecting our sense of hearing, is nothing but a form.

But all forms, as patterns of relatedness, are analyzable. Most basically, the structure of a form may be said to consist of two determinants: the things related and the relationship itself; philosophers refer to them as relata and relation, and mathematicians, as variables and a function. Traditionally, art critics use the term *form* in this sense (but there are at least four other denotative senses of the term in current usage within art criticism) when they describe the structure of a work as a design containing both "elements" and "principles," as I did earlier (see p.128, this volume).

The difficulty with this broad-brush approach to the analysis of forms may be understood if we reflect upon my description of the tonal structure of musical compositions. Readers with a penchant for concreteness and an active aural imagination have no doubt already imagined what was being talked about by running through a phrase of their favorite pieces of music as I was describing the ever-growing complexity of the reticulate forms of a musical structure.

If a theme is a recognizably uniform development of a musical motif, and a motif is a recognizably uniform musical pattern, and a pattern is a relationship between component tonal qualities, and every tonal quality is already itself a simple contrast between sound and a background of silence, then it is obvious that musical structures are describable as contexts of interrelated tonal elements and that these elements are themselves formal in their essence. And so, a musical piece is a complex structure of forms (or patterns of relatedness) made up of forms of a simpler type. And within a context where everything discriminable is of the nature of a form, it is hardly meaningful to distinguish between the elements and the principles of a design. Both are discriminable, and their difference is in the higher or lower orders of the perceived forms.

We may solve the difficulty caused by the simultaneous likeness of and differences between elements and principles merely by changing frames of linguistic reference. Let us consider the grandest of patterns imaginable—the context within which discriminations may be made, and then describe that context as being composed of those discriminations. I call these latter "counters." We have arrived here at the point where we may postulate the definition of an aesthetic context: as being composed, not of elements and principles, but of counters, that is, anything at all discriminable within that context.

Sooner or later, of course, we should like to be able to define "aesthetic expressiveness" as that property of perceptual objects that determines their aesthetic value, still defined here as whatever fulfills an interest or drive of a living organism (Dewey, 1934). But, on the way to that definition, we may merely stipulate another postulate, actually the first in my list of postulates (see Chapters, 6, 7, and 8 of this volume; Kaelin 1964a), namely, that all aesthetic expressiveness is context-bound. This definition merely associates the properties of a genus with those of its component species, since context-boundness is a property of the genus of meanings, and expressiveness is a species of meaning.

No sooner have we made these stipulations, however, than we discover another difficulty. If our experiences of artworks constitute an aesthetic context, then we soon discover that the "counters" of these contexts are not only reticulate, progressing from simplicity to complexity, but that they actually differ in kind. We made our case too easy by beginning with music, where usually the counters of the first order are all of the same kind. What is the case in painting? By way of preparing an answer, I shall give an actual perceptual experience to contemplate (see Figure 10.1, Whistler's *Arrangement in Grey and Black, No. 1: The Artist's Mother,* and Figure 10.2, Whistler's *Arrangement in Grey and Black, No. 2: Thomas Carlyle*). In my critical descriptions, I shall be trying to guide my readers' perceptions of the works.

Surely you recognize that both these paintings are portraits, the one of a woman and the other of a man, and that the surroundings in which the models sat are strikingly similar, at least upon a cursory glance. I shall postpone the sustained analytical probing of one of these arrangements until a later, more appropriate moment of my demonstration.

From your active perusal of the two reproductions, consider the figures of the man and the woman. If we say, as some art critics do (Feldman, 1967), that we see "a man" and "a woman" in the painterly composition, we are obviously misusing the English language. For what we see is a representation of a man and a woman. And we note further that each of these images or figures has been managed by a reticulate set of visual counters that are lines, colors, and shapes. We interpret these lines, colors, and shapes as images of a man and a woman because the perceptual image of a man and a woman has been abstracted into a composite array of purely visual forms that are, so to speak, projected upon the canvas.

If this description is correct, as I think it is, then it should seem apparent on reflection that the art of making a representational painting is an act of thought by which the painter transposes the visual image—what he or she sees of the subject—from the context of real life into a second context, that of the composition—itself now a physical thing—in which that subject is represented by the organization of visual counters. And our aesthetic perception is of that second context.

FIGURE 10.1 James McNeill Whistler's *Arrangement in Grey and Black, No. 1 (The Artist's Mother)*. Canvas, 171 × 143.5 cm. (67⅜ × 56½ in.) Musée d'Orsay, Paris, France. Photograph courtesy of the Service Photographique de la Réunion des Musées Nationaux de France, Paris. Cliché des Musées Nationaux.

FIGURE 10.2 James McNeill Whistler's *Arrangement in Grey and Black, No. 2 (Thomas Carlyle)*. Canvas, 145 × 164 cm. (57⅛ × 64⅝ in.) Photograph courtesy of the Glasgow Art Gallery and Museum, Scotland.

There is another way to make representational paintings, of course. A "constructivist" creates a composite image by merely combining visual counters, usually of interrelated shapes. And we still call such paintings "abstract," since we ourselves practice the change of contexts definitive of artistic abstraction in perceiving the constructed image as an aggregate of relatively primitive counters. On this account, even a surrealistic painting, with its dual representation of a real and a dream object, is abstract. Our perceptions of surrealistic paintings are not of the represented objectivities as real or even as dreamed, but of the respective images as transposed into the new "painterly" context wherein they have been rendered as visual counters depicting objects and their relationships. The difference between a realistic and a surrealistic representation will turn out to be negligible in the complete listing of postulates, to be given later.

Whistler's titles inform us that the model for the one arrangement was Thomas Carlyle, the Scottish philosopher, and that the model for the other was his mother. For those of you who prefer art-historical trivia to reflective art criticism, I should tell you that when the portrait of his mother was made, the artist's mistress of the moment was forced by the morality of the situation to move from his house; that when Carlyle viewed the portrait of the artist's mother, he expressed a liking for the painting; and that, in consequence, Whistler made a similar portrait of Carlyle himself.

But back to critical relevance. Although the paintings are similar in that they are both portraits of seated figures in full profile in a remarkably similar setting, and the painter chose identical titles for them: *Arrangement in Grey and Black,* he acknowledged the differences between them with the numerical references. We should keep in mind here that titles serve different functions in our commerce with paintings; they may only designate the painting and serve as a means for cataloguing the artist's total *oeuvre;* or they may designate the painting and give a clue for how the painting may be interpreted.

Since *The Artist's Mother* and *Thomas Carlyle* are subtitles, they may be used for cataloguing purposes and to indicate who served as models for the portraits. *Arrangement in Grey and Black,* as applied to both, would not suffice for cataloguing purposes without the added numerals; and it serves as the artist's invitation for us to interpret both paintings as a modulation of the spatial forms achieved through the arrangement of the value differentiations of color, as opposed to hue and saturation.

The moral of my story is that the difference between the title of these portraits and their subtitles may predispose a viewer to look at each painting in two different ways: as an organization of purely visual counters, or as a more complex organization of these same counters overlaid with a conceptual interpretation. The difference, corresponding to the distinction philosophers draw between percepts and concepts (see James, 1911), allows us to differentiate between kinds of counters discriminable within visually aesthetic contexts.

Following D. W. Prall (1929/1967a), I refer to the organization of perceptual counters as an "organized sensuous surface," which is a field phenomenon having all the characteristics already described for musical compositions. They may likewise be referred to as "medial counters," since the perceptual counters selected by an artist to make a composition or "arrangement" define the medium he or she is working with. Music and painting are differentiated primarily by the medial (perceptual) counters each art uses for aesthetic purposes.

Has Whistler, following Pater, succeeded in confusing what analysis has clearly separated? Listen to his personal testimony: "By the names of the pictures . . . I point out something of what I mean in my theory of painting" (Spalding, 1979, p. 19). His interpreter, continuing the testimony, explains: "With music, the listener responds to the relationship of sounds which, except in occasional instances, have no representational content. Whistler wanted to create in his art an experience as disinterested and pure as that offered by music (p. 19)." The point seems clear enough. Even when paintings obviously represent natural objects of any kind (including those of pure fantasy or naked dreams), they fulfill a purely visual interest and thereby possess aesthetic value. A sensuous surface possesses an expressive quality by virtue of the affective tone registered in the consciousness perceiving the organization of related sensuous counters. And, sometimes, that is all there is to our experiences of musical compositions and paintings, as when paintings are nonobjective and music is absolute.

The curious thing about the history of the two arts is the inversion practiced on the relative importance of a sensuous surface. Music from its very beginnings was an organization of sound experienced for its own sake; even when lonely shepherds played their rude flutes to while away the time, the experience of the sound gave pleasure. Painting began, if we interpret our archeological findings aright, in a more utilitarian fashion: with the representation of objects used for religious or economic purposes, such as the various forms of naturalistic and supernaturalistic deities in the form of light, animals, gods, and goddesses, or in the shape of animals sought in the next day's hunt. Representing the capture of these animals was deemed to have the magical property of facilitating their capture.

What the aesthetic attitudes of the aboriginal artists were, of course, is not available to us, since all we have to go on are the artifacts they left behind. We, as moderns, find the original cave paintings powerfully expressive; but then we have been influenced by the attitudes of the Renaissance, when the concept of art was enriched by the notion of a disinterested perception of sensuous counters.

The Greeks, we remember, had no notion for our concept of the "fine arts." Musicians had to learn that sounds could be used to imitate the effects of nature and that musical motifs could be associated with particular concepts to interpret the objects of nature to tell a story. Painters took a very long time, indeed, to discover that portraits could be viewed as arrangements in the value differentiations of color. But that fact is only a historical curiosity.

The point to be made for our aesthetic theory is that when objects are represented by means of the organization of sensuous counters, another kind of counter has entered the aesthetic context. Since we use concepts to interpret the objects of representation, we could refer to them as *conceptual*—a feature of aesthetic contexts exploited by so-called conceptual artists. But since I have adopted the term *surface* to refer to the medial counters of aesthetic contexts, I use the term *depth* to refer to the conceptual counters. We need only remember that this "depth" is not a spatial concept, but rather a psychological or experiential one. Then, as we refer to the sensuous surface of an aesthetic context, we should also refer to its "experiential depth" whenever that context includes conceptual counters.

And just as surface counters "deepen" into represented objects as we recognize the images in their abstraction from nature, a similar phenomenon operates within some organizations of depth counters. As the perceived relationships between lower-order counters are interpreted as images of objects, so the relationships between objects may represent an idea. For example, motherhood and childhood, as abstract ideas, may be represented in concrete images by the relationship between an adult female figure and an infant figure. Place a halo around the heads of the mother and child, and by conventional symbolism you have representations of the Virgin Mother and the infant Jesus.

As a last depth of representational power executed within aesthetic contexts through their experiential depth, we may note the psychological imagery associable with represented objects and ideas. An example would be all the religious associations Christians have always experienced while contemplating their icons. This psychological imagery tends to load the perception of the entire context with "depth feelings," such as filial or religious piety felt when the connection between the ideas and the psychological imagery is contemplated.

The open-endedness of the field of experiential depth demands a further concept to guarantee the relevance of our associations. That should be clearer when we have discussed the concept of total expressiveness. For the moment it should suffice to remember that psychological imagery, which makes sensuously concrete the representation of an idea, is a form of substitute sensation relatable through its affective tone to the affective tone of the surface.

In sum, we note for the moment that aesthetic contexts may be composed entirely of surface counters and their relationships, or of surface counters organized in such a way as to represent a field of depth counters. To make one thing (such as an aesthetic context) of these two fields we obviously need a third concept for the relationship between the two. For this reason I claim that any aesthetics worth its salt will generate at least three aesthetic categories: I call them "the sensuous surface," "experiential depth," and "total expressiveness."

The last of these categories refers to the way in which we experience the relatedness between the surface and depth counters of an aesthetic context. The word *total* in the concept of "total expressiveness" should connote the existence of a partial expressiveness within such contexts; and that is easy, since both the surface and the depth are field phenomena and both are the objects of experience. Following John Dewey, I suggest that expressiveness is the affective component of an experience by which we recognize an experience as *an* experience. In this way, the total expressiveness of an aesthetic context may be associated with Dewey's (1931/1968) notion of a "pervasive quality" of a(n aesthetic) situation.

In conclusion of this first theme, then, we may state that Whistler's two ways of naming his portraits point up the difference between the surface and the depth of visual patterns of expressiveness and invite us to search out a further determination of the concept needed to characterize their relationship, as we have already experienced them. Once I have elucidated this concept, I shall employ it in criticism of *Whistler's Mother*.

III

As I drop the thread of my first theme, I shall begin weaving the second by recalling the amazement with which I responded to a recent issue of *Time* magazine (1987). In the education section of that issue the psychological research of two educationists, both graduates of the University of Minnesota, is highlighted with the provocative question, "Can Colleges Teach Thinking?" The researchers were Karen Strom Kitchener, of the University of Denver, and Patricia King, of Bowling Green State University.

Although as psychologists they are interested in determining the developmental stages of reasoning, their approach is different from the better-known one of Jean Piaget. Where Piaget sought both the age of onset for the capacity to reason and then the stages through which that ability is developed, he was primarily interested in reasoning in the form of logical judgments, whether of an inductive (generalizing from particular instances to the general rule) or of a deductive sort (following some rule to draw a conclusion from a set of premises). Kitchener and King plan to do the same thing, but for something they refer to as "reflective judgment."

The key to my amazement is attributable to their use of the term *reflective judgment* as much as to the realization that at least some psychologists had become aware of the problem involved in applying the results of statistical analyses to predict the behavioral responses of very nonstatistical individuals. Are we truly educating for the predictable average? And if so, what can we do for the other 30 percent of the educable population? What is to become of the 85th-percentile and the 15th-percentile groups, when we refer to them with the educational euphemism *special students*? Obviously special curricula must be prepared for them.

Perhaps, it may be surmised, colleges have had such a dismal record in teaching reasoning, not because they have misjudged the stages of readiness in their students, but because they have been attempting to do the job with the wrong tools, that is, inductive and deductive reasoning.

"Reflective judgment" is reflective precisely because it is not susceptible to the rule governance of logical judgments. I know this from first-hand experience. In my first attempt as a fledgling instructor of deductive logic, my class was composed of "remedial" students, all of whom were signed up for courses in remedial mathematics and remedial English as well. I gave a pre-test on 10 classical syllogisms, asking the students to judge their validity on the basis of their pure intuitions. Then, after 15 weeks of intensive drilling on the rules for the validity of syllogisms, the students were post-tested on the same arguments. Comparing the results of the pre-test with those of the post-test was discouraging. Although the students had performed with 40 percent correctness on the first test, on their second go-around they could manage a mere 17 percent. It was enough to make a sensitive person look for another job. I duly reported the results to my departmental chairman, who simply replied: "What did you expect? They were remedial students." And, reflecting upon the matter, I myself mused, "and remedial students have difficulty mastering any kind of rule."

Rather than a means for discovering new kinds of knowledge—which, however it can be, but only under prescribed conditions—deductive reasoning is more fittingly considered a way of ordering the knowledge we already possess. And although inductive reasoning does allow us to discover useful knowledge, its successful use depends upon knowing where to look for evidence to be interpreted, where to look for confirming evidence, and how to test the facts tending to confirm or disconfirm our tentative conclusions.

It takes no great leap of the imagination to see that art critics make judgments on the values of particular works of art and that aestheticians have been trying from time immemorial to supply the information needed to guide the thought involved in the critical process. A good aesthetic theory, supplying acceptable categories for the interpretation of aesthetic experiences, should tell us where to look for the evidence supporting critical judgments and how to recognize confirming and disconfirming bits of evidence brought to bear in any reflective judgment. Since each work of art is a particular case (definable by its context of aesthetic significance), and since both the capacities of critics to consult with some success the conditions under which they have experienced the work being criticized and the backgrounds of education and experience they possess to make an interpretation of those conditions vary so widely, it should not be much of a surprise that critics tend to differ.

Kitchener and King ask in their "reflective judgment interviews," *How is it possible people can have such different points of view about this subject?* Ask any aesthetician the same question, and his or her answer is likely to be cast in some version of the analysis I have given above. It all depends upon the categories needed to judge the personal reactions of individual respondents.

Aestheticians have known since the last decade of the eighteenth century (see Kant, 1790/1951) that aesthetic judgments are not logical, but reflective; that is, they are based not upon any pre-enabling rule or warrant but upon experience and our capacities for reflecting upon the conditions of having aesthetic experiences. Immanuel Kant's distinction is found in his *Critique of Judgment*; it is drawn between what he called "determinant" and "reflective" judgments. Logical judgments he considered determinant, because whenever we possess a concept that serves as a general rule, any particular instance of that rule will be determined as possessing all the characteristics associated with that concept. For example, if goodness in art, or aesthetic expressiveness, were definable conceptually, then all aesthetic judgments would have the following form:

> *Rule:*   Whatever possesses the characteristics x, y, and z
>   is beautiful.
> *Instance:*   This object possesses those characteristics.
> *Therefore, verdict:*   This object is beautiful.

Even my first students of deductive logic should have been able to see that the form of this argument is a syllogism and that its conclusion is valid—at least when they were reasoning intuitively. But a valid argument is sound only when all its premises are true; and the truth of the major premise serving as a rule is always open to question—a claim that can be understood without considering an indefinite number of inductive examples when we keep in mind the fact (that is, hold as relevant within our reflections upon aesthetic experiences) that anything truly creative will incorporate some characteristics not yet formulizable within the status of our existing concepts. Critical concepts, in another way of saying the same thing, are open-textured. And that means that any rule, no matter when formulated, will foreclose on the possibility of novel experiences within the determination of aesthetic value.

Two recent aestheticians of note have exploited Kant's distinction. The first was John Dewey (1934), who called the argument form outlined above "judicial" or "legalistic," in order to deprecate its use in aesthetic judgment by critics considering themselves "classicists" (pp. 299–304). Classical critics make up their minds before all the evidence is in; their rules prejudge the verdict upon any individual case. Moreover, their critical procedures are conservative, backward looking, and needlessly restrictive.

But not all criticism is classicist in this sense. Kant was aware of this problem, too. In his famous "antinomies of taste," he showed that contradictory conclusions may be established by adducing different, yet relevant, sets of evidence for them. We could argue, he claimed, that our judgments of taste are made upon the basis of concepts, otherwise we would not continually be disputing them with the expectation that our differences of opinion would be resolved; or that such judgments are not made on the basis of concepts, otherwise by now we should have resolved our differences of taste. An antinomy, of course, only shows a weakness in the logical formulation of the disputed conclusions. I use Kant's formulation here merely to indicate that classicist criticism is one-half of the illogically conceived dispute. The other half of the antinomy is the basis for the kind of criticism we call "impressionistic" (Parker, 1945).

Impressionist critics claim that classicists are wrong because we possess no eternally fixed concepts for aesthetic goodness; and in this respect what they say is true. But when they push their argument by stating that the very nature of our aesthetic experiences is such—an isolable impression upon our consciousnesses—that no comparison is possible of different works or between different experiences of the same work, since impressions are unique to the moments we have them under the regnant circumstances, they obviously go too far. For one thing, their position claims some knowledge about aesthetic experiences in general—that they are registered as impressions; but the conclusion drawn from this putative fact does not jibe with our knowledge of conscious states.

As Dewey points out (1934), impressions endure, and enduring, they may become the object of conscious reflection. Although we shall not attempt to examine these enduring impressions (by an act of reflection) in order to abstract a universal property of goodness from them, we can reflect upon them and relate them to the conditions under which they were experienced. Such, for Dewey, is the basis for our reflective aesthetic judgments.

The second aesthetician to adopt the Kantian scheme of metacriticism—the criticism of criticism—is De Witt H. Parker (1920/1945). His discussion of aesthetic judgment begins with a statement of the Kantian antinomy of taste, proceeds to an explanation of classicism and impressionism as critical theories based upon the antinomy, and ends with a justification for his own type of "modified classicism."

Noting that Kant had solved the antinomy by appealing to an "indeterminate concept" (of the supersensuous substrate of humanity, that is, the functional unity of all the human cognitive faculties operative within an aesthetic judgment even when there is no single property of goodness shared by all objects judged aesthetically good), Parker is put off by the subjectivism of Kant's account and so modifies the accepted rules of classicism in accordance with his own, essentialist, account of aesthetic objects.

All works of art are experienced in some medium, for example; and by comparing expressions within the same medium we should be able to determine the goodness of a given work by judging the artist's use of the medium for its uniqueness, completeness, and perfection. "Perfection" means here the achievement of some specifiable aesthetic purpose. Needless to say, however, even this modified form of classicism leaves us with something to be desired. Although Parker agrees that no universal concept for aesthetic goodness is possible, his normative aesthetics is based upon a description of artworks given in essentialist terms, that is, by a set of appropriate concepts. What he has done is to switch essentialist claims from the normative to the descriptive aspects of aesthetic discourse, denying universality in the determination of aesthetic goodness but claiming it for that of our descriptive concepts.

Perhaps for this reason one of Parker's best known students, the late Morris Weitz, composed an essay entitled "The Rôle of Theory in Aesthetics" (1956) to show that the open-endedness of all aesthetic concepts—both normative and descriptive—precludes the essential determination of their use. According to Weitz, aesthetic theories merely point out what one might look for in giving reasons for our aesthetic reactions; and we follow his counsel when we maintain that aesthetic judgments consist in two components: the nature of the thing being judged and the relevance, and convincingness, of the reasons adduced for finding value in them.

When I take up this thread again, I shall return to John Dewey's account of reflective judgment and interpret it through the psychological categories of existential phenomenology. Perhaps the most suitable remark to be made here is that developmental psychologists may have something to learn from the long history of the aesthetic treatment of reflective judgment, and that the results of their studies may influence superintendents of public instruction to consider education in the arts not as a fringe but as an essential part of the school curriculum.

IV

How are we to educate for an increase in the capacity to make reflective judgments? How other, than by developing a practice to permit our students to achieve the ends of their aesthetic educations? These include the abilities to have aesthetic experiences and to formulate good and relevant reasons for valuing such experiences. And a preliminary test for the validity of our judgments may follow a single rule of thumb. Framed as a question, our rule asks, To what extent does the awareness of our reasons tend to reinforce or intensify our responses to the work being criticized?

Since the value of a work consists in our experience of it, that value is called "intrinsic" (to the experience); that is, an aesthetic experience is valuable to the extent that it fulfills our impulses to see, feel, imagine, and understand. We can, of course, treat aesthetic objects as an instrumental value, that is, as a means for the achievement of some external end; but then the values achieved are no longer strictly aesthetic. It is for this reason that some aestheticians follow the practice of critics in posing an alternative rule of thumb: a work of art is good, they say, when it repays our efforts to contemplate it. This version of the rule unites the analytic and synthetic aspects of reflective judgments with the added notion that contemplating works of successful art is a value we may experience for its own sake. Either version of the critic's rule of thumb should suffice to determine the validity of a critic's reasoning.

Educators attempt to spell out what these two rules of thumb imply by way of a pedagogical guide for instruction in the arts. In *Educating Artistic Vision* (1972), Elliot Eisner follows Dewey's experience-centered interpretation of aesthetics up to a certain point and then mysteriously abandons it. He divides critical statements into three kinds, after distinguishing them from psychological reports, which express a personal liking or disliking, a personal preference, of the objects open to criticism. He correctly points out that psychological reports are about the speakers and have nothing particular to do with an artwork's excellence. For him, critically relevant statements are either descriptions, interpretations, or evaluations.

Description establishes a first level of critical discourse, whose purpose is to increase the amount of visual information. But that information may concern either the "content" (subject matter) or the form of an artistic expression. In the terms explained above, descriptions may be of the surface, or the experiential depth of representational arts, or of the unmixed surface counters in nonfigurative arts.

Interpretations, which furnish the second stage of judgment, consist in expressions of analogues, in the making of suggested meanings, or even in the intimation of the personal feelings of the critic. At this stage, therefore, it is not uncommon for the critic to use metaphors and other figures of speech to capture the elusive features of an artwork's significance, whether they be the affective tone of some surface or of the depth or of the pervasive quality permeating their relationship.

Finally, armed with descriptions and interpretations, and after multiple experiences that permit cross-referencing, the critic may hazard an evaluation. Eisner's examples of typical evaluations—"this is one of the finest . . . ," "this is good," "this is better than that"—indicate that evaluations may be categorical or merely comparative.

The basis of the two types of evaluations is grounded primarily in the types of evidence developed in the second phase of judgment, critical interpretation. For example, one might judge one work better than another because the work makes the critic feel more strongly than does the other. Eisner refers to such evidence as "experiential." And there are other kinds of evidence: the "formal," the "material," the "thematic," and the "contextual."

These kinds of evidence are found in interpretations of the relationships between visual forms; or of the rarity or fineness of the purely surface properties of a medium, such as marble, oil, water color, and the like; or of the idea or ideas expressed in the depth of the representation; or finally, of the relevance a work might possess to a particular place or time or to a possible psychological analysis of the artist or a typical viewer.

According to Eisner, whether the evidence for an evaluation is found on experiential, or formal, or material, or thematic, or merely contextual grounds, critical judgments based upon that evidence consists in the careful weighing of as much of the evidence as the critic possesses. But here is where he departs from the Deweyan scheme of reflective judgment. Although the first four kinds of critical evidence— the experiential through the thematic—may be found in works of art, the so-called contextual evidence surely would constitute an example of what Dewey (1934) called "the fallacy of confusing categories" for when we begin to identify works by their effects upon history or society, or by their possible use in other social institutions, such as religion, science, mathematics, or philosophy, we have momentarily switched critical points of view—from the aesthetic to another category with which the aesthetic has been confused.

Eisner's contextual evidence likewise leaves him open to having committed that other fallacy of aesthetic judgment delineated by Dewey (1934) as "reductive." The reductionist fallacy consists in justifying an evaluation of a work of art on the basis of a single counter or set of counters. If, for example, we tend to prize works of art because we acknowledge the existence of the historical, economical, or political conditions under which they were created, or psychological state of the artist, or the structures of the societies which may have influenced the particular work under discussion, then we will have reduced the value of that work to its being an effect of those conditions or influences.

There are disciplines with an interest in artworks—the psychology of art, the sociology of art, the history of art in its widest interpretation—but none of these will explain aesthetic value. And none will replace the disciplined experiencing of the works. We might as well assume that the patronage of the church or of the aristocracy that replaced it in the Renaissance determined the goodness of a crucifixion or of a nobleman's portrait. What the patronage explains is why such subjects were chosen for artistic representation, not the goodness or the badness of the paintings embodying such motifs.

Two conclusions may be drawn from Eisner's account. First, that it remains unclear how the first two stages of criticism (description and interpretation) permit the critic to handle the supposed relationship between descriptive and interpretive evidence in the formulation of a critical judgment. And unless they are related, within the experience by the critic of the artwork's value, the relevancy of the critical judgment founded upon the two types of evidence has been seriously compromised.

To explain this critical remark I shall have to formulate two more postulates to complete the set begun in section II of this chapter. The first postulate, you recall, was the stipulation of the context-boundness of aesthetic expressions; the second defined an aesthetic context as a field of interrelated counters—of surface counters alone, or of surface counters and depth counters in their relationship.

My third postulate, which I formulate as independent, is actually a correlate of the other three, being deducible from them. It states that no one counter has an absolute significance; or, stated positively, any counter has only that significance that accrues to it by virtue of a relationship to some other counter. This postulate permits me to avoid the reductionist fallacy named by Dewey. It also explains why the experience of both the descriptive and interpretive kinds of evidence noted by Eisner must be grounded in an actually deepening experience of the critic's judgment: the relationship between the two is the object of the experience.

My fourth postulate merely states what is obvious on reflection: that the significance of an aesthetic context is the felt expressiveness of all the counters as they fund into our experience of them. What we reflect upon, in an attempt to describe the goodness of a given work of art, is the manner in which the characteristics of a complex work are felt as a determinate quality. Once such qualities have been experienced, comparisons of them may be made; but it is useless to compare two works of art to discover the value of either one of them.

So, while Eisner's qualitative evaluations of the simple positive stage ("this object is good") are not beyond the pale, the basis for comparative and superlative attributions of aesthetic value seems groundless. Perhaps what he needs is a clear distinction between aesthetic (ends-) value and artistic (technical or means-) value. But that is the second conclusion I draw from his description of critical statements.

As I view the matter, the value of Edmund Feldman's metacriticism is its faithfulness to the empirical method. His case is presented in *Art as Image and Idea* (1967). Like Eisner, he explains what he takes to be reflective judgments as developing in stages of conscious preparation; but his list contains four, not three, distinct activities.

The first of these is, again, "description," primarily of the figures in a representation, but also possibly of the free forms of a nonrepresentational piece. Along with the figures and the forms, critics are advised to note the characteristics of the artistic execution they may exemplify (as, for example, the same painting being of one's mother or an arrangement in grey and black). Next, critics are admonished to secure the above in a formal analysis. By noting more specifically how figures or forms are technically rendered within the work, one cannot help noticing the "formal" elements of an artistic construct, such as the lines, colors, and shapes of the artist's sensuous surface. This second stage of critical involvement with a work is therefore a continued search for ways of interpreting the elements isolated in the descriptive stage.

The third phase is composed of the interpretation itself. Upon the basis of the perception of determinate themes managed by the relationships between meanings suggested within the arrangement of the formal and imagistic content, the critic formulates a hypothesis for explaining the effect that the perception of the work will have upon a viewer. In this way, the hypothesis serves as an "idea," or principle, for unifying the elements discovered within the first two levels of critical analysis. Good explanatory hypotheses in general enable us to interpret paintings as symbolizing an idea.

So far, so good. What Feldman has achieved thus far is to make accessible the insight introduced into visual-art criticism by Erwin Panofsky through his distinction of "iconology" from "iconography" (1939). Where iconology studies the similarity between the structures of images and their corresponding perceptual objects, iconography studies the symbolism of these images. The title of Feldman's book indicates his debt to Panofsky. His modernism creeps in when he attempts to give an empirical description of the different kinds of criticism and the varied types of judgment one may find in the various kinds. For example, there are journalistic critics, pedagogical critics, scholarly critics, popular critics, and so on. With respect to each of these Feldman plays the role of metacritic.

In examining the techniques of first-order critics, Feldman finds that their judgments are either formalist, that is, concerned with the relationships of counters, be they surface or depth; or expressivist, that is, evaluating paintings on the basis of the intensity of the feelings expressed or the vividness of the represented image or idea; or, again, instrumentalist, that is, concerned with art as a tool in the service of some other institution, such as the church, the state, economic class, and the like.

It is obvious, of course, that instrumentalist critics violate Dewey's canons of criticism in the same way as Eisner's have been noted as promoting the confusion of categories, or the substitution of some nonaesthetic value for the aesthetic; but it cannot be denied that some "popular" critics operate in this way. All an aesthetician can say in playing the role of metacritic is that such criticism is not aesthetic: instrumentalist critics do not report on the quality of an experience of an artwork but on one possible nonaesthetic use to which aesthetic objects may be put.

The fourth and last stage in Feldman's account is evaluation proper. Evaluative judgments are, according to Feldman, the assessing of a rank to artworks. In order to make such assessments it is necessary for critics to compare a work under criticism to the "widest possible" set of comparable works. They also entail a good deal of artistic connoisseurship. For example, besides relating works to the widest possible comparison group, the connoisseur is noted for having ascertained the purpose or function of the present work, for noting any departures from historical precedents, and for relating the work as a record of its own time in the history of our culture. Here, obviously, the best source of information is the discoveries of art history.

But since not even the best historians of art can be familiar with the entirety of the history of our culture, the evaluations of art connoisseurs must be simplified. And in order to accomplish this, Feldman concludes his chapter on "The Critical Performance" with a rule of thumb of his own. The summary evaluation on particular works of art, he tells us, is a balanced judgment of the artist's originality—arrived at by reflecting upon the elements of connoisseurship noted above—as that originality has been determined by the artist's craftsmanship.

Applying this rule of thumb, he suggests, will enable us to note the correspondence—or lack thereof—between overall appearances of artworks and their putative function, whether that function be the aesthetic one of gratifying our perception or some instrumental function imposed upon the work by an additional nonaesthetic purpose. I need only point out here that the only "proper" aesthetic function of a work of art is to provide an aesthetic experience.

What this account of Feldman's metacriticism makes clear, at least to myself, is that he, too, has been guilty of confusing categories, if not the artistic with the aesthetic, then at least to some degree the instrumental with the intrinsic use of an aesthetic product. Thus a more apposite account of our reflective judgment seems to be in order.

V

The time has come to weave the threads spun from the cordage I have been preparing in the three themes heretofore discussed. I shall do that by indicating the various levels at which aesthetic literacy may be said to function within the cognitive behavior of human beings. The first, and indispensable, condition is the existence of aesthetic experiences, the values instituted by the creation of works of art.

I have avoided the description of this process, developed by both David W. Ecker (1963) and Elliot Eisner (1979), as qualitative problem solving, not because I reject the notion that an artist thinks by manipulating qualitative counters, but because emphasis upon the manipulation or arrangement of such counters itself needs some kind of explanation. That notion was discussed in my first theme.

I suggested in my preparatory remarks that the general process of "abstraction" by which an artist selects from the natural and cultural environment whatever seems useful for constructing an aesthetic expression is a proper explanation of artistic thinking. The artist does this by arranging the selected materials into a new context wherein those materials take on a new significance by virtue of the relationships obtaining between the qualities resulting from the arrangement.

Criticism is the use of language to describe or evaluate the expressiveness of the novel context. What it describes is, first of all, the counters of that context, whether they be experienced as a sensuous surface or as a field of depth representation interpreted iconologically and iconographically. Both surfaces and depths control the affective responses of the critic, and the total expressiveness of the context is the pervasive quality of all the counters as they fund into a single determinate experience.

The distinctiveness of the pervasive quality is the affective aspect of a conscious reaction to the perceived relations of the aesthetic context. Since the "value" of the expression is the experience we have of its total expressiveness, there is no need to look beyond the qualities of that experience to justify our evaluations from the strictly aesthetic point of view.

When critical descriptions are of depth counters and their relations, the "descriptions" are usually called "interpretations," but that term imports into the analysis a distinction within aesthetic experiences that tends to separate what remains fused within our aesthetic awareness. The phenomenon I refer to here is the "deepening" of the experience from a state of pure perception (of the surface) to an involved imagination (the depth) and a broadened understanding (the symbolism of the first-order depth images). The deepening of an aesthetic experience calls forth all the sedimented meanings of our past experience and brings them into focus within a single experience of this context.

Evaluation is another thing; it is the second aspect of criticism. I should like to suggest that it, too, may be considered a form of phenomenological description. To see evaluation in this light, we must first distinguish between the aesthetic value of the expression and the technical means employed by the artist to pull it off. These latter are referred to as "artistic values."

Artistic values are means; aesthetic values are ends. But given the nature of perceptual qualities, there is a one-to-one correlation between the expressiveness of the aesthetic context and the actual materials and techniques employed by the artist. It is for this reason that they are easy to confuse, as both Eisner and Feldman were noted above to have done. But if having the experience is the only way to consummate aesthetic value, then comparing two contexts in order to determine the value of either, whether relatively or absolutely considered, is a decision made on the basis of a logical confusion. Expressed as an adjective, the term *aesthetically good* has no comparative or superlative form.

However, if two aesthetic contexts are compared after an experience of their pervasive qualities, then it becomes possible to compare them—not indeed aesthetically, but by virtue of something else the two contexts have in common. Judgments on the originality of aesthetic expressions are such comparative judgments, but they concern either the materials or the competency of the artist to work in some heretofore unknown manner. These judgments are not aesthetic, but technical or means oriented.

A knowledge of techniques as the ordering of means toward an end may be relevant to the discovery of an aesthetic value—whether by an artist or by a viewer—but without an experience of the ends-in-view guiding the use of the available means, there would be no way of evaluating their use. Evaluation is, therefore, something other than giving a rank to works of art. But if so, then what?

I make bold to suggest that this process is descriptive, too. In judging the effectiveness of technical means one must have an experience of the end—the perception of the aesthetic quality pervasive of the artistic creation. Keep in mind the fact that the correlation between technical means and aesthetic end is one-to-one. Therefore, in describing both the surface and the depth counters and the ways in which they are related in the particular case, the critic is putting his or her reader into a position to follow how the technical competency of the artist has controlled an aesthetic response to the work. So, when, in this technical sense, a work of art is judged good, it is evaluated as effectively controlling an aesthetic response. The evidence for the judgment, however, is given in a description of the funding counters.

There is still a difference between the aesthetic value found in the experience and the artistic values by which that experience is controlled. But the logic of the situation is such that these means values are judged only in relationship to the given end—the aesthetic experience itself. Any ranking of compared aesthetic experiences changes the categories of discourse from those governing the description of qualitative aspects of experience to those governing quantitative measurement. We can compare qualities, of course, but then we are presented only with another quality—that of likeness of difference, two possibilities of a purely formal relatedness.

The description and evaluation of criticism is metacriticism; and as these efforts indicate, that, too, is a matter of reflective judgment in Kitchener's and King's sense of the term. Indeed, we have already witnessed three versions of reflective metacriticism: Eisner's, Feldman's, and my own. But it should be clear by now that my own metacriticism is practiced upon the basis of an aesthetic theory, or generalized description of aesthetic experiences in terms of the three categories exemplified in the confusion embedded within the ambiguous titles of Whistler's twice-named works.

I turn now to a criticism of his *Arrangement in Grey and Black, No. 1: The Artist's Mother* (refer to Figure 10.1).*

The dominant form of the composition, both by its size and its position, is the figure of a woman, portrayed in full seated profile, situated within the middle ground of the represented space. This space,

---

* Black-and-white reproductions of the paintings discussed in this chapter are included for the convenience of the reader, who is encouraged to refer to Frances Spalding's *Whistler*, pp. 46–47 [figs. 36 & 37] (Oxford: Phaidon Press, Ltd., 1979) for museum-quality color reproductions of the works. Figures 10.1 and 10.2 used with permission of the Service Photographique de la Réunion des Musées Nationaux de France, Paris, France, and the City Art Gallery and Museum, Glasgow, Scotland.

not being filled, is "negative." The figure itself contrasts to its background, the greenish-grey wall, in two respects: both in the value of the black dress against the grey of the wall and in the differences between the human body as a biomorphic form and the architectural forms determining the shape of the room. On the surface and in the depth, a contrast that establishes a perceptual tension.

But, looking only at the central figure, one perceives the same gradation in value already noted on the surface contrast between figure and ground within the overall shape of the woman, where the black of the dress grades up to the greys of the lace headpiece, falling gently onto the left shoulder, and the lace of the cuffs, extended into slightly darker grey of the handkerchief. So the gradual value differences between the greys of her clothing and the highlight of the footrest establish a descending diagonal pattern through the space of the middle ground. This same pattern may be viewed as rising from the value intensity of the footrest to the less intense greys of the headpiece—from the lower left to upper right of the diagonal.

The two pulls—of the figure against its ground and the rise or fall of the graded intensities of value within the figure—modulate the surrounding negative space behind, in front of, and around the figure, whose face, rendered in flesh-toned pink, is complementary to the greenish grey of the wall: another contrast that creates an additional tension, pulling the gaze through the negative space between the two concentrations of color. So, the figure rests where it is by the force of the double contrast.

Attending to the background now—the three-dimensional spatial form of the room—the viewer may observe the harmonious repetition of earthtones: the brown of the floor darkened in the wainscotting and in the curtain, the verticality of the curtain balancing the horizontality of the wainscotting, and within that balanced positive space, a similar balance repeated in the frames of the prints. But once again this figure and its ground are related, this time harmoniously by the repetition of the browns in the far ground and the reddish brown of the lady's auburn hair. Here the gradation is in the hue of the colors.

Repeated gradations—both in hue and in value—establish a harmony. The reception of this harmonious relationship is kinesthetic, as attention moves along the degrees of the graded distinctions of discriminable color phenomena. The overall pattern of the earthtones is circular, as various patches surround the figure, itself now perceived as a hemisphere of positive three-dimensional space defining its complementary hemisphere in the surrounding negative space. The two half spheres are divided by the extended sine curve linking the rhythmical rise from the highlights of the footrest to the hands and the head—all greys against a black ground—to its shadowy presentation in the negative space it shapes.

The laterally undulating plane of the hanging curtain is broken up by the flowing floral pattern imprinted in its cloth: another repetition here in the continuous sine curve delineation of the curtain's folds, intercut by a contrasting pattern of the seemingly random location of the individual floral patterns, which themselves become positive spaces as their lighter grey pulls from the surrounding darker ground.

The highest value—the highest light—is registered in the matting of the print, which contains a representation within a representation, here perceived as a negative space modulated into four mainly rising planes of foreground, middle ground, background, and horizon that may represent a near shore, a body of water, a far shore, and a sky. That space and its representations, whatever they are, remain indeterminate as to their experiential depth, even as they repeat the variations in the hue and value of the colors of the woman's hair and lace headpiece, but in muted form, just hanging there on the wall.

The woman's head is canted in a crossing pattern to the diagonal rise of the three tones in the grey chordal mass (footrest, hands, head); the position of the head puts it, the framed print, and the hands into a triangular pattern, isolating the negative space above and below the undulating sine curves of the woman's silhouette. That space is, so to speak, illuminated by the originally perceived double contrast between greys and blacks—the figure itself and the surrounding space of the wall; the wainscotting and the curtain show a similar gradation of value in the earthtones.

And there she sits, a woman of more than a certain age, at rest with herself and the living, breathing, space of her surrounding world, serenely resigned to her place in this world. As she sits there she is bathed with the little light streaming into her negative space as from an invisible window. Her single dominant moral quality is of quiet repose; it is expressed in the demeanor of her pose, the starkness of the Victorian clothing, and the impeccable rightness of her placement in the middle of this closed universe, where the skirt of her dress cuts a black wedge between two equal negative spaces above the floor in front of and behind her body.

These negative spaces are further modulated by the legs of the chair behind and the footrest in front of the figure. The thrust of the chair legs is upward to her back, which is gently curved so as to leave another negative space between her back and the back of the chair. The chair continues the upward thrust toward her head and the opening onto the two patterns into which the head figures: either the fall toward the footrest via the hands or the triangulation with the hands and framed print on the wall.

The serenity of the figure is the moral quality of the person represented in portrait. That is the second level of experiential depth, the "idea" properly to be associated with the represented figure. But as we continue to contemplate the muted contrasts in the variations between first-order images (woman, chair, curtain, prints, and so forth) when they are perceived through their surface qualities, the artist's arrangement in grey and black, we discover the relationship between the surface and experiential depth—the feeling of the harmony between the gently modulated contrasts in blacks and greys, the browns and pinks (this latter relationship highlighted by the reddish brown of the auburn hair), and the feeling of the serenity generated by the character of the woman perfectly at ease with her environment.

But good things come in threes: repetition of the contrasts in the central figure and her immediate environment; the relations between the figure and the ground that create both the positive and negative spaces of the creation; and, lastly, the serenity of the lady's golden age.

So serenely is this harmony felt that it is difficult to reflect that the artist's mistress had to move out to permit the model to sit for the portrait!

Portrait of the Artist's Mother? Or *Arrangement in Grey and Black?* Obviously both, each expressing the same feeling—the poised balance of opposed forces. Once we trace the meaning of the image to the serenity of the woman's character, we see that serenity repeated in the double contrasts of the color gradations discernible in the hues and the values of the painter's chosen palette. And the same contrasts are apparent within the figure and its surrounding ground of gently modulated negative spaces.

In this painting, the perceptual field of the sensuous surface melds harmoniously with the conceptualized experiential depth. Is it any good? I think so. It rewards our every attempt to contemplate it; and analysis of its structure enhances our original impression that here there is something to be reckoned with. Mock it as we may, the structure maintains its cohesiveness and fulfills an interest we find in visual perceptual fields.

VI

What, then, are the parameters of aesthetic literacy? On the lower end, technical proficiency in the construction of an expressive context;

and on the upper end, the discipline of criticism as informed by an effective metacriticism that is itself informed by an adequate aesthetic theory.

And all the rest, as the painter once told me in confidence, is for the birds. I was later told that this was Barnett Newman's favorite jibe against aesthetics and aestheticians.

AFTERWORD

Selecting 10 essays written during the past 30 years on the subject of philosophical aesthetics and its relationship to the problems of art and aesthetic education would constitute a meaningless gesture—unless there were a present need for a clarification of that relationship; unless that aesthetics were both coherent and practical; and, finally, unless the teachers of our art teachers can succeed in translating the categories described in the theory into a set of behavioral patterns by which their students, the teachers of our children, themselves can succeed in aiding their students to participate in the wondrous world of art.

If we start tracing the areas of responsibility in this "translation" process, we could begin with the professional competencies of philosophers (usually, certified skill in the analysis of concepts or categories) and then move on to the tasks of educators and schools of education in managing the transmission of the foundational knowledge supplied by competent philosophical analysis. In such a way, we might expect to produce teachers capable of interacting with their students, whose behavior would be so modified in the interaction as to prepare them for further participation in the activities controlled by the institutional fabric of our society.

It matters little, in a democratic system of education, whether the end of that process is thought to be the "growth" of the individual (Dewey, 1916) or the "enrichment" of our society. Depending upon the scope of our original philosophical analysis and the accuracy of our descriptions of the various stages of the process, we should be led to expect just that degree of success in the venture as would be permitted by the further accuracy of the communicative system by which philosophical categories are turned into educational concepts and these, in turn, into effective skills of teachers and students. In every case, and at every level, effective communication is the key to educational success.

But this does not mean that the activities composing the process must necessarily begin at the top—as if philosophers had some privileged insight into the nature of things that would permit them to dictate what must be done, educationally, to achieve the ends of a good society or to permit the growth of individuals therein. That indeed was an idea of Plato, perhaps the first of our Western philosophers to formalize the relationship between philosophy considered as a rational explanation of all that is and public education as a means of social control.

Plato wrote his *Republic* in an attempt to show the connection between human nature and the state and to indicate what must be the educational practices of the state that would promote the virtues of its citizens. But he made one serious mistake. Since he misconceived the role of poetic creation as an aesthetic phenomenon, he decided to banish the poets from the Republic. Were the ancient poets necessarily liars, who on the one hand dealt in third-rate realities and on the other tended to stir up the unruly passions of innocent citizens? We all know, from reading the 10th book of the *Republic*, that Plato thought so; and we all know that he was wrong.

Some of us claim to know why, and those of us who substantiate our claim by pointing to Plato's imposition of a metaphysics upon his epistemology and of that epistemology upon his aesthetics as the source of his error are not wholly deluded. If we still read him, it is to learn a lesson, that is, not to commit his errors; accordingly, our investigations will proceed from the bottom up, so to speak, rather than from the top down—from the arts to an aesthetics rather than from aesthetics to the arts. We shall begin by observing just how poets and other artists actually function in a democratic society to communicate a value to the general society. (See Madeja & Onuska (1977) for a contemporary application of this idea.)

Whatever value is created in the arts may or may not become an enduring part of the social structure (depending upon the related institution of criticism), but the institution within which it is created—art—nevertheless functions to liberate the human impulse to self-expression. And as such it is good.

But just as Karl Marx once argued that Hegel's idealistic philosophy had to be stood right side up in order to be made thereby both materialistic and socially realistic, so Friedrich Nietzsche argued that all the values established in traditional philosophy had to be transevaluated for an understanding of the process by which the original values had become established in the first place. Plato, too, needed to be set right side up. Values, Nietzsche argued, are not imposed upon us from without, by some external authority, nor from within, by the fixed nature, or essence, of our being; they can only be created in the process of living, and with no more authority than the individual decision to create them.

And if Nietzsche is right about the creation of values, that fact must be reflected in our account of an art education based upon student participation in our aesthetic institutions. How this is to be reflected in the program proposed within these pages should already be clear: he classroom must be the focus of the social interaction between teacher and student. Each of these players in the game must learn their roles of self-expressing, creative student and sympathetic, critically responding teacher. Working together, they share the experience of an aesthetic value.

I

A number of years ago David Ecker and I were invited by the officers of the National Society for the Study of Education to participate in a project that was given the name *Philosophical Redirection of Educational Research*. Given our specific competencies, we were asked to limit ourselves to proposing a foundational study in aesthetic education. Putting our heads together, we came up with the essay entitled "The Limits of Aesthetic Inquiry: A Guide to Educational Research" (1972). The plan was to describe the structure of aesthetic knowledge and thereby to suggest all the areas of research relevant to education in the arts. Since the resultant typology constituted only an interpretive frame for locating the relevant disciplines, it could not be thought of as a substitute for the research of specialists in the various fields but only as a guide to educational specialists for structuring the relevant competencies into a coherent, practical educational program.

It may be of some use to recapitulate the scheme here. We began with the question, What should be included in a well-designed program of instruction in the arts? Immediately we opted for a basic level of aesthetic experiences (whether creative or appreciative) as the ultimate reference of any language system used to describe aesthetic phenomena. And, of course, courses in the making and appreciating of artworks were already staples in the art educational curriculum. Our point was to insist that these courses be taught in such a way as to permit maximum self-expression on the part of students consistent with the proper critical appreciation of the "works" created in those acts of self-expression. Within the classroom, teachers were to play the role of critic in relation to the student playing that of artist.

We were not unaware of the difficulties of imposing an undue amount of concern for the value of the created product, since our first joint venture in aesthetic education had been a proposal to achieve a workable balance of attention to be paid to both the process and the product of the art process in teaching "art" to very young students (Ecker & Kaelin, 1958).

Our approach in the earlier work was to show the relevance of aesthetics for the teaching of art—a project, as I indicated in the Preface to this work, that was begun at the suggestion of Fred Logan at the University of Wisconsin. The 1972 project had as its aim to describe the entire range of philosophical interest in the teaching of art. Whether we had learned anything about the subject in the interim of 14 years might be determined by considering the success or lack thereof in relating philosophy to aesthetics and aesthetics to art experiences in such a way as to reveal the "structure of aesthetic knowledge." As a method for achieving this end, we chose to describe the relationships obtaining between the languages used to talk about the primary interest of art educators, which we still assumed to be the creation and appreciation of works of art.

The results were arranged in a five-step ordering. Where the objects and events of aesthetic experience constitute the most basic level of "content" for aesthetic education courses, it does so by establishing the facts to be clarified in further theoretical interpretation.

The first level of interpretation—the first exclusively linguistic rendering of the facts created by artists and their appreciators—is criticism. That, too, has long been a staple of higher education; it thus needed only revision—out of consideration for the readiness of students—to be applied as a tool for the instruction of elementary and secondary school students. Critical language may be either purely descriptive or evaluative, as it is when it is used to express judgments of the worth of individual artworks.

Metacriticism is to criticism what criticism is to art. It either describes acts of criticism or evaluates them. When either of these levels of language is used merely to describe, the justification of its use is in the truth of the statements promulgated. The normative use of language at either level would be justified by the nature of the reasons given for the judgment enunciated.

Another function of metacritical discourse is the prescription of a method for making critical judgments, and justification for such prescriptions may stem from a theory of aesthetic judgment, such as the reflective account of Immanuel Kant (1790/1951), the one proposed in Chapter 10 of this collection; a theory of aesthetic objects and their structure and functioning within aesthetic experiences, such as those offered by Dewey (1934) and Pepper (1955) in the tradition of American pragmatism; a theory of artistic creation, such as the one found in Croce (1909/1972), as corrected by Collingwood (1938/1958); or a theory of aesthetic response, such as that proposed by Aristotle in ancient times and Roman Ingarden in the recent past (1931/1973a,1937, 1968/1973b).

For the best extant example of American metacriticism, one should consult *Aesthetics: Problems in the Philosophy of Criticism*, by Monroe C. Beardsley (1958). Professor Beardsley became the dean of American aestheticians following the decline of Stephen Pepper. In the passage of the mantel, the subject lost its pragmatic tinge and passed over into the full-fledged color of linguistic analysis.

The title and the subtitle of Beardsley's principal treatise places the locus of aesthetic inquiry between aesthetic theory proper and its application, as a metacritical tool for describing and evaluating critical uses of language, and, in his discussion of the "canons" of criticism, for prescribing a method to be used in justifying one's own critical pronouncements.

Much of the debate in philosophical aesthetics during recent years, however, has not been metacritical; it has been metatheoretical. When it was argued by such analytical philosophers as Morris Weitz (1956), Paul Ziff (1953), Maurice Mandelbaum (1965), and others, whether a theory of art were possible owing to the so-called indefinability of the concept of art, or to the "open-textured"nature of that concept, the argument was not over the merits of a particular suggested definition for *art*, but rather over the "wrongheadedness" of any attempt to formulate such a theory.

Analytic philosophers have always preferred to be wrong than to be wrongheaded, since they cannot conceive that any wrongheaded person could possibly be right about anything. And for this reason they paid little attention to the work of continental aestheticians. Besides, if they were to do that, they would have to improve on their linguistic competence. But their obvious choice was for a philosophy of language rather than for the languages others used to enunciate aesthetic judgments, with or without the blessing of an aesthetic theory.

Weitz, who set the tone for the debate, seemed to be the only person convinced that the kind of definition that would permit the construction of a theory would have to be what used to be called a "real definition," that is, one which sets out the necessary and sufficient conditions for the correct use of the terms used to formulate the theory. And his argument was deceptively simple: since aesthetic concepts are open-textured, they cannot be used to formulate a theory. His metatheoretical assumption: only "real" definitions may be used to construct a coherent theory.

That assumption was first challenged by Maurice Mandelbaum (1965) and later by George Dickie (1984). Nelson Goodman contended that the Weitz–Mandelbaum debate harbored a red herring in that the open-textured nature of aesthetic terms did not preclude our talking about the necessary and sufficient conditions of their use, since a careful consideration of the symbolic functioning of the arts, themselves considered a kind of language, exhibited a set of aesthetic "symptoms": in one account (1968, pp. 252–255), four in number; and in another (1978, pp. 67–68), five, which disjunctively considered would be necessary and conjunctively, sufficient, for determining the "aesthetic" nature of that symbol system. This means that if any symbol system shows none of the four (or five) symptoms, then it is not used for aesthetic purposes; and if it shows all four (or five), then it is used for an aesthetic purpose. But Goodman denies that his work is in aesthetics. His investigations are into the properties of the arts considered as symbol systems.

As for Mandelbaum's criticisms of the indefinability thesis, we may recall the nature of his objections to Weitz and Ziff: they failed to distinguish between the exhibited properties of works of art and their purely relational, or "nonexhibited," properties, such as "having been created by someone for some actual or possible audience" (Mandelbaum, 1965, p. 222). Another such purely relational quality, not unrelated to Mandelbaum's example, is "interpreted as a gesture," the making or experience of which gesture is considered a value in itself.

Dickie, following up the suggestions of Arthur Danto that one of the most apparent purely relational properties of works of art was their function within an active "artworld" (1964, 1973), conceived of his "institutional theory" of art as a counterexample to refute Weitz's contention. What better way to refute a (meta)theory concerning the impossibility of aesthetic theory than to produce such a theory that works? What Dickie's theory does is to capitalize on the Meadean notion (1926, 1934) that aesthetic activities, as creative acts of communication, are institutionalizable within the functioning of our other social institutions.

Danto's "artworld" referred to such institutionalized behavior as that exhibited by critics, art historians, museum directors, gallery owners, and the habitués of museums, galleries, and other agencies for the creation and appreciation of artworks. Why not include our schools in this institutional network of behavior?

I have been proposing that this has already happened in the happier moments of art instruction within our public schools and that, if
we keep our wits about us, we can do something to improve that situation by designing a program in the instruction of the arts that would
permit both teacher and student to fulfill their social roles, as defined
by the formal relationships of the school, and thereby to integrate
within our aesthetic educational programs the same relative role structure that is embedded within the institutional patterns of the artworld.
It is this feature of the proposals developed in the previous 10 articles
that would guarantee that the development of human potential (see
Scheffler, 1985) and, simultaneously, the enrichment of our society's
democratic institutions (Dewey, 1916/1966) were proper aims of our
aesthetic education.

Permit me to recapitulate the argument here: if we consider aesthetic experiences to be the proper content of a general educational
program, we may make some progress toward establishing the social
goals of our educational policies if we consider these experiences to be
mediated by the works of art that are created by students and appreciated and criticized by the teacher.

The act of creation itself is both creative and communicative. If it
is aesthetic, it is so because the value communicated is created in the
act of communication. In this sense, the experience is itself an intrinsic value. But as uniting creator and critic, the completion of the communicative act serves to build a social dimension of meaning: as
appreciated, the work is preserved, or sold, or embedded within our
cultural backgrounds as the "allusionary base" of sedimented knowledge structures by which future attempts at creation become interpreted (Broudy, 1987). So, interpreted from the socially psychological
point of view adopted in these essays, the initial base for instruction
in the arts is considered to be the phenomena of creative communication.

Criticism either describes or evaluates the aesthetic experiences
embedded within the original acts of creative communication.

Metacriticism either describes or evaluates the critical discourse of
teachers who help students evaluate their own works.

Aesthetic theory is prescriptive of metacritical procedures just to
the extent it correctly describes the general properties of artworks, acts
of creation, or appreciative responses to the works created in acts of
creative communication.

And metatheory is the use of language to prescribe the rules for the
construction of a workable aesthetic theory.

II

The claim, made by Ecker and myself, that all the relevant discourse interpretive of our aesthetic experiences finds its place somewhere on this ascending order of "stacked languages" has been denied by some of our critics on the ground that it leaves no place for art criticism. Acknowledging the complexity of our claims, that a program of instruction to be built upon our assumptions would leave place for both the explicit and implicit structuring of aesthetic knowledge, they ask where art history would fit into the scheme. As for the "explicit structure" of such knowledge, the movement up the ladder from art experiences to criticism, metacriticism, theory, and metatheory describes the conditions by which truth-claims at a lower level are judged as categorically correct: in this way, the requirements of sense making are fulfilled. The reverse direction, from theory down to art creation and appreciation, fulfills the requirement of empirical adequacy, in that the application of higher level language use is specific in a particular context. The lower levels are implicit in the higher (Ecker & Kaelin, 1972, p. 267).

So, where do the art historian's labors fit?

Apply the ladder in answer to the question. Ar historians sometimes describe properties of works of art; when they do, they are performing criticism. At other times, they attempt to evaluate works of art by applying a historical canon; and when they do, they are doing normative criticism. When they criticize other critics for using an "inappropriate" critical norm—one not fitting the time of the artist, say—they are doing normative metacriticism. When they merely describe the criticism of other critics—as they often do, since the "art" in art criticism is often broadly enough interpreted to include the reception of artworks by the contemporary critics of their artists—they are obviously doing descriptive metacriticism. And lastly, when they enunciate a general theory of art, as Gombrich (1960) did in formulating his notion of art as illusion, they are functioning at the level of aesthetic theory.

The only difference between the "ladder" of aesthetic discourse and that of art historical discourse is the intrusion of historiology at the level of theory. But another way of showing the relationship between aesthetic theorizing and art-historical theorizing is to accept the entire ladder of aesthetic discourse as the primary rung of the art-historical ladder and to add two additional rungs of peculiar significance to art historians. Their metatheory is still a mixture of logical and empirical canons and still has as its purpose a description of the conditions to be met for anyone to have achieved a successful theory. And the set of those descriptive enunciations still constitutes the prescription of the rules to be followed for constructing a theory. Only, here, the theory is a theory of history; and the metatheory is properly called *historiology* (the methodology of history and of historiography).

And so, if our program of education in the arts is to include the four disciplines of art production, art criticism, art history, and aesthetics, it would appear that the "Ecker–Kaelin typology" of aesthetic discourse would cover all the necessary bases. We only insist that our instruction in art production not be limited to *knowledge about* artistic creation—which is, indeed, a subject for both aesthetics and art history and would seem, then, to have claim to the right of entry on its own.

In general, our programs of instruction in the arts cannot be limited to the transmission of *knowledge about* the arts from a peculiar point of view, no matter how many points of view, no matter how so many "disciplines" are thought to be relevant to the model program. The model program has as an essential component the *knowledge how* to perform a peculiar task—whether that be to make a work of art, or to criticize it, or to criticize criticisms of it, and so forth.

A phenomenological account of aesthetic education merely describes what conditions are to be fulfilled if we are to claim that these behavioral tasks have been performed in the manner prescribed for the given order of performances. And that, I hope, is the virtue of the theory proposed in the collected essays of this volume.

III

Is there currently a present need for such a theory?

As long as the competing philosophical or psychological schools have produced no viable program of aesthetic instruction for our public schools there would seem to be such a need. Logical positivism produced no coherent aesthetic theory; philosophical analysis declared such a theory impossible. For these reasons, perhaps, philosophers of education working in those traditions had nothing of significance to say about aesthetic education. The best of the analytical philosophers of education have not as yet got beyond epistemology, science, and ethics as pertinent to the conception of their task (Scheffler, 1958).

But Scheffler (1958) betrays his provincialism when he writes:

> Such a purpose [to stimulate the application of newer philosophical approaches to education], natural though it is, flies in the face of both

> institutional and intellectual custom in calling for serious converse
> between professional philosopher and professional educator. For al-
> though such converse is fairly frequent between philosopher and
> scientist, between philosopher and man of letters, and between phi-
> losopher and theologian, the philosopher and educator typically face
> each other as relative strangers on the academic landscape, who when
> they do talk to each other, speak with the distant politeness of those
> who have urgent business elsewhere. (p. 1)

Readers of these words should remember that Scheffler is both professor of philosophy and professor of education at Harvard University. At
least he could not pretend in one of his roles to have more urgent
business in the other.

In another of his books, however, Scheffler clarifies what he takes
the profession of philosophy to be: not the history of the philosophical
study of education, the study of what has been concluded by other inquirers in the history of our philosophical culture; but the application
of the "newer" philosophical method, the posing of "philosophical"
questions for the purpose of clarifying certain pervasive features of educational thought and argument. Central among such concerns are the
nature of teaching and the discussion of the language used by educators to formulate the programs and aims of their educational systems
(Scheffler, 1960). As examples of such language uses, he cites statements of definitions, educational slogans, and metaphorical descriptions.

Scheffler's posture repeats that of our earlier idealists (the St. Louis
Hegelians) and pragmatists (Dewey and Mead), and even that of our
contemporary phenomenologists, both in declaring their own novelty
of approach and in using some form of conceptual analysis of the categories used to sort out the aspects of experience to be incorporated into
an educational program (indeed, all these philosophical schools would
have cheerfully agreed with his suggestion that the aim of "systematically reflecting" upon educational policy and the education of educational policy makers is the proper route to take). But he is not confident
enough of his method to show the connection between the categories
of interpretation and the concepts they authorize as descriptions or
prescriptions of functioning educational policy. As Max H. Fisch (1970)
pointed out, the slogan of the analytic movement became *Mind your
language!* But he spoke as an historian of philosophy.

We can sympathize with Scheffler's desire to avoid the errors of
history without dignifying his ignoring of history—of the history of
philosophy as a guide to education; for, as in the case of Plato considered above, we can surely learn, by recognizing the error of a histori-

cal doctrine, that something else is the truth. What distinguishes the age of analysis (White, 1955) should not be its provincial, parochial nature but the conscious abandonment of the idea that philosophy is itself an independent philosophical discipline with a subject matter all its own. It was that historical assumption that permitted philosophers of all ages to make prescriptions for educational behavior on the basis of some kind of external authority—metaphysical, moral, religious, and so forth—whose truths were to be propagated through our educational systems. Philosophy is a technique, indeed a technique of categorial and conceptual analysis, without a subject matter to call its own.

Or so one conception of the discipline has it. For this reason, in recent times philosophy has become a second-level discipline borrowing its content from a more primary, first-order discipline. Instead of philosophy as the love of wisdom or the mother of sciences, as the institution had developed in the history of our culture, it has become the reflective study of a primary institution; instead of philosophy as metaphysics, epistemology, ethics, and aesthetics—the study of the True, the Good, and the Beautiful—as it had been throughout history, it has become the philosophy of science, of conduct and law, and, as apropos to the present case, of art. And if we are asked to show the range of the two disciplines, we should be able to point to the three upper levels of "aesthetic discourse"—metatheory, theory, and metacriticism, each directed in a downward focus upon the two lower—criticism and art creation and appreciation, within which activities the institutions of the artworld are observed to function.

Aesthetic education consists, within this scheme, of bringing to bear upon the lower levels the rational techniques of the three higher. There is no claim being made that there is only one way to perform at each of the five levels of the distinctively human activities associated with the structure of aesthetic knowledge, only that such a structure exists and that research is required at every level to perfect our approach to education in the arts.

Although the now-classic text for graduate art education courses edited by Eisner and Ecker (1966) may appear dated, its chief rival at the time was the text of Irving Kaufman (1966); and they may have both been superseded by two giant volumes published since. Hastie and Schmidt (n.d.) and Lansing (1969) have produced tomes that, at the time, appeared to enrich the profession: the first of these texts points up the discordancies found among philosophical aestheticians; and the second purports to be a philosophy of art turned into a practical guide to art education.

But all three of these volumes—the Kaufman, the Hastie and

Schmidt and the Lansing—contain materials for the instruction of art education rather than a program for building the structure of a program that may be "completed" by the cooperative activity of teachers and students. Each assumes that the content of the field is already known.

Still more recently, the discipline-based aesthetic education program was developed by the Getty Center for Education in the Arts (see Preface to this volume), the report of which appeared in a special issue of the *Journal of Aesthetic Education*, edited by Ralph A. Smith. Two articles of special interest for my own study are those prepared by Clark, Day, and Greer (1987), entitled "Discipline-Based Art Education: Becoming Students of Art," and by Donald W. Crawford, whose piece is entitled "Aesthetics in Discipline-Based Art Education" (1987). Although the entire collected contents of this special issue were accompanied by the usual disclaimer of funding institutions—that the views expressed by the authors were those of the authors, and not necessarily those of the J. Paul Getty Trust—the entire issue was copyrighted by that same trust, leaving no doubt as to who controls the rights on the publication of those ideas.

IV

To answer the question that motivated this portion of my inquiry—whether there is a need for this collection of essays—I can only suggest that my readers consider the alternatives. After all, Thomas Munro, who for 25 years held the position of curator of education at the Cleveland Museum of Art while simultaneously holding the rank of professor of art in the Graduate School of Western Reserve University and the editorship of the *Journal of Aesthetics and Art Criticism*, had attempted to define the philosophy and psychology of art education as early as 1956 (Munro, 1956a). But not many practicing art educators were capable of granting him the "scientific" pretentions of his aesthetic theorizing (Munro, 1956b), especially since they were undergirded largely by the Spencerian doctrine of evolution (Munro, n.d.). Presumably, one of the reasons for rejecting such an educational theory was the lack of clarity in Munro's formulation of his aesthetic theory. And no unclear formulation of any aesthetic theory may be turned into a practical guide to education in the arts. Indeed, Munro's aesthetics in retrospect now seems more scientistic than scientific.

The second criterion suggested for judging the worth of the educational program being proposed in these pages is the practicality of the theory. I have attempted above to make the phenomenologically grounded theory as clear as the facts of the matter appear to me. And the use of a single philosophical viewpoint to structure both the proposed aesthetic theory and its application to the classroom activities of the graduate school (in the training of the teachers of teachers) and of primary and secondary schools (in the interaction between teachers and students of the arts) gives the educational theory a stamp of simplicity when it is compared to the eclectic accounts given the four participating disciplines of the discipline-based art education (DBAE) program. That simplicity makes the theory all the more practical.

What is still lacking in making this existential-phenomenological account of aesthetic education completely practical is a delivery system for translating the categories of the theory into the concepts used to describe their application to the educational setting, where eventually those same categories will have been introduced, via the educational concepts, into the behavioral patterns of teachers and students. For an example of this latter sort of educational research, the recent dissertation of Margaret Johnson (1988) supplies us with a model for developing her own program of instruction in art appreciation and criticism as a dialogue between teachers and students. Chapter IV of that dissertation bears the title "Dialogue and Dialectic in a Model for Teaching Visual Art Criticism as Making a Reflective Aesthetic Judgment." And once such a model has been defined, it can be tested empirically in a classroom situation. A similar project was attempted earlier by E. Louis Lankford (1980) of the Ohio State University.

The lines of communication seem open, and the institutional structures already exist within schools for permitting the ultimate pragmatic test of any educational theory: Does the theory applied in practice achieve its anticipated results?

Only a careful application of the theory will allow us to make that ultimate judgment. In the meantime, we can only hope for the best and, coincidentally, stop pretending that more pressing business calls us elsewhere.

GLOSSARY

BRACKETING. A metaphorical expression for the equivalent terms, listed below, *epoché* and *phenomenological reduction*. Bracketing consists in suspension of our previous knowledge or beliefs concerning the existence of the world or any of its aspects while attending to an object of consciousness. Rather than referring to a tree that is perceived, in bracketing we refer only to the properties of the tree-as-perceived, that is, how the tree appears to consciousness. Instead of referring to the physical artifact, the bracketing critical consciousness will refer to what appears in its phenomenal field, that is, a structured set of appearances either sensuous or conceptual or both. Bracketing thus corresponds to the demands of relevance in critical reaction to works of art.

CONSCIOUSNESS (an act). Not, primarily, a stream, but a single act within the stream of a single subject's awareness. As an act, it is always directed to an object, whether that object be found in the world (a transcendent object) or within the subject's stream of consciousness (an "immanent transcendency"). For example, perception is a consciousness directed to the objects that make up our world; reflection is a consciousness directed to previous acts of consciousness. Both types of consciousness are necessary for an explanation of aesthetic judgment, by which, in general, we reflect upon what is perceived of an artifact.

EIDOS (pl. EIDĒ). An *eidos*, Greek for *essence*, is a repeatable characteristic of experience, general rather than specific. According to Husserl, consciousness may intuit an essence by voluntarily changing its conscious modes, from perception to imagination, say, and attending to the invariant characteristics exhibited by the corresponding objects of consciousness. The relationships between such essences are said to constitute the "noematic nucleus," or essential meanings, by which a consciousness intends its objects. See NOEMA, below.

EPOCHĒ. Greek for *suspension*. The subject who suspends knowledge or beliefs about the world, by bracketing them out of relevance, has practiced the phenomenological reduction (q.v.). The *epoché* isolates the quality of a given conscious experience, which in turn becomes the object of aesthetic judgment.

ESSENCE. The repeatable characteristic of human experience considered as necessary for the constitution of an object's meaning and found in the structures of conscious intention (see Consciousness). A critic's description of what there is to be perceived in a work of art is given in terms of such "necessary determinants" of human knowledge.

FORESTRUCTURE. In Heidegger, a replacement for the Husserlian phenomenological reduction. Every human experience, for Heidegger, is open to interpretation. We always interpret what we do not know in terms of what we do. What we do know is itself interpreted according to three component moments: a forehaving (all our past knowledge plus our present situation); a foresight (a particular item intended within the present situation); and a foreconception, or essential determinant in terms of which the foresight, or particular subject of attribution, becomes interpreted.

A forestructure is used by every critic making an interpretation of the "meaning" of a representational work of art. Consider a Picasso synthetic cubistic piece: the represented object is viewed in multiperspectival aspects, frontally and in profile simultaneously. Or consider a simple case of impressionism: the object is displayed as an amalgamation of luminous particles. Without a critical forestructure, the critic would have something to be interpreted but no means of making the interpretation.

HERMENEUTICS. The science or art of making interpretations. In Heidegger, as opposed to the historical movement of Biblical interpretation, all interpretations exhibit circularity of reasoning. What one interprets is already known, in some sense, but only implicitly; the purpose of the interpretation is to make explicit what one has already been acquainted with. Making the implicit explicit is the business of interpretation, which is effectuated by application of the "forestructure" (q.v.).

In terms of artistic criticism, the person making an aesthetic judgment always has already experienced the qualities that must be interpreted in a reflective judgment. In more specific detail, every iconological key must be written in terms of a given critical forestructure.

INTENTION. An act by which a consciousness is related to some object; a synonym for intending, the difference being the abstraction of intention as opposed to the concreteness of intending.

Every intention, and hence every act of intending, is a consciousness taken in relationship to the object intended, or meant. On the consciousness side of the relationship one finds a noesis (q.v.) correlated to a noema (q.v.). Within the art-critical domain, intentions are either primary, having as objects the characteristics of artworks, or secondary, having as objects our previous experience of such characteristics.

INTENTIONAL OBJECT. The phenomenologically reduced work of art (see Noema); epistemologically, the object of an intention qua meant; aesthetically, the work of art as structured in our conscious experience of an artifact. Intentional objects are contrasted to the real objects of the world and the ideal objects of the purely formal sciences. Following the phenomenological reduction, the critic describes the structures of the intentional object. It is not to be confused with an artist's intention prior to the construction of an artwork, although a relationship may exist between the two senses of the term.

INTENTIONALITY. The property by which consciousnenss is related to an object, the structures of which constitute the basis for a phenomenological description. In phenomenological methodology, the defining property of purely conscious events as opposed to the physical or physiological substructures of our conscious experience. In reflection, the object of our critical appraisal of works of art.

NOEMA (pl. NOEMATA). The intentional object by which consciousness relates itself to some transcendent object; an object *qua* meant, composed of a nucleus of essential structures; can be intuited only in an act of reflection. Works of art, as opposed to simple physical artifacts, are composed of noematic structures.

NOESIS (pl. NOESES). The subjective character of an act of consciousness intending an object, correlated with a given noema. For every *noema* there is a correlated *noesis* whose character as act is to be related to a transcendent object via that *noema*. "Red" is a noematic essence by which consciousness, in an act of perception, intends a colored space. This perceiving is a noetic act. Both *noesis* and *noema* may be intended by a reflective consciousness.

ONTIC ANALYSIS. The analysis of an existent or entity according to the properties displayed by that entity under characteristic circumstances; for example, an analysis of things in terms of substance and attribute, cause and effect, and the like. Opposed to an ontological analysis, which aims at the "being" of an entity: its substantiality or presence to some contemplating subject. Ingarden gives an ontological analysis of works of art in terms of their intentional structures; Heidegger gives an ontological analysis of artworks as loci for the presencing of Being, as special regions in which Being is "brought to a stand."

ONTOLOGICAL ANALYSIS. See ONTIC ANALYSIS, above.

ONTOLOGY, FUNDAMENTAL. The ontology by which Heidegger attempted, in *Being and Time*, to interpret the scope and validity of the "derivative" ontologies had developed in the history of philosophy from the pre-Socratics to his own time. The basic phenomenon of this ontology is *Dasein*, or human being, which has both ontic and ontological characteristics; indeed, one of *Dasein's* ontic characteristics is to pose the ontological question: What is the meaning of Being, of my own being? Another is to reflect upon the meaning of its aesthetic experiences.

PHENOMENON. The appearance of an object to a consciousness; it is open to investigation, within phenomenology, by application of bracketing, reflection, description, and interpretation. Defined as "how an object appears," phenomena constitute the essence of aesthetic qualities that are found in their purity in an act of phenomenological reduction (q.v.).

PHENOMENOLOGICAL REDUCTION. A synonym for *bracketing* and *epoché*. The phenomenologist performs the phenomenological reduction by suspending all belief and knowledge in the worldly existence of the real object and by attending only to the conscious correlates, noetic or noematic, by which consciousness intends such objects. It is the first stage of Husserlian analysis of human knowledge and a necessary stage for intuiting aesthetic qualities of natural objects or artistic creations; the source of the common distinction between artifact (a real object created by an artist) and an artwork (an intentional object that may be intuited by either the artist or an art appreciator).

PHENOMENOLOGY. A method for the analysis of conscious experience, either descriptive, as per Husserl and Ingarden, or hermeneutical, as per Heidegger. An expanded version of the methodology, given by myself, attempts to apply both descriptive and hermeneutical techniques to our appreciation of works of art.

PSYCHOLOGISM. According to Husserl, a fallacy of explanation by which the properties of logical concepts and theorems depend upon the conditions of the human psyche according to which they are constructed or intuited. The psyche, like any other object of nature, must be phenomenologically reduced before an interpretation may be given of the meanings associated with this term. When reduced, the psychological subject becomes the transcendental ego.

TRANSCENDENTAL EGO. What remains, in reflection, of the subject of experience when all elements of psychological or bodily experience have been bracketed. Meanings attributed to this concept are, among others, "the subjective pole of human experiences" and "the unity expressed in a variety of conscious acts." Husserl's *Cartesian Meditations* gives at least seven more meanings associated with this purely phenomenological concept. Happily, none of the nine is directly relevant to aesthetic analysis.

TRANSCENDENTAL REDUCTION. The procedure of a reflective consciousness by which it attempts to intuit its own essential structures as an object unto itself; that stage in the phenomenological program of Husserl by which the transcendental ego is made manifest. Not a necessary procedure for aesthetic analysis.

REFERENCES

Austin, J. L. (1961). A plea for excuses. In *Philosophical papers* (pp. 175–204). Oxford, England: Clarendon Press.

Barkan, M., Chapman, L. H., & Kern, E. J. (1970). *Guidelines: Curriculum development for aesthetic education*. St Louis: CEMREL.

Beardsley, M. C. (1958). *Aesthetics: Problems in the philosophy of criticism*. New York: Harcourt & Brace.

Beardsley, M. C. (1965). On the creation of art. *Journal of Aesthetics and Art Criticism, 23*, 291–304.

Brentano, F. C. (1973). *Psychology from an empirical standpoint* (A.C. Rancurello, D.B. Terrell, & L. McAlister, Trans.). London: Routledge & Kegan Paul; New York: Humanities Press. (Original work published 1874.)

Broudy, H. S. (1987). *The role of imagery in learning*. Los Angeles: Getty Center for Education in the Arts.

Cary, E. L. (1971). *The works of James McNeill Whistler*. Freeport, NY: Books for Libraries Press.

Chapman, L. H. (1978). *Approaches to art in education*. New York: Harcourt Brace Jovanovich.

Clark, G. A., Day, M. D., & Greer, D. (1987). Discipline-based art education: Becoming students of art. *Journal of Aesthetic Education, 21*, 129–193.

Collingwood, R. G. (1958). *The principles of art*. New York: Galaxy Books. (Original work published 1938)

Crawford, D. W. (1987). Aesthetics in discipline-based art education. *Journal of Aesthetic Education, 21*, 227–239.

Croce, B. (1972). *Aesthetic* (D. Ainslie, Trans.). New York: Farrar, Strauss & Giroux. (Original English translation 1909)

Danto, A. (1964). The art world. *Journal of Philosophy, 61*, 571–584

Danto, A. (1973). Art works and real things. *Theoria, 39*, 1–17.

Dewey, J. (1910). *How we think*. Boston, New York, and Chicago: Heath.

Dewey, J. (1934). *Art as experience*. New York: Minton, Balch, & Co.

Dewey, J. (1950). *Reconstruction in philosophy*. New York: Mentor Books. (Original work published 1920.)

Dewey, J. (1966). *Democracy and education*. New York: The Free Press. (Original work published 1916.)

Dewey, J. (1968). Qualitative thought. In *Philosophy and civilization* (pp. 93–116) Gloucester, MA: Peter Smith. (Original work published 1931.)

Dickie, G. (1962). Is psychology relevant to aesthetics? *Philosophical Review, 71,* 285–302.

Dickie, G. (1964). The myth of the aesthetic attitude. *American Philosophical Quarterly, 1,* 56–65.

Dickie, G. (1966). Attitude and object: Aldrich on the aesthetic. *Journal of Aesthetics and Art Criticism, 25,* 89–91.

Dickie, G. (1979). What is art? An institutional analysis. In M. Rader, (Ed.), *A modern book of aesthetics* (5th ed.) (pp. 459–72). New York: Holt, Rinehart & Winston.

Dickie, G. (1984). *The art circle: A theory of art.* New York: Haven.

Ecker, D. W. (1963). The artistic process as qualitative problem solving. *Journal of Aesthetics and Art Criticism, 21,* 283–290. (Reprinted in Eisner & Ecker, 1966)

Ecker, D. W. (1967). Justifying aesthetic judgments. *Art Education, 20,* 5–8.

Ecker, D. W., & Kaelin, E. F. (1958). Aesthetics in public school art teaching. *College Art Journal, 17,* 382–391.

Ecker, D. W., & Kaelin, E. F. (1972). The limits of aesthetic inquiry: A guide to educational research. In *Philosophical redirection of educational research* (pp. 258–86). (71st Yearbook of the National Society for the Study of Education). Chicago: NSSE.

Eisner, E. W. (1965). Curriculum ideas in a time of crisis. *Art Education, 18,* 10.

Eisner, E. W. (1972). *Educating artistic vision.* New York: Macmillan.

Eisner, E.W. (1979). *The educational imagination.* New York: Macmillan.

Eisner, E. W., & Ecker, D. W. (1966). *Readings in art education.* Waltham, MA: Blaisdell Publishing.

Feldman, E. B. (1967). *Art as image and idea.* Englewood Cliffs, NJ: Prentice-Hall.

Fisch, M. H. (1970). The critic of institutions. In R. Tursman (Ed.), *Studies of philosophy and the history of science* (pp. 182–192). Lawrence, KS: Coronado Press. (Originally a presidential address delivered before the Western Division of the American Philosophical Association, 1956.)

Ghiselin, B. (Ed.). (1955). *The creative process.* New York: Mentor Books.

Gombrich, E. H. (1960). *Art and illusion.* New York: Pantheon Books.

Goodman, N. (1968). *The languages of art.* Indianapolis and New York: Bobbs-Merrill.

Goodman, N. (1978). *Ways of world making.* Indianapolis and Cambridge, MA.: Hackett Publishing.

Hastie, R., & Schmidt, C. (n.d.). *Encounter with art.* New York, St. Louis, San Francisco, London, Sydney, Toronto, Mexico, and Panama: McGraw-Hill.

Heidegger, M. (1962). *Being and time* (J. Macquarrie & E. Robinson, Trans.). London: SCM Press. (Original work published 1927.)

Heidegger, M. (1964). The origin of the work of art (A. Hofstadter, Trans.). In A. Hofstadter & R. Kuhns (Eds.), *Philosophies of art and beauty* (pp. 649–70). New York: Modern Library. (Original work published 1935/6.)

Heyl, B. (1957). The critic's reasons. *Journal of Aesthetics and Art Criticism, 16,* 169–179.

Hospers, J. (1956). The Croce-Collingwood theory of art. *Philosophy, 30,* 3–20.

Hume, D. (1911). *A treatise of human nature* (Vol. II in Everyman's Library edition). London: J.M. Dent & Sons. (Original work published 1738.)

Hume, D. (1951) An enquiry concerning the principles of morals. Sec. 1 in L.A. Selby-Bigge (Ed.), *Hume's enquiries.* Oxford: Clarendon Press. (Original work published in 1777.)

Husserl, E. (1962). *Ideas* (W.R. B. Gibson, Trans.) New York: Collier Books. (Original work published 1913.)

Husserl, E. (1963). *Cartesianische Meditationen und Pariser Vorträge* [Cartesian meditations and Paris lectures] (S. Strasser, Ed.). The Hague: Martinus Nijhoff. (Original work published 1926.)

Husserl, E. (1965). *Philosophie als strenge Wissenschaft* [Philosophy as a rigorous science]. In the series *Quellen der Philosophie* (R. Berlinger, Ed.). Frankfurt-am-Main: Klostermann. (Original work published 1910–11.)

Husserl, E. (1969). *Cartesian meditations* (D. Cairns, Ed.). The Hague: Martinus Nijhoff. (Original work published 1926.).

Ingarden, R. (1962a). *Untersuchungen zur Ontologie der Kunst* [Investigations into the ontology of art]. Tübingen: Max Niemeyer Verlag. (Original essays published 1933, 1946, 1947.)

Ingarden, R. (1962b). Das Musikwerk. In *Untersuchungen zur Ontologie der Kunst* [Investigations into the ontology of art] (pp. 3–136). Tübingen: Niemeyer.

Ingarden, R. (1967). Aesthetic experience and the aesthetic object. In N. Lawrence and D. O'Connor (Eds.), *Readings in existential phenomenology* (pp. 303–323). Englewood Cliffs, NJ: Prentice-Hall. (Original work published 1961.)

Ingarden, R. (1973a). *The literary work of art,* (G.G. Grabowicz, Trans.). Evanston: Northwestern University Press. (Original work published in 1931).

Ingarden, R. (1973b). *The cognition of the literary work of art* (R.A. Crowley & K. R. Olson, Trans.). Evanston: Northwestern University press. (Original work published 1937.)

Ingarden, R. (1983). in *Selected papers in aesthetics,* ed. by P.J. McCormick. Washington: D.C.: The Catholic University of America Press. (Original work published 1961.)

James, W. (1911). Percepts and concepts. In *Some problems in philosophy* (pp. 47–74). New York: Longmans, Green, & Co.

Johnson, M. H. (1988). *Dialogue and dialectic: Developing visual art concepts through classroom art criticism.* Unpublished doctoral dissertation, Florida State University Dissertations, Tallahassee.

Jowett, B. (Trans.). (1937a). *Symposium.* In *The dialogues of Plato.* New York: Random House.

Jowett, B. (Trans.). (1937b). *The republic.* In *The dialogues of Plato.* New York: Random House.

Joyce, J. (1956). *Portrait of the artist as a young man.* New York: Viking Press Compass Books. (Original work published 1916.)

Kaelin, E. F. (1959). The arts and communication. *Arts-in-Society, 1,* 71–85.

Kaelin, E. F. (1962). *An existentialist aesthetic: The theories of Sartre and Merleau-Ponty.* Madison: The University of Wisconsin Press.

Kaelin, E. F. (1964a). Method and methodology in literary criticism. *School Review, 72* 289–308.

Kaelin, E. F. (1964b) Aesthetics and the teaching of art. *Studies in Art Education, 5,* 42–56. (Reprinted in Eisner & Ecker, 1966)

Kaelin, E. F. (1965). The visibility of things seen: A phenomenological view of painting. In J. Edie (Ed.), *An invitation to phenomenology* (pp. 30–58). Chicago: Quadrangle Books.

Kaelin, E. F. (1966). The existential ground for aesthetic education. *Studies in Art Education, 8,* 3–12.

Kaelin, E. F. (1967). Notes towards an understanding of Heidegger's aesthetics. In E. Lee and M. Mandelbaum (Eds.), *Phenomenology and existentialism* (pp. 59–92). Baltimore: The Johns Hopkins Press.

Kaelin, E. F. (1968a). An existential-phenomenological account of aesthetic education. *Penn State Papers in Art Education,* No. 4. University Park: The Pennsylvania State University.

Kaelin, E. F. (1968b). Art and existence. *Humanitas, 4,* 181–210.

Kaelin, E. F. (1968c). Aesthetic education: A rôle for aesthetics proper. *Journal of Aesthetic Education, 2,* 51–66.

Kaelin, E. F. (1968d). Isness and oughtness: Reasoning about values. *Art Education, 21,* 6–10.

Kaelin, E. F. (1970a). *Art and existence.* Lewisburg, PA: Bucknell University Press.

Kaelin, E. F. (1970b). *Epochē* and relevance in aesthetic discourse. In R.A. Smith (Ed.), *Aesthetic concepts and education* (pp. 135–163). Urbana, IL: University of Illinois Press.

Kaelin, E. F. (1980) Between the innocent eye and the omniscient mind. In D. W. Ecker (Ed.), *Qualitative evaluation in the arts* (pp. 19–60). New York: Division of Arts and Art Education, New York University.

Kaelin, E. F. (1986) Why teach art in the public schools? *Journal of Aesthetic Education, 20,* 67–71.

Kant, I. (1951). *The critique of judgment,* (J.H. Bernard, Trans.). New York: Hafner Publishing. (Original work published 1790.)

Kaufman, I. (1966). *Art education in contemporary culture.* New York: Macmillan; London: Collier-Macmillan.

Kennick, W.E., ed. (1976). *Art and Philosophy,* 2d. ed. New York: St. Martin's Press.

Langer, S. K. (1953). *Feeling and form.* New York: Scribner's Sons.

Lankford, E. L. (1980). Merleau-Ponty's concepts of perception, behavior, and aesthetics applied to critical dialogue in the visual arts. Unpublished doctoral dissertation, Florida State University, Tallahassee.

Lansing, K. M. (1969). *Art, artists, and art education.* New York, St. Louis, San Francisco, London, Sydney, Toronto, Mexico, Panama: McGraw-Hill.

Lindsey, A. (1982). *A phenomenologically based aesthetic theory with application to teacher preparation in accordance with adult education principles.* Unpublished doctoral dissertation, Florida State University, Tallahassee.

Logan, F. M. (1955). *Growth of art in American schools.* New York: Harper & Brothers.

Madeja, S. S., & Onuska, S. (1977). *Through the arts to the aesthetic.* St. Louis: Central Midwestern Regional Educational Laboratory.

Magliola, R. R. (1977). *Phenomenology and literature.* West Lafayette, IN: Purdue University Press.

Mandelbaum, M. (1965). Family resemblances and generalization concerning the arts. *The American Philosophical Quarterly, 2,* 219–238.

McKeon, R. (Ed.). (1941). *The basic works of Aristotle. De Poetica* [The Poetics.] (I. Bywater, Trans.). New York: Random House.

Mead, G. H. (1926). The nature of the aesthetic experience. *International Journal of Ethics, 36,* 382–392.

Mead, G. H. (1934). *Mind, self and society from the standpoint of a social behaviorist* (Charles Morris, Ed.). Chicago: University of Chicago Press.

Merleau-Ponty, M. (1962). *The phenomenology of perception* (C. Smith, Trans.). New York: Humanities Press. (Original work published 1945)

Merleau-Ponty, M. (1964a). The philosopher and sociology. In *Signs* (R. McCleary, Trans.) (pp. 98–113). Evanston: Northwestern University Press.

Merleau-Ponty, M. (1964b). *The primacy of perception* (C. Dallery, et al., Trans.). Evanston: Northwestern University Press.

Merleau-Ponty, M. (1965). Le doute de Cézanne. In *Sens et non-sens* [Sense and Nonsense] (5th ed.) (pp. 15–44). Paris: Nagel. (Original work published 1948.)

Merleau-Ponty, M. (1969a). Cézanne's Doubt. In A. L. Fisher (Ed.), *The essential writings of Merleau-Ponty* (pp. 233–51). New York: Harcourt, Brace, and World. (Original work published 1948.)

Merleau-Ponty, M. (1969b). Eye and mind. In A.L. Fisher (Ed.), *The essential writings of Merleau-Ponty* (pp. 252–86). New York: Harcourt, Brace, and World. (Original work published 1961.)

Munro, T. (1956a). *Art education: Its philosophy and psychology.* Indianapolis, New York, Kansas City: Liberal Arts Press.

Munro, T. (1956b). *Towards science in aesthetics.* New York: Liberal Arts Press.

Munro, T. (n.d.). *Evolution in the arts.* Cleveland: The Cleveland Museum of Art.

Nietzsche, F. (n.d.). The birth of tragedy from the spirit of music. In *The philosophy of Friedrich Nietzsche* (C. Fadiman, Trans.) (Secs. 1–8). New York: Modern Library. (Original work published 1871.)

Panofsky, E. (1939). *Studies in iconology.* New York: Oxford University Press.

Parker, D. H. (1945). *The principles of aesthetics* (2nd ed.). New York: F.S. Crofts & Co. (Original work published 1920.)

Passmore, J.A. (1951). The dreariness of aesthetics. *Mind, N.S., 60,* 318–325.

Pater, W. (n.d.) *The Renaissance.* New York: Modern Library. (Original work published, 1873)

Peirce, C. S. (1940). How to make our ideas clear. In W. Muelder & L. Sears (Eds.), *The development of American philosophy* (pp. 341–46) New York: Houghton, Mifflin.

Pepper, S. C. (1949). *The basis of criticism in the arts.* Cambridge, MA: Harvard University Press.

Pepper, S. C. (1953). Emotion. In E. Vivas & M. Krieger (Eds.), *The problems of aesthetics.* (pp. 376–386). New York and Toronto: Rinehart (Original work published 1937).

Pepper, S. C. (1955). *The aesthetic work of art.* Bloomington: Indiana University Press.

Prall, D. W. (1967a). *Aesthetic judgment.* New York: Crowell Apollo Editions. (Original work published 1929)

Prall, D. W. (1967b). *Aesthetic analysis.* New York: Crowell Apollo Editions. (Original work published 1936.)

Quiller-Couch, A. (Ed.) (1939). *The Oxford book of English verse* (new ed.). John Keats's "Ode on a Grecian urn" (pp. 745–746). Oxford: Clarendon Press.

Santayana, G. (1955). *Sense of beauty.* New York: Modern Library. (Original work published 1896.)

Sartre, J.P. (1948). *The psychology of the imagination* (no translator cited). New York: Philosophical Library. (Original work published 1940.)

Scheffler, I. (Ed.). (1958). *Philosophy and education.* Boston: Allen & Bacon.

Scheffler, I. (1960). *The language of education.* Springfield, IL: Thomas.

Scheffler, I. (1985). *Of human potential.* London, Boston: Routledge & Kegan Paul.

Smith, R. A. (Ed.). (1966). *Aesthetics and criticism in art education.* Chicago: Rand, McNally.

Spalding, F. (1979). *Whistler.* Oxford, England: Phaidon.

Time magazine. (1987, February 16). Can colleges teach thinking? p. 61

Urmson, J. O. (1962). What makes a situation aesthetic? In J. Margolis (Ed.), *Philosophy looks at the arts* (pp. 13–27). New York: Scribner's Sons.

Weitz, M. (1950). *Philosophy of the arts.* Cambridge, MA: Harvard University Press.

Weitz, M. (1956). The rôle of theory in aesthetics. *Journal of Aesthetics and Art Criticism, 15,* 27–35.

White, M. (1955). *The age of analysis.* New York: Mentor Books.

Wimsatt, W. K., & Beardsley, M. C. (1946). The intentional fallacy. *Sewanee Review, 54,* 468–488.

Wimsatt, W. K., & Beardsley, M. C. (1949). The affective fallacy. *Sewanee Review, 57,* 458–488.

Wittgenstein, L. (1953). *Philosophical investigations* (G.E.M. Anscombe, Trans.). New York: Macmillan. (Published posthumously.)

Ziff, P. (1953). The task of defining a work of art. *Philosophical Review, 62,* 58–78.

Ziff, P. (1954). Art and the 'object of art.' In W. Elton (Ed.), *Essays in aesthetics and language* (pp. 170–186). Oxford: Blackwell.

Ziff, P. (1958). Reasons in art criticism. In W. Kennick (Ed.), *Art and philosophy,* 2d ed. (pp. 669–86). New York: St. Martin's Press.

ANNOTATED BIBLIOGRAPHY

The entries in this bibliography have been selected for their relevance to the unifying theme of this volume covering the fields of aesthetics, art criticism, art and aesthetic education, phenomenology, and symbolic interactionist social psychology. It makes no claim to exhaustiveness; I include it in order to facilitate quick reference back to the horse's mouth for those who would find such a thing useful for their own purposes.

Brentano, Franz Clemens (1973). *Psychology from an Empirical Standpoint*, trans. A. C. Rancurello, D. B. Terrell, and Linda L. McAlister; ed. L. L. McAlister. London: Routledge & Kegan Paul; New York: Humanities Press.
    Arguably, the beginnings of modern phenomenology, but most assuredly the source of Husserl's notion of "intentionality," which Brentano brought forward from medieval epistemology.

Dewey, John (1934). *Art as Experience*. New York: Minton, Balch, & Co.
    The primary source for American pragmatic aesthetics and principal source of my notion of the "depth" counters of an aesthetic experience.

Dewey, John (1968). *Philosophy and Civilization*, reprint edition. Gloucester, MA.: Peter Smith. (Originally published 1931.)
    A collection of essays containing two of Dewey's capital contributions to aesthetics prior to the publication of *Art as Experience* in 1934. The first, originally published in 1931 is "Qualitative Thought" (pp. 93–116), which describes the process of artistic creation as an act of problem solving; the second, "Affective Thought" (pp. 117–25), which describes artistic creation as guided by the emotions controlled in the discovery of an aesthetic object, was originally published in 1926.

Dickie, George (1962). Is Psychology Relevant to Aesthetics? *Psychological Review, 71*, 285–302.
    His answer is a surprising "no." But that should be interpreted as a refutation of arguments made for a mysterious "aesthetic attitude," not to be confused with the "natural" or "phenomenological" attitudes. The argument is heavily influenced by the work of Wimsatt and Beardsley listed below.

Dickie, George (1969). The Myth of the Aesthetic Attitude. In *Introductory Readings in Aesthetics,* ed. John Hospers. New York: The Free Press, pp. 28–44.
  A more specific refutation of claims made for a special attitude either favorable to or necessary for the existence of an aesthetic object.

Dickie, George (1974). *Art and the Aesthetic: An Institutional Analysis.* Ithaca, NY: Cornell University Press.
  The most fully developed institutional theory of aesthetics, built as an alternative to the "undefinability thesis" concerning art objects.

Dufrenne, Mikel (1953). *Phénoménologie de l'expérience ésthétique* (The Phenomenology of Aesthetic Experience). Paris: Presses Universitaires de France. 2 vols.
  An account, like my own, derived from the "aesthetic" works of Sartre and Merleau-Ponty, which draws upon the correlation between the experience—the subjective side—and the structures of aesthetic objects making their appearance in a three-fold way: as sensuous constructs (presence), as representative of imaginary objects (imagination), and as expressive of a uniquely felt "world" (reflection).

Ecker, David W. (1963). The Artistic Process as Qualitative Problem Solving. *Journal of Aesthetics and Art Criticism, 21,* 283–290.
  Dewey's essay on qualitative thought applied to art education; originally, a doctoral dissertation defended at Wayne State University.

Heidegger, Martin (1962). *Being and Time,* trans. John Macquarrie and Edward Robinson. London: SCM Press, Ltd. (Originally published 1927.)
  The fountainhead source of existential phenomenology and of the hermeneutical methodology following upon the author's use of it to explain it as an "existential" structure of the human understanding. I have employed the same method in this text for interpreting the depth signification of artworks.

Heidegger, Martin (1964). The Origin of the Work of Art, trans. A. Hofstadter. In *Philosophies of Art and Beauty,* ed. Albert Hofstadter and Richard Kuhns. New York: Modern Library. Pp. 649–701.
  Heidegger's analysis of three works of art, looking for a sense of their origins and discovering their internal workings as a strife between "earth" and "world." I find in these metaphors reference to the surface and depth structures of an aesthetic experience.

Husserl, Edmund (1969). *Cartesian Meditations,* trans. Dorion Cairns. The Hague: Martinus Nijhoff. (Originally published 1926.)
  A description of the phenomenological *epoché* as a single layered, continuous process. Also contains the fullest description of the functions fulfilled by the "transcendental ego" in giving sense to human experiences. The translator rather idiosyncratically personalizes the transcendental ego.

Husserl, Edmund (1962). *Ideas,* trans. W. R. Boyce Gibson. New York: Collier Books. (Originally published 1913.)

Middle-vintage Husserl, containing a description of the phenomenological *epochē* as a triply layered process of consciousness reduction, along with
his account of an etching by Albrecht Dürer. Perhaps the best introductory source for an understanding of "descriptive phenomenology."

Ingarden, Roman (1973). *The Literary Work of Art*, trans. G. G. Grabowicz. Evanston: Northwestern University Press. (Originally published 1931.)
An eidetic description of a literary work of art as an intentional object built
up of four distinct levels of conscious meaning structures.

Ingarden, Roman (1973). *The Cognition of the Literary Work of Art*, trans. Ruth
Ann Crowley and Knneth R. Oslon. Evanston: Northwestern University Press.
(Originally published 1937.)
The noetic side of our consciousness intending literary works of art, writ-
ten to complement the noematic analysis of the previous text.

Ingarden, Roman (1962). *Untersuchungen zur Ontologie der Kunst* (Investigations into the Ontology of Art). Tübingen: Max Niemeyer Verlag.
Analysis of the artworks in other media: music, painting, architecture, and
the film. The works are still intentional objects, analyzable into strata,
which, however, differ from medium to medium. The distinction between intentional and real objects allows the author to draw a correlative
distinction between the "aesthetic values" of the intentional work and the
"artistic values" of the physical artifact. Paul Ziff, in the article listed below, attacks this distinction.

Ingarden, Roman (1975). Phenomenological Aesthetics: An Attempt at Defining its Range. *Journal of Aesthetics and Art Criticism, 33,* 257–269.
An overview of the topic containing a special introduction to the author's
own aesthetic methodology.

Kaelin, Eugene, F. (1962). *An Existentialist Aesthetic.* Madison: University of
Wisconsin Press.
An aesthetic theory culled from the philosophical works of Sartre and
Merleau-Ponty. The former stresses the phenomenology of the imagination; the later, of perception. Taken together, they provide the concepts
necessary for a description of the surface and depth characteristics of artworks.

Kaelin, Eugene F. (1970). *Art and Existence.* Lewisburg, PA: Bucknell University Press.
Application of the surface/depth distinction to the works of various art
media: literature, painting, music, dance, and film.

Kaelin, Eugene F. (1967). Notes toward an Understanding of Heidegger's Aesthetics. In *Phenomenology and Existentialism,* eds. Edward N. Lee and Maurice
Mandelbaum. Baltimore: The Johns Hopkins Press. Pp. 59–92.
The source of Heidegger's ontological description of the working of a work
of art, ending with a generalized account of such works as the strife between "earth" and "world."

Kant, Immanuel (1951). *Critique of Judgment*, trans. J.H. Bernard. New York: Hafner Publishing. (Originally published 1790.)
> The classical statement of aesthetic judgment as "reflective," used by both Dewey and Parker to refute the claims of classicism and impressionism in criticism.

Langer, Susanne K. (1948). *Philosophy in a New Key*, paperback reprint. New York: Penguin Books. (Originally published 1942.)
> Her first attempt at an aesthetic theory based upon "the studio point of view." Concentrates on the medium of music, introducing the notion of a symbol as a means for making an abstraction. According to this theory, musicians create a "virtual image" of time expressive of the patterns of human feeling. Largely influenced by the philosophy of Ernst Cassirer.

Langer, Susanne K. (1953). *Feeling and Form*. New York: Scribner's Sons.
> Generalization of the theory of expression developed in the previous entry to cover the media of painting, dance, architecture, poetry, prose, dramatic literature, and the film.

Mead, George Herbert (1913). The Social Self. *Journal of Philosophy, 10,* 374–380.
> A pioneering work in social psychology by the founder of "symbolic interactionism."

Mead, George Herbert (1922). A Behavioristic Account of the Significant Symbol. *Journal of Philosophy, 19,* 157–163.
> A description of the process of finding significance in gestures. The foundations of a theory of communication between social individuals.

Mead, George Herbert (1926). The Nature of Aesthetic Experience. *International Journal of Ethics, 36,* 382–392.
> Aesthetic value as the consummatory aspect of distinctively human acts.

Mead, George Herbert (1934). *Mind, Self and Society from the Standpoint of a Social Behaviorist*, ed. Charles W. Morris. Chicago: The University of Chicago Press.
> The fountainhead of symbolic interactionism, prepared from notes taken by students in the author's famous course in social psychology at the University of Chicago in 1927 and 1930.

Merleau-Ponty, Maurice (1964). *The Primacy of Perception*, trans. Carleton Dallery et al. Evanston: Northwestern University Press. (Originally published 1961.)
> Volume edited by J.M. Edie, to include the title essay, which was the synopsis of the author's early work prepared to defend his candidacy for a chair at the Collège de France, along with others in phenomenological psychology, philosophy of art, history, and politics. The essay in aesthetics is "Eye and Mind," both references symbolic of empirical and rationalistic philosophy and of a possible solution of the disputes between these schools of thought entertainable from a phenomenological reading of the art of painting. This same essay is as close as Merleau-Ponty ever

got to expressing the relationship between the "surface" and "depth" of a painting.

Merleau-Ponty, Maurice (1962). *The Phenomenology of Perception*, trans. Colin Smith. New York: Humanities Press. (Originally published 1945.)
The author's completest account of the primacy of perception in human expressive acts.

Merleau-Ponty, Maurice (1969). *The Essential Writings of Merleau-Ponty*, ed. Alden L. Fisher. New York: Harcourt, Brace & Co.
Contains both "The Eye and the Mind" and "Cézanne's Doubt," the best sources for the author's theory of painting.

Parker, DeWitt H. (1945). *The Principles of Aesthetics*, 2d. edition. New York: F. S. Crofts & Co. (Originally published 1920.)
The text of a course taught many years at the University of Michigan, enormously influential in American aesthetics owing primarily to its inclusion of both a general theory of aesthetic objects and a number of special theories for the different media. Marred by its essentialism and the derivative solution to the argument between classical and impressionistic critics that the author calls a "modified classicism." Had the psychology of this text been more phenomenological, the need for a text such as my own would have been less pronounced. Not many American aestheticians have heeded the author's suggestion that their work should be supported by the relevant portions of social psychology.

Prall, David W. (1967). *Aesthetic Judgment*. New York: Crowell Apollo Editions. (Originally published 1929.)
Naturalism in aesthetics by the author who coined the expression *aesthetic surface* to emphasize the medial values of expressive acts.

Sartre, Jean-Paul (1948). *The Psychology of the Imagination*, no trans. New York: Philosophical Library. (Originally published 1940.)
The phenomenology of the imagination from beginning to end, with a conclusion dedicated to aesthetic objects as imaginative constructs. Given an ontological interpretation, these latter founded the author's future speculations on human nature as "radical freedom."

Sartre, Jean-Paul (1948). *Being and Nothingness*, trans. Hazel Barnes. New York: Philosophical Library. (Originally published 1943.)
The phenomenological ontology that became the bible of the French existentialist "café rats."

Urmson, J.O. (1962). What Makes a Situation Aesthetic? In *Philosophy Looks at the Arts*, ed. Joseph Margolis. New York: Scribner's Sons, pp. 13–26.
A landmark, of sorts, illustrating the difficulty in defining the aesthetic dimension of human experience when one is convinced there is no essence for the same.

Wimsatt, William K., Jr., and Beardsley, Monroe C. (1946). The Intentional Fallacy. *Sewanee Review, 54*, 468–488; and Wimsatt, William K., Jr., and

Beardsley, Monroe C. (1949). The Affective Fallacy. *Sewanee Review, 57,* 458–488.

The two articles together have provided American aesthetics with some of its most lively debates. For George Dickie, who accepts the descriptions offered, they formed the basis of his doctrine of the irrelevance of psychology to aesthetics; for myself, they show the way toward a proper psychology of art—the phenomenological, along with its characteristic "return to the things [artworks] themselves!"

Ziff, Paul (1954). Art and the 'Object of Art.' In *Essays in Aesthetics and Language,* ed. William Elton. Oxford: Blackwell. Pp. 170–186.

Contains the denial of the existence of a special object of art, which is supposedly the correlate of an aesthetic attitude and distinct from the physical artifact. According to Ziff, the "intentional" objects of the phenomenologists are merely the results of a different kind of description—which, upon reflection, turns out to be a phenomenological description, as opposed to a purely physical one. This last interpretation, of course, is a restatement of Husserl's famous phenomenological reduction of consciousness.

INDEX

Aesthetic analysis
  and aesthetic judgment, 34
  and linguistic theory, 44
Aesthetic attitude, Aldrich-Dickie
  debate on, 130
Aesthetic behavior, as principle of
  autonomy, 188–119
Aesthetic categories, 174
  in aesthetic education, 110
  surface and depth of, 75
Aesthetic context, postulates for
  interpreting, 76–77
Aesthetic creation, in idealistic
  aesthetics, 39
Aesthetic depth, 34, 92, 93
  analyzed, 19
  and association, 24–25
  and content, 20
  and iconic meanings, 19–20
  and psychological imagery, 172
  and representational art, 18
  significance of, 97
Aesthetic discourse, Ecker-Kaelin
  typology of, 200–201
Aesthetic education
  aims of, 25–27
  autonomy and creativity of, 120
  autonomy and permissiveness of, 119
  autonomy principle and freedom of,
    119
  autonomy principle of, 118–26
    summarized, 135–36
  and communication theory, 113
  completeness, and criticism of, 121,
    135
  completeness principle of, 131–35
    summarized, 136

  concept of, 65–66
  and creative communication, 193
  criticism in, 132
  defined, 111–12
  the discipline of, 108–9
  ends and means in, 114
  every student's right to, 81–82
  institutional structure of, 26
  and normative aesthetics, 132
  objectives of, 109–10
  permissiveness in, 119–20
  phenomenological limits of, 137
    summarized, 135–37
  principles of, 112–13, 135–37
  projectional principle of, 114–18, 120
  relevancy principle of, 126–31
    summarized, 131, 136
  and socialization of individuals,
    114–15
  and society, 111
  theory and practice of, 137
  values of, 79–82
Aesthetic inquiry, scope of, 119
Aesthetic institution, analyzed, 112–13
Aesthetic judgment
  in art education, 25–27
  context of, in D.W. Ecker, 35
  contextual, 80
  "good reasons" school of, 33
  institutionalized, 78
  objectivity of, 24
  optimal expertise in, 134
  vs. psychological preference, 34, 67
  and psychological reports, 67
  and qualified liking, 34–35
  and referential adequacy in language, 35
  as surface and depth description, 20

223

Aesthetic literacy
  concept of, 190–91
  as goal of art education, 163
Aesthetic object, theory of, 98
Aesthetic objects, intentional
  in Ingarden, 149–51
  in Langer, 148
  in Sartre, 148
Aesthetic relevance, and contextual
    significance, 74
Aesthetic response, relevancy of, 35
Aesthetic significance
  postulates of, 77, 160–62, 182–83
  vs. signification, 96
Aesthetic surface, 17–18, 20, 33, 92, 93
  deepening of, 139, 148–49, 173, 186–87
  thickening of, 75–76
Aesthetic theory
  and analytical philosophy, 201
  definitions' role in, 56
  methodology of, 108–9
  and positivism, 201
  thin and thick, 18–20
  Weitz's view of, criticized, 43–44
Aesthetic valencies, and value
    determinants, in Ingarden, 150
Aesthetic values
  and culture, 71–72
  and goals of art education, 30
Aesthetics
  analytic, criticized, 44–46
  and beauty, 7
  classicism in, 8
  and consummatory values, 3
  as criticism of criticism, 60, 101
  Crocean, criticized, 40
  and eidetic description, 141
  existentialist, in Sartre and Merleau-
    Ponty, 148–49
  and expression, 7–8
  and the facts of taste, 31
  Greek, 3, 4–8
  idealistic, summary evaluation of, 42
  love and beauty in, 4
  as meta-aesthetics, 86
  phenomenological, as a method for
    art education, 102–3
  phenomenological and pragmatic, 94
  as philosophical discipline, 31, 67
  and philosophy, 3
  as philosophy of art, 11, 193
  role of paradigms in, 43, 46
  role of theory in, 42–46
  romanticism in, 8
  thick and thin, 18
Aesthetics proper
  and philosophy of art, 71
  defined, 70, 71
Affective fallacy, 84
  and aesthetic meanings, 126
  and expressiveness, 160
  and infinity hypothesis, 24–25, 84, 27
  phenomenological resolution of, 129
Aldrich, Virgil, 130
Aristotle
  and aesthetics, 197
  on catharsis, 6
  and censorship, 6, 7
  on form, 6
  and poets, 6
Armstrong, Louis, on defining jazz, 55
Arnold, Matthew, and touchstone
    theory of criticism, 128
Art
  as aesthetic institution, 30, 54
  as institution among institutions, 59
  institution of, in Dickie, 58–59
  from nonobjective to representational,
    19
  process of, in Croce, 39
  as social institution, 7
  technical instruction in, 15
  and technique, 39
  and technique, in Kant, 45
  and visibility, 53
Art appreciation, in art education, 16
Art criticism
  concept of, 185
  expertise in, 158
  and "good reasons" school, 133
  history of, 157–58
Art curriculum, and aesthetic inquiry,
    195–99
Art education
  in adult education, 16
  beginning where students are, 15–16
  in Clark, Day, and Greer, 204
  cognitive development in, 27
  and control of feelings, 26–27
  discipline based (DBAE), 60, 62, 204
  ends-values in, 61–62
  founding a program in, 15

improvement of taste in, 27
justifying normative judgments in,
    29–30
pedagogical principles of, 86
and pedagogy, 66
predicament of, 164
production of art in, 15
social functions of, 29
stacked languages in, 196–99
and the structure of knowledge, 196
works of art in, 15
Art elements, classified, 21–22
Art for art's sake, reinterpreted, 61–62
Art genres, as surface and depth, 12–13
Art history
    and aesthetic categories, 85
    as discourse on art, 200–201
Art institution, federal support of, 70
Art interpretation. *See also* aesthetic
        significance
    postulates of, 130
Art media, in aesthetic inquiry, 17
Art process
    and aesthetic judgment, 41
    analogized with the scientific, 49–51
    in Ecker, 47–49
    in neo-pragmatism, 53
    role of pervasive qualities in, 52
Art theory
    Danto-Dickie institutional, 57–59
    institutional, 54, 56
    role of definitions in, 58
Artist
    as teacher, 16, 36–37
    and teaching of art, 15, 16
Artistic techniques and aesthetic
        judgment, 186
Arts
    classified, 18–19
    musical, and time, 21
    nonobjective, 21
    visual, and space, 21
Attitude modification, methodical, 140
Attitudes
    aesthetic, 93, 130
    natural, 130, 140
    phenomenological, 130
Austin, John L., and phenomenology,
    100

Baumgarten, Alexander, 37

Beardsley, Monroe C.
    on aesthetics as metacriticism, 197
    as critic of Ecker, 89
    and local qualities, 95
Behavior prediction, and essential
        determination, 116
Berenson, Bernard, 85
Botticelli, Alessandro, *Birth of Venus*,
    149
Bracketing, 139–40
    as aesthetic method, 75
    and aesthetic significance, 95
    in aesthetics proper, 81
    as analysis of conscious acts, 105
    in art criticism, 160
    defined, 207
    in educational practice, 83
    effect of, 78–79
    and *epochē*, 143
    Husserl's practice of, 91, 93
    in or out, 74–75, 84, 149
    in Ingardenian aesthetics, 149
    and relevance in critical discourse,
        128–29
Brentano, Franz
    as proto-phenomenologist, 142
    psychologism of, 142

Carlyle, Thomas, as Whistler's subject,
    171
Categories, aesthetic
    as critical tools, 102
    educational use of, 131
    of phenomenology, 102, 130–31, 174
    traditional, 128
Censorship, 70
Cézanne, Paul, and gestalt features, 145
Champlin, Nathaniel, 47
Classroom, as locus of aesthetic
        communication, 117
Closure, aesthetic
    and aesthetic evaluation, 162
    as funding counters, 132
    in perception and judgment, 134
Closure, perceptual, in aesthetic
        contexts, 98
Collingwood, Robin G.
    and aesthetic theory, 197
    differences with Croce, 41
    as follower of Croce, 42–42
Communication, aesthetic

Communication, aesthetic (*continued*)
  in aesthetic education, 115
  and autonomy, 136
  existential model of, 122
  measurement of, 121
  Platonic model of, 121, 136
Communication, nonverbal, in aesthetic
    education, 110
Concepts
  open, in aesthetics, 46, 177, 179, 197
  open and closed, in aesthetics, 43–46
Consciousness
  defined, 207
  Husserlian concept of, 91
  and meaning constitution, 141
  as temporality, in Heidegger, 106
Consciousness modification
  in artistic process, 106
  in linguistic analysis, 100
  in logical positivism, 100
  in Merleau-Ponty, 100
Contemporary philosophy, age of
    analysis, 203
Contextualism. *See also* aesthetic
    significance
  and aesthetic expressiveness, 168
Counters, aesthetic. *See also* aesthetic
    context
  in contextual significance, 78, 128, 182
  and Ecker's "component qualities,"
    104–5
  elements of perceptual forms, 167–68,
    171–73
  kinds of, 128, 130, 133–35, 185
  and significance, 95, 96
Crawford, Donald W., aesthetics in
    DBAE, 204
Creative process
  in Beardsley, 103
  in Ecker, 103
  in Ghiselin, 103
Critical concepts
  and aesthetic categories, 164–65
  open textured, 43–46, 177, 179
Critical evaluation, in Eisner, 181
Criticism
  and aesthetic preferences, 133–34
  in art education, 165
  classical, falsely deductive, 177
  concept of, 185
  concepts of, open textured, 177, 179

evaluation as descriptive, 160–62
  functions of, in Eisner, 180–81
  "good reasons" school of, 72–73
  impressionistic, 178
  as institutional control, 79–80
  instrumentalist, in Feldman, 184
  judicial or impressionistic, in Dewey,
    159
  kinds of, in Feldman, 183–84
  and the liking standard, 133–34
  ontological, in Merleau-Ponty, 146
  and phenomenological description,
    141
  range of, 165
Croce, Benedetto
  and aesthetic theory, 197
  as idealistic aesthetician, 32, 38–40
Cubism
  compared to futurism, 96
  defined, 96
  style of, 103
Cultural values, in art, 71–72
Culture, two senses of, 71

Danto, Arthur
  and the artworld, 198
  as institutional theorist, 57
Descartes, René
  on difference between science and
    arts, 31–32
  and error of substance theory, 87–88
  hyperbolic doubt in, 87–88
  influence on Husserl, 142
  and philosophical method, 87
Description, art critical deepening of,
    185–86
Description, eidetic, in aesthetic theory,
    101, 131, 140
Description, ontological, as educational
    alternative, 115–16
Description, phenomenological, as
    aesthetic evaluation, 186
Descriptions, phenomenological and
    eidetic, 141
Dewey, John
  on aesthetic closure, 162
  on aesthetic judgment, 158–59, 162
  and aesthetic theory, 197
  on art as an experience, 139
  compared to Heidegger, 162
  on educational theory, 68

on fallacies of criticism, 161
on impressionistic criticism, 178
on individual and society, 193
on the live creature, 159
on logical and reflective judgments, 177
on making aesthetic judgments, 134
and means-ends continuum, 115, 117
on perception and criticism, 131–32
as philosopher of education, 199
as pragmatic aesthetician, 38, 46–47, 90
on problems and tasks, 116
on total expressiveness, 174
on value as interest, 167
Dickie, George
on aesthetic attitude, 130
as anti-psychologisitic aesthetician, 93
anti-psychologism of, criticized, 94–95
on defining art, 198
as institutional theorist, 57–59, 198
Dürer, Albrecht, *Ritter, Tod und Teufel*, 143, 147

Ecker, David W.
on aesthetic value, 33
as critic of Horowitz painting, 51–52
and Dewey, on problem solving, 47–48
and limits of aesthetic inquiry, 195–99
as pragmatic aesthetician, 47–49, 89
Education, defined, 112
Educational theory
adequacy of, 108
and behavioral sciences, 120
and linguistic puzzle solving, 68–69
and philosophy, 67–68
and phenomena of experience, 69–70
pragmatic ends of, 66–67
use of statistics in, 116
Educators and educationists, 65–66
Eidos, defined, 207
Eisner, Elliot W.
as analytic philosopher, 32
on critical uses of language, 32–33
on criticism, evaluated, 182–83
on criticism in art education, 163, 180
on theory in art education, 31
Eisner, Elliot W., and Ecker David W.
as art educators, 28, 29, 31, 36, 203

on criticism in aesthetics, 89
as critics of scientism, 82–83
on qualitative problem solving, 185
Epochē, defined, 207
in Descartes, 87–88
Epochē, phenomenological
as aesthetic procedure, 65
and aesthetic significance, 102
in aesthetics, 94–95
ambiguities of, in Husserl, 91
art critical method, 84
art critical procedure, 99
and critical reflection, 102
by Husserl, 74, 129, 142
method in aesthetics, 99, 102
and reduction, 140
Essence, defined, 207
of an individual, object of criticism, 98
Essences
aesthetic and family resemblances, 99
as *eidē*, 140
and eidetic description, 140
and essentialist fallacy, 99
and invariant characteristics, 140
Platonic, 99
and social classification, 116
Evaluation, as assignment of worth, 184
Evaluation in criticism, in Eisner, 181
Existential phenomenology
in educational theory, 82–83
as method for aesthetic education, 111
Existentiality, 115
Expression
in Collingwood, 40
in Croce, 38
Croce-Collingwood theory of, 38–42
and expressiveness, 72
and intentional fallacy, 22–24, 159–60
Expressiveness
aesthetic value of, 167
in Feldman's metacriticism, 184
as felt tension, 13
surface and depth of, 185
total, and funding counters of, 174

Facticity, 120
Family resemblances
and aesthetic essences, 99
in Croce, 44–45
in Weitz, 43
in Wittgenstein, 57, 99

Feldman, Edmund B., 163, 183–85
Fisch, Max H., 202
Forestructure, analyzed, 154
    defined, 208
Form
    abstract representational, 171
    aesthetic, 12
    aesthetic, perception of, 167
    and aesthetic analysis, 166–67
    and content, 12
    musical, 167
    senses of, 167
Forms, representational, 168
Fundamental ontology, defined, 209

Genius
    concept of, 23–24
    and intentional fallacy, 23–24
Ghiselin, Brewster, on creative process,
    103
Goodman, Nelson, on defining art, 198

Hastie, Reid; and Schmidt, Christian,
    203
Heidegger, Martin
    aesthetic categories of 156–57
    as aesthetician, 155–57
    on architecture, 156
    Being and Time, 73–74
    and Dewey, on significance, 162
    on disclosedness, 73
    and educational theory, 106
    and existential analysis, 74
    and existential openness, 115
    as fundamental ontologist, 153
    as hermeneutical phenomenologist,
        139, 153
    and human disclosedness, 154
    on individual essences, 98
    influence on Merleau-Ponty, 145–46
    on openness, 73
    on poetry, 156
    on temporality of consciousness, 159
Hermeneutical circle, 154–55
Hermeneutics
    defined, 208
    and description of aesthetic depth,
        157
    as method of understanding, 154–57
    as science of interpretation, 153
Horowitz, Saul, 49, 51–52

Hospers, John, 41, 103
Hume, David
    as critic of substance theory, 88
    on judgments of taste, 28–29, 30
    and phenomenology, 91
    and relativity of taste, 30
Husserl, Edmund
    on bracketing, 74–75, 91, 129
    as critical phenomenologist, 13
    and Descartes, 90, 91
    descriptive phenomenology of, 139–44
    and educational theory, 106
    idealism of, criticized by Ingarden,
        149
    and phenomenological *epochē*, 74
    phenomenological methodology of, 90
    against psychologism, 142
    on regional ontologies, 90
    on return to phenomena, 89
    as Sartrean precursor, 147

Idealism. *See also* expression
    in aesthetic theory, 38–42
Ingarden, Roman
    and aesthetic theory, 197
    aesthetics of, criticized, 152–53
    on aesthetics of painting, 151
    eidetic description in aesthetics,
        98–99
    as phenomenological aesthetician, 90,
        129, 146
    scope of aesthetic writings, 149, 153
Inspiration
    and artistic execution, 125
    in Ghiselin, 123
    in Kant, 123
    limitations of, 125–26
    opposed models of, in aesthetic
        education, 123
Intelligence, in aesthetic education, 110
Intention
    ambiguities of, 124–26
    defined, 208
Intentional fallacy, 84, 160
    and aesthetic inspiration, 124
    analyzed, 124
    and expression, 159–60
    and null hypothesis of meaning, 23, 84
    phenomenological resolution of, 125
    re-evaluated 104–5
    and Sartrean intentionalism, 148

Intentional object, defined, 208
Intentionalism
  and artistic imagination, 104
  in theories of creation, 103
Intentionality, as conscious act, 105
Intentionality, defined, 209
Intentions, 142

Johnson, Margaret, 205
Joyce, James
  on Christian artists, 10
  Portrait of the Artist as a Young Man,
    12
Judgment, reflective
  in criticism, 176
  in Kant, 176, 196
  and logical inference, 175–76
Judgments, practical and cognitive, 164

Kant, Immanuel
  on aesthetic judgment, 11, 41, 122,
    158–59, 162
  and creation as discovery, 11
  on genius, 37
  on genius and taste, 11
  and phenomenology, 91
  on reflective judgment, 196
  on subjectivity of aesthetic judgment,
    178
Kaufman, Irving, 203
Keats, John, on truth and beauty, 5
King, Patricia, 175, 176
Kitchener, Karen Strom, 175, 176
Kristeller, Paul O., criticized by
    Mandelbaum, 57

Langer, Suzanne K., 148
Language
  defining range of aesthetic inquiry
    by, 196–99, 200–201
  uses of, in aesthetic education, 199
Lankford, E. Louis, 205
Lansing, Kenneth M., 203
Leonardo da Vinci, and religious
    paintings, 152
Lessing, Gotthold Ephraim, 8
Lindsey, Anne, 14
Logan, Fred, 196

Madeja, Stanley, and Onuska, Sheila,
    194

Magliola, Robert, 155
Mandelbaum, Maurice
  as critic of analytic aestheticians, 57
  on defining art, 198
  on definitions in aesthetics, 57
  as meta-theorist, 177
Marx, Karl, on inverting Hegel, 194
Mead, George H.
  and creative communication, 122
  and social theory of art, 59
Meaning in art, 22–25
Meanings
  as concepts and categories, 101
  and essences, in phenomenology,
    101–2
Merleau-Ponty, Maurice
  on art of painting, 146
  and consciousness modification, 100
  gestaltism of, 144–45
  and limits of phenomenology, 144–45
  as phenomenological aesthetician, 90,
    144
  and primacy of perception, 144, 152
  theory of forms in, 144
Meta-theory
  in aesthetics, 107
  principles of, 107–8
Metacriticism
  concept of, 187
  Feldman's, criticized, 185
  language about criticism, 196
Metaphor, as phenomenological
    description, 141
Methods, objective and subjective, in
    aesthetic education, 111
Meyer, C.F., criticized by Heidegger,
    155–56
Mondrian, Piet
  and abstract art, 18
  Broadway Boogie Woogie, 18
Munro, Thomas, 204
Music, form in, 166

Newman, Barnett, on aesthetics and
    aestheticians, 191
Nietzsche, Friedrich, 8, 9, 194–95
Noema
  concept of, 141
  conscious structure of, 105
  defined, 209
Noemata, and sedimented meanings, 141

Noematic strata, in Ingarden, 150–51
Noesis, defined, 209
Noesis, as structure of consciousness, 105
Noetic acts, concept of, 141

Ontic analysis, defined, 209
Ontological analysis, defined, 209
Ontology, existential
  as principle of education, 118
  and aesthetic categories, 146

Panofsky, Erwin
  as art historian, 85
  iconology and iconography of, 183
Parker, DeWitt H.
  on elements of aesthetic experience, 14
  on logical and reflective judgments, 178
  "modified" classicism of, 179
  on obstacles to art, 55
  social psychology in aesthetics of, 26, 56
Passmore, J.A., on the dreariness of aesthetics, 88
Pater, Walter, on formalism in art, 166
Peirce, Charles S.
  and aesthetic theory, 197
  and object of criticism, 77, 95
  pragmatic maxim of, 88
Percepts and concepts, in William James, 172
Pervasive qualities
  and aesthetic contexts, 186
  in criticism, 185
  and ordered aesthetic counters, 174
  and total expressiveness, 105
Phenomenological reduction, defined, 209
Phenomenology
  and aesthetic analysis, 73
  defined, 210
  descriptive and hermeneutical, 139
  method for art education, 108
  tested in meta-theory, 108
Phenomenology, existential. See also Heidegger, Martin
  and aesthetic judgment, 179
  in art education, 63, 68
Phenomenon, defined, 209

Phenomenon, as object of phenomenological analysis, 139
Philosophies, applied to education, 202
Piaget, Jean, 175
Picasso, Pablo
  communism of, 24
  Guernica, 24, 76
Plato
  aesthetic method of, 72
  as aesthetician, 4–8
  and Beauty, 70, 72
  on censorship, 5, 7, 62, 194
  as complete philosopher, 70
  and imitation, 72
  on inspiration, 37, 121
  Ion, 121
  on philosophical aesthetics, 194
  on poets, 5
  as social engineer, 194
Platonism, and romantic poets, 5
Prall, David W. See also aesthetic surface
  on aesthetic surfaces, 75, 144
  as phenomenologist, 92–93
  and sensuous surface, 172
Psychologism, in aesthetics, 93
Psychologism, defined, 210
Public schools, social aims of, 61–62

Reasoning, deductive and inductive, 176
Reduction, phenomenological. See also epochē, phenomenological
  in aesthetic perception, 106
  eidetic, in aesthetics, 98, 140
  transcendental, in Husserl, 142, 144
Relevance
  in critical discourse, 84
  as principle of aesthetic education, 112, 126–31
Rosenberg, Harold, 85

Santayana, George, 92
Sartre, Jean-Paul
  on aesthetic image, 105
  aesthetics of, criticized, 147–48
  and existentialist aesthetics, 147
  on imagining the absent, 144
  as phenomenological aesthetician, 90, 144
Scheffler, Israel, 199, 201–2

Schopenhauer, Arthur, 8
Science
  practical uses of, 81
  and technology, 81
Sensuous surface. *See also* aesthetic
    surface
  in music and painting, 172
Shaw, George B.
  on marriage, 55
  on teaching, 37
Significance
  contextual, 97–98
  vs. signification, 77, 96
Smith, Ralph A.
  on criticism in aesthetics, 89
  as editor, 85, 204
Socialist realism, 7, 70
Surrealism, 97

Taste, education of, 27
Teaching
  in existential situation, 117
  modeled on art, 82–83
Thomas Aquinas, St., 10–11
Tragedy
  in Aristotle, 6
  Christian, 10
  Hellenic, 6, 10
Training, vs. educating, 116
Transcendence, 115
  as subject of education, 117–18, 135
Transcendental ego, defined, 210
  functions of, 143
Transcendental reduction, defined, 210

Urmson, J.O., on aesthetic situations,
    146

Values
  aesthetic, 165, 180
  in educational arguments, 29
Van Gogh, Vincent
  and depth significance, 97
  criticized by Heidegger, 155–56
Villemain, Francis, 47

Weitz, Morris
  as analytic aesthetician, 42
  on definitions in aesthetics, 197–98
  early organicism of, 56
  influence of Wittgenstein on, 56
  as meta-theorist, 177
  and open concept of art, 123
  as organicist aesthetician, 42
  as student of D.H. Parker, 56
Whistler, James A.M., 163
  Arrangement in Grey and Black, No. 1,
      168–69, 187–90
  Arrangement in Grey and Black, No. 2,
      169, 170
  artistic legacy of, 166
  and musical values in painting, 151
  on theory of painting, 172
  significance of titles, 171
White, Morton, 203
Whole child, 19, 29
Work of art
  and aesthetic expression, 17
  and aesthetic judgment, 11–12
  ambiguity of, 16–17
  as artistic discovery, 71
  and creative discovery, 46
  as intentional object, 98
  as intentional object, in Prall, 92
  from nonobjective to representational,
      60
  as physical analogue, 148
  as polyphonic harmony, in Ingarden,
      151
  relational nature of, 20
  as stratified noema, in Ingarden,
      150–52

Ziff, Paul
  on aesthetic descriptions, 129
  criticized by Mandelbaum, 57
  as meta-theorist, 177
  on ordinary language in aesthetics,
      127
  as phenomenologist *manqué*, 93–94
  on reasons for liking artworks, 133

ABOUT THE AUTHOR

E. F. KAELIN holds a master's degree from the University of Missouri (1950), a diploma of higher studies in social psychology from the Université de Bordeaux, France (1951), and a Ph.D. from the University of Illinois (1954). He has taught at the University of Missouri, and the University of Wisconsin at Madison. He currently teaches philosophy of art and criticism, and recent continental philosophy, at Florida State University in Tallahassee, where he was former chairman of the Department of Philosophy.

Professor Kaelin has been an associate editor, editor, and contributing editor of *Arts-in-Society*, a journal of the arts in adult education at the University of Wisconsin, and, in the recent past, was a contributing editor of *The Journal of Aesthetic Education*. He was also a member of the National Advisory Board of the Aesthetic Education Program, the Central Midwestern Educational Laboratory (1968–1976). He is the author of *An Existentialist Aesthetic* (1962), *Art and Existence* (1970), *The Unhappy Consciousness: The Poetic Plight of Samuel Beckett* (1981), and *Heidegger's Being and Time: A Reading for Readers* (1988).